CORRUPTION AND DEMOCRATISATION

BOOKS OF RELATED INTEREST

The Resilience of Democracy: Persistent Practice, Durable Idea
Edited by Peter Burnell and Peter Calvert

Civil Society and Democracy in Africa
Edited by Nelson Kasfir

Democracy in Argentina: Hope and Disillusion
By Laura Tedesco

Civil Society: Democratic Perspectives
Edited by Robert Fine and Shirin Rai

Democracy and North America
Edited by Alan Ware

Democratisation and the Media
Edited by Vicky Randall

Corruption and Democratisation

Editors

ALAN DOIG
ROBIN THEOBALD

FRANK CASS
LONDON • PORTLAND, OR

First published in 2000 in Great Britain by
FRANK CASS AND COMPANY LIMITED
Newbury House, 900 Eastern Avenue, London IG2 7HH, England

and in the United States of America by
FRANK CASS
c/o International Specialized Book Services, Inc.
5804 N.E. Hassalo Street, Portland, Oregon 97213-3644

Copyright © 2000 Frank Cass & Co. Ltd

Website: www.frankcass.com

British Library Cataloguing in Publication Data

Corruption and democratisation
    1. Political corruption 2. Political corruption – Case
    studies 3. Representative government and representation
    4. Representative government and representation – Case
    studies
    I. Doig, Alan II. Theobald, Robin
    364.1'323

ISBN 0 7146 4996 1 (hb)
ISBN 0 7146 8057 5 (pb)

Library of Congress Cataloging-in-Publication Data

Corruption and democratisation / editors, Alan Doig, Robin Theobald.
        p.   cm.
    ISBN 0-7146-4996-1 (hb). – ISBN 0-7146-8057-5 (pb)
    1. Political corruption. 2. Democratization. I. Doig, Alan.
    II. Theobald, Robin.
    JF1081.C656   1999   99-40344
    364.1'323 – dc21   CIP

This group of studies first appeared in a Special Issue of the *Journal of
Commonwealth & Comparative Politics*, Vol.37, No.3 (November 1999),
[Corruption and Democratisation].

Printed in the UK by Antony Rowe Ltd., Chippenham, Wilts.

Contents

Introduction: Why Corruption?   **Alan Doig and Robin Theobald**   1

In the State We Trust? Democratisation, Corruption
and Development   **Alan Doig**   13

Democratisation or the Democratisation of
Corruption? The Case of Uganda   **David Watt,
Rachel Flanary and
Robin Theobald**   37

Causes and Consequences of Corruption:
Mozambique in Transition   **David Stasavage**   65

The Changing Context of Corruption Control:
The Hong Kong Special Administrative
Region, 1997–99   **Jonathan Moran**   98

Combating Corruption in Botswana: Regional   **Robin Theobald
Role Model or Deviant Case?   and Robert Williams**   117

Democracy, Development and Anti-Corruption
Strategies: Learning from the Australian
Experience   **Robert Williams**   135

Conclusions: Prospects for Reform in a
Globalised Economy   **Robin Theobald**   149

Abstracts   160

Index   163

Introduction: Why Corruption?

ALAN DOIG and ROBIN THEOBALD

Towards the end of his first year in office, World Bank president, James Wolfensohn, identified corruption as a major global problem. In the 50 odd countries Wolfensohn had visited during his debut year, corruption was the most predominant issue of public concern. In July 1996, whilst visiting the G7 summit in Lyons, Wolfensohn warned that the extent of corruption in developing and transitional economies was undermining public support for spending on overseas aid. 'When voters think that their money is going into a few peoples' pockets and Swiss bank accounts, that erodes the whole quality of the assistance package.' In fact, by 1996 there were already signs of serious aid fatigue, with the US cutting overseas aid by around one-third and major donors such as Britain and France reducing aid budgets by four to six per cent. The US decided not to contribute at all during the period 1997–99 to the International Development Agency, the UN's soft lending arm aimed at funding projects in the poorest countries (mainly in Tropical Africa).[1] In addition to its effects on aid, corruption is also widely held to deter investment, undermine good government, distorting government policy and leading to a misallocation of resources:

> In a corrupt environment, resources may be directed towards non-productive areas – the police, the armed forces and other organs of social control – as the elite move to protect themselves, their positions and their material wealth. Resources otherwise available for socio-economic development will be diverted into security expenditure. This, in turn, can cause the weakening of market institutions as rent-seeking, rather than investment becomes the major objective of policy makers.[2]

Corruption, in addition, bears down most heavily upon the poorest sections of society who must ultimately bear the cost of the distortions and deprivations it produces.[3]

The importance of combating corruption was also signalled in one of Kofi Annan's early interviews after his appointment as Secretary General of the United Nations. Economic development on the continent of Africa, the Secretary General affirmed, 'implies good governance, competent elites, and above all, the disappearance of corruption'. In December 1996 the

United Nations adopted a declaration against international corruption and bribery enjoining member nations to strive to eliminate these and associated pathologies. To this end, states should criminalise the bribery of foreign officials as well as end the situation in which bribes are tax deductible.[4]

With regard to this last point, the United States has for some time been pressing other developed countries to outlaw foreign commercial bribery by their corporations along the lines of the Foreign Corrupt Practices Act (FCPA) of 1977. The view of the Clinton administration is that US firms lose tens of billions of dollars every year because foreign rivals are able to pay bribes to win contracts. In many OECD countries, not only is bribery not illegal, such payments can be offset against tax.[5]

Other international organisations that have recently inveighed against the evils of corruption are the International Monetary Fund, the World Economic Forum (which in 1995 established the Davos Group), the World Trade Organisation, the International Chamber of Commerce, the Organisation of Latin American States, the 29-member Organization for Economic Co-operation and Development, the G7 group of industrialised nations and the European Union.[6] In November 1997 the UK government in a major policy document, *Eliminating World Poverty: A Challenge for the Twenty-First Century*, affirmed its support for World Bank and IMF efforts to curtail corruption. The White Paper noted, *inter alia*, that it is the poor who bear the heaviest cost through the higher prices and fewer employment opportunities that are the principal consequences of the distortions that corruption can produce.[7]

In addition to governmental and public international organisations working against corruption are NGOs (non-governmental organisations), probably the best known and most active in this field being Transparency International (TI). Established by former World Bank employees in 1993, TI's mission is 'to curb corruption through international and national coalitions encouraging governments to establish and implement effective laws, policies and anti-corruption programmes' as well as to 'strengthen public support and understanding for anti-corruption programmes and enhance public transparency and accountability in international business transactions and in the administration of public procurement'.[8] TI's basic strategy is to work both at the international level with such agencies as the World Bank, the United Nations and aid organisations, as well as locally by establishing national chapters. The aim of the latter is to bring together diverse local interests – political, professional, business, citizens groups and suchlike – who have an interest in combating corruption in that particular country. To local chapters TI offers advice and assistance on organisation, how to monitor the actions of various departments of state, the role of the media and other related areas. To this end TI produces a source book which is designed to serve as a manual of institutionalised measures which can be mobilised to reduce corruption.[9] By the middle of 1998 there were 70 such national chapters.

As many commentators have noted, until the 1990s the term 'corruption' figured hardly at all in the discourse of international organisations both public and private. On the contrary, many states that were known to be thoroughly corrupt were in receipt of very substantial loan and aid packages. Why then this tidal wave of concern about a phenomenon that according to many commentators has always existed? Have the 1990s seen a sudden upsurge in corruption? If so, why?

WHY CORRUPTION?

First, we need to try and identify the phenomenon with which we are concerned, unfortunately by no means an easy task. However, in order to short-circuit an interesting but none the less time-consuming debate, it will be helpful to identify the essence of political corruption as 'the abuse of public authority for private profit'.[10] Although such a 'definition' leaves much to be desired, it will serve to demarcate the general phenomenon with which we are concerned: the public official, appointed or elected, who uses his/her authority illegitimately or illegally to advance his/her own interests. The diverse manifestations of corrupt transactions have been identified as ranging from:

> acceptance of money or other rewards for awarding contracts, violations of procedures to advance personal interests, including kickbacks from development programmes or multinational corporations; pay-offs for legislative support; and the diversion of public resources for private use, to overlooking illegal activities or intervening in the justice process. Forms of corruption also include nepotism, common theft, overpricing, establishing non-existent projects, payroll padding, tax collection and tax assessment frauds.[11]

At this point it would also be useful to distinguish between 'grand corruption' on the one hand, and routine or 'petty corruption' on the other. Grand corruption has been defined as 'the misuse of public power by heads of state, ministers and senior officials for private pecuniary gain'.[12] With grand corruption we are dealing with highly placed individuals who exploit their position to extract large bribes from representatives of transnational corporations (TNCs); arms dealers, drug barons and the like, who appropriate significant pay-offs from contract scams, or who simply transfer large sums of money from the public treasury into private (usually overseas) bank accounts. Examples of grand corruption in recent years have become all too familiar: the late Felix Houphouet-Boigny's boast that he had 'billions abroad', 'Citoyen' Mobuto Sese Seko's reputed US$5 billion in overseas bank accounts, the alleged £3 billion – a conservative estimate – siphoned out of Pakistan by the family of former prime minister, Benazir Bhutto, and the billions accumulated by 'Suharto Inc', the vast business empire controlled by the former Indonesian president's family and cronies – are but the tip of the iceberg.[13] One Swiss banking source has estimated that more then US$420 billion is held in that country's banks by African heads of state alone.[14]

Grand corruption in the form of unashamed looting of the public treasury has hitherto not been as obvious in developed countries primarily for two related reasons: the existence of a large private sector and the opportunities it offers for irregular self-enrichment; and, second, the obverse in the form of the smaller size and lesser strategic position of the public sector in their respective economies. Accordingly, fraud in the form of illegally using, diverting or simply stealing funds from private firms and other non-governmental organisations is much more evident in developed countries than in their less developed counterparts. Indeed banking fraud, illegal share operations, insider dealing, complex company frauds, major insurance scams and suchlike seem recently to have become virtually the daily fare of the business press. This does not of course mean that the public sector in the developed world is immune to predation. Everywhere the state is active in economy and society presents an opportunity for rent-seeking. This is particularly apparent in the case of the European Union coffers, which seem to be a favourite target with reportedly more than US$6.4 billion going adrift every year.[15] Under the headline 'Brussels reels from endless scandals', a piece in *The Guardian* (UK) related how the European Parliament threatened to withhold the discharge of the 1996 EU Budget unless the Commission (that is, the European Union bureaucracy) could account for £1.5 million of humanitarian aid destined for Rwanda and Burundi. Another case involved the apparent disappearance of over £40 million designed to build relations between the EU and its Mediterranean neighbours. In these two cases and 20 others the Commission's financial controllers had refused to divulge information or access to relevant documents. In February 1999, under a sustained barrage of criticism from the European Parliament all 20 of the EU's commissioners were eventually forced to resign.[16]

In western Europe and the United States a good deal of public concern has also been expressed about the ancillary interests of elected politicians, both whilst in office and after leaving. There have been numerous cases of often audacious self-enrichment through such mechanisms as company directorships, outside consultancies, selling information and contacts, lucrative book deals or lecture tours or good old fashioned bribery. In the United Kingdom members of the House of Commons are required to register their outside interests as well as the earnings which flow from them. However, hitherto nothing serious seems to have happened to them when they have not.[17] Cronyism, a term habitually associated with the Third World, is clearly pervasive among political and business elites in the north. In his masterly account of 'how Washington works', Hedrick Smith has catalogued the multifarious exchanges – federal employment, access to key figures and information, free flights on private jets, holidays overseas, tickets for major sporting events, invitations to dinner with 'big shots' and so on – which constitute the core of 'the power game' in the United States.[18] In November 1996 a British national newspaper, the *Daily Mail*, carried a piece entitled 'Peddling Family Assets' which in no uncertain terms suggested that the son of a former British prime minister had been able to amass his estimated £40 million fortune largely because of his parent's influence. Interestingly, the article maintained that had such advantages accrued to the son or daughter of a US president whilst in office, then the law would have been clearly contravened.[19] The fact that a newspaper which is commonly regarded as a staunch supporter of that prime minister's Conservative government ran this story reflected growing public concern in Britain over 'sleaze' in national politics. In fact the sleaze factor played a major role in the massive defeat suffered by the Conservatives in the general election of 1997. Ironically, its Labour successor, after a honeymoon period, found itself confronting similar accusations. One much publicised case involved a donation of £1 million to Labour Party coffers from a motor racing magnate whose sport was then said to have benefited from a relaxation of restrictions on tobacco advertising.[20] In relation to such cases, the observation is often made that the increasing costs of electioneering in mass democracies, and the primacy this places upon fundraising, render such informal exchanges virtually inevitable. The point about such exchanges, however, is that although often leading to substantial gains, material or otherwise, for one or more of the parties concerned, many of them would probably not fall within the purview of a legal conception of corruption.

Turning now to petty corruption, we are dealing here with the soliciting or extortion of small payments by low level officials in order to expedite business by cutting through red tape; or to do what they are supposed to do anyway. Petty corruption in this form is often referred to as 'speed' or 'grease' money. Whilst from one point of view trifling when compared with the vast sums plundered by the powerful, petty corruption is no less significant precisely because it bears most heavily on the poorest and weakest sectors of society who can least afford to make payments for services to which they are anyway entitled. The burden is even more apparent when we take into account the fact that petty corruption often involves swindling members – often the most vulnerable members – of the public out of their rightful dues – pensions and disability payments, for example; or outright extortion by police or customs officers or members of the armed forces.[21] Countries in which petty corruption is pervasive must in addition endure disablingly low levels of trust in public institutions, with all the extremely negative consequences for commitment to collective projects, civic behaviour, levels of crime and public order.

So far as the actual incidence of corrupt behaviour is concerned this is even more problematic than the task of definition. It is widely accepted that the measurement of crime in general is fraught with difficulty. Even more is this the case with a pattern of behaviour which in many countries is neither illegal nor even regarded as illegitimate. Our thinking about the level of corruption in this or that society tends therefore to be somewhat impressionistic, based upon our own perceptions (or prejudices), or those of journalists, diplomats, politicians, businessmen and the like. Along these lines, Transparency International regularly publishes an index, developed at the University of Göttingen, under which a number of countries are ranked according to perceptions registered in a range of relevant surveys. In 1996 and 1997 Nigeria was perceived as the most corrupt of the 52 countries included, with Denmark the least.[22] Does this mean that Nigeria is the most corrupt country in the world?

In so far as the survey included less than a third of the world's nation states it would obviously be unwarranted to reach that particular conclusion (as the compilers of the index readily recognise). The fact that there were no other West African countries in the survey prompts us to ask whether Nigeria is in reality more corrupt than neighbouring Chad, Niger, Benin, Togo and so on. With a population that more than exceeds these and most of the rest of West Africa, and proportionately more business transactions – as well as a higher volume of these with the West – Nigeria is for these reasons alone more likely to display a higher incidence of *perceived* corrupt transactions. This is not, of course, to argue that corruption is not a problem in Nigeria. The point being made here is that such ranking exercises, interesting and useful though they may be, tell us relatively little about the actual incidence of corruption in specific countries and even less about whether this incidence has increased over time. In other words, we cannot say unequivocally that the problem of corruption is more serious in 1998 than it was in 1978. All we can say is that it is generally perceived as being more serious. Why is this the case?

First, the ending of the Cold War has permitted, if not necessitated, the serious scrutiny of foreign policy on the part of the great powers, in particular the support of manifestly corrupt regimes. Heads of state who in the interests of political expediency were permitted to use the public treasury as their personal piggy bank are now being put under increasing pressure, especially by creditor nations and institutions. Or, like Mobutu, they were unceremoniously dumped. Currently, the curtailment of grand corruption is seen as essential for good government which, in turn, is regarded as a *sine qua non* of sustainable economic development.

Second, also a consequence of the ending of the Cold War, the speed with which the Soviet economic system was dismantled and market capitalism introduced has had a number of unanticipated and undesirable consequences. A high level of initial optimism, not to say triumphalism, has been confounded by the onset of acute economic and political instability, large-scale unemployment and poverty, alarming levels of crime and gangsterism, all of them interwoven with pervasive political corruption.[23]

Third, increasing globalisation in ratcheting up the level of competition also raises the threshold for corrupt transactions. Those demanding corrupt payments in a context where an increasing number of agencies are bidding for high cost public works contracts can play each off against the other by raising the required levels of the 'commission'. As a headline in the *Financial Times* put it: 'Goodbye Mr. 10 per cent', referring to a growing tendency for demands for side-payments to escalate even as high as 30 per cent. Clearly, there comes a point when TNCs and business interests generally have a powerful interest in arresting the spiral.[24]

Fourth, the revolution in information technology and the parallel expansion of financial services has made possible the movement of trillions of dollars across the world at the push of a button. This has vastly expanded the scope for corruption and fraud as well as the laundering of the proceeds of ancillary illegitimate activities.

Fifth, the upsurge of a series financial scandals in developed countries has shaken Western governments and business out of their 1980s 'greed is good' complacency. The Savings and Loans fiasco, the involvement of prestigious Wall Street finance houses in illegal trading, the collapse of Bank of Credit and Commerce International (BCCI), of newspaper tycoon Robert Maxwell's empire, together with a whole raft of other financial scandals, dramatically highlighted the need for developed countries to put their own houses in order. One may add here that the increasing scrutiny of the behaviour of public figures by the mass media, the relentless quest for a juicy story – this in turn a consequence of escalating media competition – has exposed the deeply flawed character of many national institutions and persons. Both reflecting and driving the apparently insatiable public appetite for details of peccadilloes of the rich and the powerful, has been a declining confidence in those in authority, especially politicians.[25]

Sixth, the chilling expansion of the trade in illicit drugs, the growth of narco-economies and even narco-states, has focused attention on the threat, not simply to financial institutions, but to the integrity of the state itself. In 1996, a former head of Interpol warned a conference of law enforcement officers in Cambridge that the stupendous profits from drugs enables perpetrators to 'reach the highest levels of our institutions'.[26] Such apprehensions were dramatically realised the following year when the Mexican general put in charge of that country's war against drugs was found to be deeply implicated in the trade himself. After police searched three of his properties, General Gutierrez was charged with corruption and accused of having close links with one of the major drugs cartels.[27] In January 1998, a minister at the UK Home Office, confirming that 80 per cent of the heroin seized in Britain flowed through Turkey, went on to express concern about rumours that Turkish police and even members of the government were implicated in the trade.[28] Overall, the annual proceeds of the drug trade are estimated to be in the region of US$400 billion, only slightly less than the GDP of the UK![29]

Last, but by no means least, is the depressing growth in world poverty. Under the neo-liberal ethos of the 1980s many less developed countries were constrained to adopt structural adjustment programmes, the aim of which was to deregulate their economies, allowing greater scope for the operation of market forces. The thinking behind these programmes was that drastically curtailing the dead weight of an overblown public sector would release hitherto suppressed productive forces and engender significant growth. As a consequence of the 'trickle-down' effect, economic gains would gradually percolate through to the less well off, so reducing the overall level of poverty.

It is extremely difficult to evaluate the consequences of such programmes. However, there seems to be a consensus that, at best, their gains have been modest. So far as the sub-continent of tropical Africa is concerned, more than a decade of structural adjustment has produced little growth whilst the problem of poverty remains as urgent as ever.[30] Many of the states of Latin America, by contrast, have registered high levels of growth (Argentina, Chile, Peru, Uruguay), as well as other economic gains, not least drastic reductions in inflation. None the less, such progress is widely acknowledged to have been at the expense of growing social inequality as well as increases in absolute poverty. By 1992, 46 per cent of the population of Latin America was estimated to be living below the poverty line.[31] According to the *United Nations Human Development Report of 1998*, 20 per cent of the global population was accounting for 88 per cent of consumption. The 225 richest people in the world had a combined wealth – US$1 trillion – equal to the annual income of the poorest 47 per cent of the earth's population – some 2.5 billion people.[32]

The seriousness of the situation was acknowledged by James Wolfensohn in October 1997. In a keynote speech, Wolfensohn referred to the 'poverty time bomb'. With three billion of the world's population now living on less than $2 per day, this time bomb 'could explode in our children's faces'.[33] One significant consequence of the scale of the crisis has been a realignment in official thinking about the role of the state in development. Whereas, according to the neo-liberal view, the state was regarded as, at best, an impediment to development, the 1990s saw its partial rehabilitation, with the notion of good governance now considered to be a *sine qua non* of macro-economic stability and growth. Good governance requires that the state be both efficient and effective, which can be achieved only by the state limiting its activities to those which it is best qualified to perform. However, this slimmed down state must also be generally perceived as legitimate. That is to say, the process of government should be open and honest as well as meeting the needs of its citizens. In order that these needs be met, the state must be constrained by, as well as work with, a vigorous civil society.[34] Thus, through the resurrection of a hitherto somewhat neglected concept, the issues of 'democracy' and 'democratisation' have been reincorporated into the official development lexicon.

Accordingly, we open this collection with Alan Doig's discussion of the interrelationships between democratisation and development. Doig begins by examining the standard components of democracy and the principal factors that underpinned its emergence in the West. Recognising that LDCs are embarked upon a radically different developmental trajectory, Doig moves on to ask whether a democratic regime is compatible with the exigencies of much needed rapid economic growth. Does the developmental state need to be insulated from the pressures of a burgeoning and increasingly importunate civil society? If development and democracy are compatible, what policies and strategies, if any, might further the latter? Doig concludes by emphasising the necessity of the careful sequencing and co-ordination of reform policies both across sectors and between donors.

It would be churlish to dissent from the view that Uganda has made extraordinary progress over the past decade and half. From the dreadful bloodletting and economic chaos of the early 1980s, the country has experienced impressive economic growth in an overall context of remarkable political stability. Because of these achievements, the National Resistance Movement (NRM) regime of Yowerri Museveni, although reluctant to move to a multi-party system, seems to enjoy a high degree of legitimacy. Despite these undoubted gains, Uganda continues to endure widely acknowledged and unacceptably high levels of corruption. David Watt, Rachel Flanary and Robin Theobald examine the major reforms which have been undertaken in an attempt to reconstruct Uganda's state apparatus and estimate the chances of reconciling the need for continued regime legitimacy with the quest for good governance.

David Stasavage addresses the problem of why corruption in Mozambique appears to have increased significantly over the last decade or so, especially when the adoption of structural adjustment should have reduced the opportunities for abuse. Based upon interviews carried out with private sector and donor representatives in Mozambique, as well as the analysis of recent reports on the business environment, Stasavage emphasises the transitional nature of Mozambican society. In particular, he highlights the decline and eventual disappearance of controls on public servants formerly imposed centrally by the FRELIMO regime. This decline needs to be set alongside the absence of a major programme of civil service reform, together with the failure to simplify excessively complex commercial regulations. Such failures have created ample opportunities for a kind of 'anarchic' corruption which Stasavage believes to be particularly damaging for commerce and investment.

Given the current upsurge of concern about corruption, it is not surprising that the operations of Hong Kong's Independent Commission Against Corruption has attracted much attention. Not only has the ICAC had 25 years' experience in dealing with the problem, but it is also widely acknowledged to have enjoyed considerable success both with investigation and prosecution and education and prevention. For these reasons the Hong Kong ICAC has tended to take on the status of a model which is held up for other countries to emulate. By way of considering the transferability of the ICAC model, Jonathan Moran emphasises the political economy of the context in which the agency is constrained to operate. Moran addresses himself specifically to the radical change which Hong Kong has undergone with the transfer of sovereignty to the Peoples' Republic of China. Will the effectiveness of the ICAC be undermined by the former colony's increasing integration with a state that has no co-ordinated corruption strategy, whose legal system is heavily politicised, and whose civil society is manifestly weak? Moran concludes that the increasing politicisation of the Hong Kong legal system, a shift in the balance of power away from pro-democracy elements and the growing influence of organised crime, foreshadow problems with the Special Administrative Region's future anti-corruption strategy.

For many, Botswana is regarded as an island of stability in a sea of turbulence, a long-standing democracy which has never known military government. In addition, Botswana's record on administrative probity is unequalled in tropical Africa. However, during the late 1980s and early 1990s, Botswana experienced a series of financial scandals which led to the creation of a Directorate on Corruption and Economic Crime. Robin Theobald and Robert Williams discuss the background to the emergence of the Directorate, examine its operations and speculate on the likely problems it will face in the future. In particular, Theobald and Williams address the question of the transferability of the DCEC to other states in tropical Africa.

Robert Williams renders a useful service in reminding us that corruption is by no means a problem that is restricted to less developed states. Whilst industrialised societies, with their developed institutions, are in theory better placed to expose and deal with corruption, they are by no means immune to the contagion. In his examination of a number of high profile cases in the states of Australia, Williams brings out the essentially political nature of anti-corruption discourse. He also highlights the difficulties of reconciling and incorporating into policy the different perspectives of administrators on the one hand, and politicians on the other.

NOTES

The editors would like to record their appreciation of the funding provided by the British government's Department for International Development for research projects on which a number of the contributions are based, and in particular the corruption and anti-corruption strategies research project. The contributions, of course, reflect the views of the authors.

 1. *Financial Times* (UK), 2 July 1996. See also, M. Celarier, 'Corruption: The Search for the Smoking Gun', *Public Fund Digest*, 8, 1 (1997), 37–45.
 2. F. Stapenhurst and P. Langseth, 'The Role of Public Administration in Fighting Corruption', *International Journal of Public Sector Management*, 10, 5 (1997), 311.
 3. *TI Newsletter*, June 1997, 5.
 4. *TI Newsletter*, Sept. 1996, 7.
 5. In Denmark, France, the Netherlands and, according to some interpretations, the UK bribes are tax deductible. In March 1999, Germany passed a law which ended tax deductibility. See *TI Newsletter*, June 1999, 5.
 6. *Financial Times*, 22 July 1997.
 7. *Eliminating World Poverty: A Challenge for the Twenty-first Century*, UK Department for International Development (1997), 30.
 8. *TI Mission Statement*, Transparency International, Berlin, 1995.
 9. J. Pope (ed.), *National Integrity Systems: The TI Source Book* (Washington, DC: Transparency International, 1997).
10. For an extended discussion of the problems of defining corruption, see A.J. Heidenheimer, M. Johnston and V.T. LeVine (eds.), *Political Corruption: A Handbook* (New Brunswick: Transaction Publishers, 1989).
11. *United Nations Human Development Report 1998* (New York: Oxford University Press, 1998), 11.
12. G. Moody-Stuart, *Grand Corruption in Third World Develoment* (Berlin: Transparency International, 1994), 1.
13. Houphouet-Boigny's confession (boast?) is recorded in *West Africa*, 9 May 1983, 1142. On Benazir Bhutto see the *Financial Times*, 25 Sept. 1997; on 'Suharto Inc.' see *The Guardian Weekly*, 31 May 1998. See also *TI Newsletter* 12 June 1997 on the missing Marcos millions.
14. P. McCauslan, 'A New Deal for Africa ?', Royal African Society/Institute of Commonwealth Studies Conference 'Corruption in Africa', Institute of Commonwealth Studies (London), November 1993.

15. *The Times* (UK), 4 Dec. 1996.
16. M. Walker, 'The Commission Gets its Come-uppance', *The Guardian Weekly*, 24 Jan. 1999.
17. See A. Doig, *Corruption and Misconduct in Contemporary British Politics* (Harmondsworth: Penguin, 1984), and F.F. Ridley and A. Doig (eds.), *Sleaze: Politicians, Private Interests and Public Reaction* (Oxford: Oxford University Press, 1998).
18. H. Smith, *The Power Game: How Washington Works* (New York: Random House, 1988).
19. *Daily Mail* (UK), 16 Nov. 1998.
20. J. Freedland, '"Culture of Cronyism" Spells Woe for Labour', *The Guardian Weekly*, 19 July 1998.
21. For a shocking catalogue of such abuses see T. Lodge, 'Political Corruption in South Africa', *African Affairs*, 97, 387 (1998), 157–88.
22. Transparency International and J.G. Lamsdorff, University of Goettingen, *Internet Corruption Ranking*, 1997. See also *TI 97 Corruption Perception Index. Frequently Asked Questions* (Berlin: Transparency International, 1997). Internet: http://www.transparency.de. In the 1997 Index the UK and the USA were situated at positions 15 and 16 respectively. By 1998, with 85 countries now included, Nigeria had moved up to position 81 alongside Tanzania. Bottom of the list was Cameroon. *TI Newsletter* (Dec. 1998).
23. On gangsterism in Russia see, J. Lloyd, 'The New Class', *Prospect*, Jan. 1998, 34–9. On corruption in eastern Europe generally, see A. Klich, 'Bribery in Economies in Transition: The Foreign Corrupt Practices Act', *Stanford Journal of International Law*, 32, 121 (1996), 121–47.
24. *Financial Times*, 22 July 1998.
25. See Ridley and Doig, *Sleaze*, and M. Punch, *Dirty Business: Exploring Corporate Misconduct* (London: Sage, 1996).
26. *The Guardian*, 10 Oct. 1996.
27. *TI Newsletter*, March 1997.
28. K. Nezan, 'La Turquie, Plaque Tournante du Trafic du Drogue', *Le Monde Diplomatique*, July 1998.
29. 'Drugs Trade Dwarfs all but Three of Biggest Economies', *The Guardian Weekly*, 8–14 July 1999.
30. See R. Lensink, *Structural Adjustment in Sub-Saharan Africa* (London: Longman, 1996), and D. Rimmer, 'Adjustment Blues', *African Affairs*, 94, 374 (Jan. 1995).
31. D. Green, *Silent Revolution: The Rise of Market Economies in Latin America* (London: Latin America Bureau, 1995), 202–3.
32. L. Elliot and V. Brittain, 'The Rich and Poor are Growing Further Apart', *The Guardian Weekly*, 20 Sept. 1998. *Human Development Report, 1998*, United Nations. Internet: www.undp.org/undp/hdro.
33. *The Guardian Weekly*, 5 Oct. 1997.
34. See especially *World Development Report 1997: The State in a Changing World* (New York: Oxford University Press for the World Bank, 1997).

In the State We Trust? Democratisation, Corruption and Development

ALAN DOIG

The global political changes that have taken place since the late 1980s and early 1990s have had a profound impact on the political systems of many developing countries. These changes stemmed from both domestic political forces and changes in the external environment, with developing governments no longer able to rely on uncritical donor support to secure a bulwark against communism, as well as communist countries exposed both to the rigours of the market and to demands for democratisation. Since this period, democratisation and multi-party systems have increasingly been promoted to replace the authoritarian single-party and military regimes of Soviet Bloc countries, Africa and Latin America. But, from the outset, the fundamental question must be whether democratisation is 'a gamble worth taking, not only for its intrinsic value as a defence against tyranny but for its instrumental value in institutional change and improved policy? Or is democracy another false start in poor countries attempting costly economic reforms?'[1]

Democratisation is seen by Western governments, international donors, academics and commentators as a significant developmental step[2] that could (or, more conjecturally, should) provide the impetus needed to resolve such countries' political, economic and social problems and lead the way to the establishment and eventual consolidation of democratic governance, including universal political association and participation alongside a limited, transparent and responsive state and an end to the debilitating impact of corruption, misappropriation and waste that characterised earlier regimes. Many 'new democracies', not unlike their predecessors, have yet to deliver significant sustainable social, economic and political change. This begs the question of whether the promotion of democratisation is enough to achieve such goals, whether it fosters new types of corruption, and how the engagement of the public can be achieved to ensure the effectiveness of the role of democracy in promoting political, social and economic development.

Alan Doig, Liverpool Business School, Liverpool John Moores University.

WHAT ARE WE VOTING FOR? THE STATE AND THE
PURPOSE OF DEMOCRACY

The 'history of the states system' was part and parcel of 'the growing coincidence of territorial boundaries with a uniform system of rule'; 'the creation of mechanisms of law-making and enforcement'; 'the centralisation of administrative power'; 'the alteration and extension of fiscal management'; 'the formalisation of relations among states through the development of diplomacy and diplomatic institutions'; and 'the introduction of a standing army'.[3] Given that in the history of most countries the 'the state preceded democracy by some four or five centuries', and that its core functions of 'external security, internal law enforcement, and the management of the country's finances'[4] were exercised primarily for the benefit of the ruler or ruling elite, the history of democratisation has been concerned with the control of the state and the ends to which the state has been put.

Democratisation is thus not simply 'electoral democracy'[5] where the visible and formal trappings of political participation mask the continuing control of the state by rulers and ruling elites who manipulate the electoral process (from electoral fraud through to the creation of parties that are mobilised, funded and controlled by the elites) to legitimise their retention of power and their continuing use of the state machinery in pursuit of their own interests. The *purpose* of democratisation is to engage the participation of the public in the activities of the state, and the consequential nature and roles of the state: 'democracy is one form of the state' in which 'the state is seen as the institutional embodiment of a concern with the identification and realisation of public interest, with a rational analysis of norms in a disinterested and benevolent manner'.[6] Its most commonly promoted ideal – the liberal democratic or representative democracy model – 'is essentially a decision-making system, assuming certain absences of restriction on free expression, with a hugely developed form of citizenship. Democracy combines freedom of criticism of authority with the rights to organise in opposition to authority and to participate in the making of decisions for the whole community'.[7] In addition to defining the relationships between the public and the state – the nature of participation – democratisation should therefore also shape what the state does, and why it does it, by defining both principles *and* process:

> policymakers are selected through elections ... There is a strong element of popular control in this model. Though the people don't actually make policy, they do, through their representative, have some kind of broad influence on policy decisions. Clearly then it is the role of government, according to the conventional view, to carry on the

demands of the citizenry as interpreted by their representatives ... Conformity with citizens' demands is ensured through periodic elections and through contact and consultation with citizens in their local community.[8]

There may be no single checklist of a democracy but the textbooks repeat lists of common principles and themes reflecting the reciprocal relationship between the state and the public through the mediation of the 'political society':[9] political legitimacy for the state through universal suffrage and regular elections; the peaceful transfer of power; an effective political opposition and representative government; accountability through transparency of decision making and the provision of information; separation of powers; effective scrutiny of financial expenditure; effective standards of conduct in public office; official competencies such as impartially recruited and well trained public servants; realistic social policies and low defence expenditure; human and civil rights as indicated by freedom of religion, association, expression and movement; impartial and accessible criminal justice systems; and the absence of arbitrary government power.

A democratic polity may be aspirational rather than actual in terms of Dahlian goals of 'effective participation' (the fullest means of expressing choice), 'enlightened understanding' (the fullest information for choice), 'control over the agenda', 'voting equality at decisive stages' and 'inclusiveness'.[10] Nevertheless, most would profess adherence to participatory, transparent and accountable procedures, to promoting economic development and liberalisation, to improving the social, health and educational prospects of the public and providing a responsible and responsive normative political and legal framework. The key issue here is the goal of governance in the democratic context. Defined as the 'use of political authority and the exercise of control over society and the management of its resources for social and economic development', governance encompasses the 'nature of functioning of a state's institutional and structural arrangements, decision-making processes, policy formulation, implementation capacity, information flows, effectiveness of leadership, and the nature of the relationship between rules and the ruled'.[11] Governance, therefore, is the *purpose* of democratisation in that it is concerned with not just the organisation and activity of government – its economy and efficiency – but also the ends to which they are put – its effectiveness and impact – in terms of achieving levels of economic, human and institutional development which 'benefit the population as a whole' and promote the 'literary, education and employment opportunities'[12] which in turn enhances the ability of the population to demand and participate effectively in the processes of government, thereby legitimising its activities and developing a reciprocity of trust.

DEVELOPING THE DEMOCRATIC STATE – REINVENTING HISTORY?

The democratic state is taken as the norm among Western industrialised countries:

> advanced, complex economies, industrial and post-industrial, with considerable mixed-economy elements; urbanised societies with relatively high living standards; extensive social services and educational provisions; liberal-democratic political values, parliamentary institutions; free elections and competitive party systems; extensive interest-group participation in policy-making; sophisticated administrative systems, diversified functionally and geographically, subject to the rule of law and other controls; large professional bureaucracies headed by elected politicians. In world perspective they form an obvious cluster.[13]

The pathway into the cluster (whose members, as donors and through their influence with international aid agencies, often espouse such goals for developmental purposes) is traceable through a number of deliberate, complementary and coincidental developments.[14]

Firstly, the process of urbanisation drew governments increasingly into the planning and provision of public amenities and municipal services and the regulation of the market economy – to facilitate production and trade as well as to check abuses. While this significant increase in the scope of government placed a premium on co-ordination, clear lines of communication, efficiency and, above all, administrative professionalism, the drive for national efficiency was then given a significant further boost by international rivalry between the Great Powers. Secondly, and inextricably bound up with this process, was the expansion of trade and commerce which both expressed and made possible the rise of a bourgeois class. This, thirdly, gave rise to the emergence of civil society and the emergence of a public domain, an area of social space between the state and the private sphere in which citizens are able to articulate and pursue their interests in association with others. The development of an effective civil society comprising a plurality of social groupings able to confront and contest with the state has played and continues to play a central role in the maintenance of an accountable and publicly available state.

The rise of the bourgeoisie was followed by the emergence of a working class in the sense of a class-for-itself, albeit reformist rather than revolutionary, in that the concentration of wage earners in large units of production engendered a growing consciousness which manifested itself in increasing pressure on the state initially for political citizenship (the extension of the franchise and other political rights). However, the admission of the working class to the political arena eventually produced an escalation of demands to incorporate social citizenship[15] – in other words, demand for greater access to the fruits of the industrial system as well as greater protection from the vagaries of the market.

Fourth, the emergence of an active, often militant, civil society raised the problem of the incorporation of the masses, particularly the working class, which, at the beginning of the twentieth century, formed the overwhelming majority of the labour force. Although its origins probably lie in Bismarck's pioneering scheme of the 1880s, the modern welfare state reached its apogee in the 30-year post-Second World War boom period. By providing social security for its citizens complemented by Keynesian demand management, the welfare state undertakes to insure them against the vicissitudes of the market economy. In underwriting the well-being of its citizens the modern state seals its contract with civil society, serving the interests of which is its primary purpose. Finally, in addition to the granting of 'civil', 'political' and 'social' rights, allegiance to the centre and identification with a national culture was further promoted by an increase in geographical and social mobility, the expansion of mass education, the development of mass markets and the mass media. These processes combined to produce both a standardised mass culture comprising common ideals, norms, idioms, modes of expression and styles of life, as well as to intensify the involvement of the people with this common culture.

Clearly the above generalisations gloss over significant differences between European societies and their widely varying routes to 'modernity' and functioning democratisation, as well as sometimes simplify, or retrospectively attach sequential sense to, wide-ranging changes, fortuitous circumstance or random events. Nevertheless, the key point being argued here is that this political reality and the confidence it has produced is the outcome of a specific historical configuration of political and economic forces. Further, this configuration is the product of a general development trajectory taken by western European, Australian and North American societies. Three further lines of thought arise from this.

First, insofar as in a general sense a specific developmental path that has been followed by developed countries has been identified, clearly those mechanisms of change that have propelled these states along this path continue to operate. In other words, developed states are not comfortably settled in a moment of rational-legal equilibrium. On the contrary, intensifying global competition has brought about a fiscal crisis in developed states necessitating public sector economies, privatisation, outsourcing, re-engineering and the like. Not only has it had an impact on the range and delivery of public service provision in developed countries but it has informed approaches to reform promoted by developed countries as part of their particular continuing development trajectory. Similarly, the global economy, legitimate or illicit, will impact on the nature of the development of transitional or developing states:

> the often weak and debt-ridden economies of many developing countries leave them vulnerable and dependent on economic forces and relations over which they have little, if any, control. Although the internationalisation of production and finance places many instruments of economic control beyond even the most powerful countries, the position of those at the lower end of the globalisation hierarchy, experiencing the stronger effects of unevenness, is substantially worse.[16]

Second, there are many developing countries, particularly those in tropical Africa and Asia, who have *not* moved along an upward economic development path and remain characterised by poorly integrated economies with large subsistence sectors, poor education and fragmented social composition, with all the concomitant issues concerning state income, capability for participation and a sense of national identity. In fact, such states tend to be caught in a permanently recurring circle of administrative underdevelopment in which the ability to appropriate resources is severely inhibited by administrative weakness, but administrative weakness is further exacerbated by difficulties of appropriation. Basic structural deficiencies are subject to inadequate scrutiny by a weak civil society, including a weak bourgeoisie. Serious communal differences further fragment the public domain and undermine national integration. Trust in the state, so vital to the discourse of public administration, is at a minimum while the balance of relative strengths between the public and the state to lead to negotiated interaction, and then to the institutionalisation of the rights to the former in relation to the latter, continues to be absent.

Third, within such a dynamic continuum there is the question of whether history can be repeated or re-invented, and whether this is either realistic or realisable given the current diversity among, and levels of development of, transitional or developing countries. Less developed countries have followed quite different developmental paths, few of which reflect (or could now reflect) the conditions outlined above. Developing countries which have succeeded in attaining a degree of successful economic development, and where the state has been able to provide services and resources for the benefit of the public, have themselves been the consequence of certain historical patterns which are distinct from, and even contradictory to, the experiences of other developing countries. In the Far East, post-1945 developments[17] – strong state elites and associated powerful bureaucracies (often as a result of Japanese colonial rule) and weak and poorly organised, civil society groups, especially entrepreneurs – allowed state elites to have the upper hand in relations which were nevertheless influenced by traditional practices and organisations, such as networks of region, family, school and other groupings – *guanxi* in Chinese. Following the Second World War these states continued to modernise. Financial systems were nationalised or under state influence and, importantly, states gained access to large amounts of foreign capital in the form of public loans and private finance.

Political authoritarianism was combined with economic controls while indigenous businesses lacked political power and access and bribed elites for favours either in the form of capital allocation or administrative support. Business communities had to negotiate with state elites to gain access to resources, whilst state elites demanded general co-operation in economic policy and also pay-offs for this assistance. State elites could even govern the form business development took. Although the patterns differed in each country the combination of strong states bolstered by large flows of foreign capital, weak business sectors, and pre-existing socio-cultural patterns of patron–client ties and networks were able to produce economic growth. What may have made an effective state in economic development terms, therefore, may not have been democratisation.

There are those, such as Adrian Leftwich, who argue from the basis of such experiences (and they are not confined to Asian countries) that the components of the 'developmental' state – the 'form and distribution of power, and the manner of its use in and through the state'[18] – have been crucial. He lists seven: *de facto* or *de jure* one-party states; *relatively* uncorrupt purposeful and determined developmental elites; the *relative autonomy* of the developmental elites and state institutions from the demands of special interests in the pursuit of the putative national interest; the creation of 'very powerful, highly competent and insulated economic bureaucracies with the authority in directing and managing economic and social development'; a weak civil society; the establishment of such features at an early point in the country's development; an intolerance of opposition.[19]

REFORMING AND REALIGNING THE STATE TOWARDS DEMOCRATISATION

In responding to the drive for democratisation, therefore, two themes have to be addressed. First, what is to be done to create or promote the conditions for democratisation has to be done within existing indigenous conditions and circumstances. Secondly, and consequentially, what must underpin democratisation is the means to secure the provision of public benefits and rights that democratisation is perceived to be bringing: 'sustaining democracy or a successful democratic transition requires that democratic regimes be capable of fulfilling the people's expectations. Failure to do so can derail the transition and bring about a serious questioning of the necessity of political change.'[20]

Without the basic ability to deliver, and without such a delivery within a realistic timescale, the linkage between democratisation, political participation and perceptible changes in the quality of life for the majority of the population will be impaired, if not broken. Here the experience of the reforms in former Soviet bloc countries underlines the importance of the state (or the importance of the failure of the state) to deliver the expectations of initial democratisation. In Russia, as elsewhere in post-soviet states, reformers struggle with the old oligarchs, in part a hang-over from the previous command economy system, while asset-strippers use their hold on state power to benefit from corrupt accumulation. Communism is re-emerging in parties which base their appeal upon the old social welfare certainties of Communist rule, under which, until 1989, 'many were cold but few were frozen'.[21] Economic deprivation combined with a failure to institutionalise political reforms has led to a general distrust of democracy and a lack of participation.

Moreover, organised crime has taken advantage of the new political space to strengthen its influence in the state with a consequential environment in which legitimacy and the proper institutionalisation and consolidation of democracy is undermined by demoralised public administration, high levels of street crime, food and utilities shortages, poor public services, a discredited political system and the pervasive presence of organised crime while mainstream groups like business now distrust the system:

> the mafya are both a cause and effect of the central state's lack of authority ... The mafya is at once a loose collection of criminal entrepreneurs, a dominant force behind the new Russian capitalism and a natural response to the failure of the state to carry out various basic social functions. As a result tax evasion has become widespread, not just because the authorities cannot adequately police the revenue,

but because businesses feel evasion is their right given that they are having to pay separately for services the state should provide. The result is a vicious circle.[22]

However corrupt and inefficient it may be, the state nevertheless has in most countries some sort of national presence, is a provider and allocator of services, resources and functions, and offers an organisational and organising shape that would be impossible to abolish and build from new. Thus the existing state machinery has a crucial role in the drive for democratisation, particularly in relation to the redirecting of its focus and activities towards the people. States, however artificial their genesis and disengaged from the aspirations and realities of most citizens, also have an identity that may sustain 'loyalty and compliance even when the delivery systems fail'.[23] They comprise existing institutions and institutionalised interests that cannot be easily ignored or bypassed:

> external agencies can force reforms on developing-country governments but the outcomes are just as likely to be negative as they might be positive. The bureaucratic organisations of developing countries have grown out of deep roots and have the legacies of pre-colonial, colonial and independence eras embedded within them. They are hybrids but they are distinctive with their own rationalities, operating structures and values. New grafts may be rejected especially when imposed on an unwilling host. Effective reforms must be indigenously owned if they are to be successful.[24]

Working with and through the state to promote a limited, transparent and responsive state, however, is fraught with difficulties, not least because many states in developing countries are not geared up to delivering many of the expectations or are in the hands of those for whom democratisation is not entirely welcome. Even if the state is not in a position to respond fully to democratisation or to provide public administration or services that are efficient and honest, it is just as important that the state is generally *perceived* to be – or has the potential to be – predisposed towards becoming so, thus inspiring a workable degree of trust in the validity and credibility of the democratisation process. The whole point of democratisation is to promote governance and, given that the state is crucial to the success of democratisation, the state *has* to be persuaded to recognise – and institutionalise – its relationship with the public. While the state has the power and the means 'to govern and regulate society', the public has to have those social, civil and political rights 'essential for the regulation of this regulator'.[25] For that to happen, the state has to address at the outset those conditions necessary for those rights to be meaningful by accepting the centrality of its obligation to help the most disadvantaged and to ensure the provision of the basic public goods – food, housing, education, primary health care – that relieve them from the political isolation, insecurity and vulnerability that basic survival engenders. Citizens of developing countries 'may enjoy formal equality, for example, before the law, but for many of them it is rendered virtually meaningless in practice by the absence of satisfactory housing, nutrition and education'.[26] There are, however, a number of constraints to this.

First, for most developing countries the state had a distorted development consequential on its status as creation or dependency of imperial powers. This meant that political boundaries were artificially created, that the economic relationship with the imperial power was often extractive, and that 'the colonial state was an outgrowth not of indigenous civil society but of metropolitan society mixed, however, with executive characteristics not tolerated within the metropolis. In other words, the colonial state was a hybrid: an alien executive instrument of a culturally different political community'.[27] The colonial state, by its nature, focused on issues of 'high politics' – issues which touch 'on the very existence of the state and the ways in which it deals with threats to that existence. Its strategies commonly (though not exclusively) involve the people who occupy elite positions in the state apparatus. Since it is involved with the questions of the state's security and broad organisation, we might think of it as dealing with state security'.[28] Not surprisingly, those areas often considered as 'low politics' – 'more mundane issues such as economic policy, public health, education, routine administration, welfare benefits and environmental protection'[29] – received much less attention and investment.

Second, the ending of colonial rule often included 'elements of the decolonisation process which were designed to ensure that government passed into the hands of conservative interests: firstly, independence constitutions concentrated power in the executive to ensure order; and secondly, hastily organised elections encouraged the development of support through ethnic and regional networks'.[30] The process introduced elite rule through the 'uniting' role of a single dominant party and the use of existing institutionalised means of coercion, suppression and force in order to protect that rule and to eliminate opponents, while the presence of widespread poverty, limited class development, particularly in the absence of a rapidly developing industrial or commercial private sector, and the clear lack of national integration meant the state was the major or only avenue for upward mobility, status, power and wealth.

Third, in such circumstances, post-independence development of the state has reflected the primacy of 'high politics' in the skewed nature of its institutional configuration – clientelist presidencies, powerful armed forces

TABLE 1
INDEPENDENCE AND THE END OF PARTY COMPETITION IN AFRICA

Country	Independence Day	Abandoning a Competitive Party System
Sudan	1956	1958
Ghana	1957	1966
Brit Somaliland	1960	1969
Nigeria	1960	1966
Sierra Leone	1961	1967
Tanzania	1961	1962
Uganda	1962	1969
Kenya	1963	1982
Malawi	1964	1966
Zambia	1964	1973
Lesotho	1966	1986
Swaziland	1968	1973

or police forces, the ceremonial and public building trappings of a nation state – with a focus on elite gain or regime survival rather than broader public needs. The consequences were invariably repressive one-party or, more likely, military control. Of the 34 British colonies and dependencies granted independence between 1954 and 1974, for example, David Sanders reports that 17 (the majority were African states) later abandoned a competitive party system (see Table 1[31]).

Four, there has been the continuing imbalance in government spending in developing countries, which tends to reflect the imbalance between high and low politics, with own-country (rather than donor) funding continuing to go on many of the high politics areas, such as the criminal justice system, defence and the cost of the public sector itself – which is the resource that underpins the exploitation of the state for personal or partisan interests. As Lawrence Cockcroft bluntly notes in relation to Africa, 'at the heart of the moral dilemma in contemporary Africa is the frequent absence of a sense of the public good, a sense of the welfare of society as a whole'.[32] There is no tradition of public service.

> The notion that politicians, bureaucrats or military chiefs should be servants of the state simply does not make sense. Their political obligations are, first and foremost, to their kith and kin, their clients, their communities, their regions, or even to their religion ... The legitimacy of the African political elites, such as it is, derives from their ability to nourish the clientele on which their power rests. It is therefore imperative for them to exploit governmental resources for patrimonial purposes.[33]

Fifth, corruption is often an integral feature of public office – as 'freehold entitlement' rather than rent-seeking – and core evidence of the self-regarding nature of state activity and the inextricable intertwining of public and private interests of those concerned. Up to the end of the 1980s, the study of corruption had largely been a preserve of academics and official inquiries until one report in 1989 from the United Nations stated that,

> as regards the various forms of corruption, it was noted that they range from acceptance of money or other rewards for awarding contracts, violations of procedures to advance personal interests, including kickbacks from development programmes or multinational corporations; pay-offs for legislative support; and the diversion of public resources for private use, to overlooking illegal activities or intervening in the justice process. Forms of corruption also include nepotism, common theft, overpricing, establishing non-existing projects, payroll padding, tax collection and tax assessment frauds. [34]

A year later another warned of its impact: 'corrupt activities of public officials can destroy the potential effectiveness of all types of governmental programmes, hinder development, and victimise individuals and groups'.[35]

Since then, nearly all international donor agencies and a number of donor countries have become increasingly insistent that the levels and pervasiveness of corruption in developing countries was a major constraint to the democratisation agenda and had to be addressed: 'while corruption is manifest in every society, and in democratic as well as authoritarian regimes, systems corruption is a deadly sign that a society can no longer effectively manage its resources for public purposes ... Every resource is privatised – appropriated for private gain at the expense of those members of the public who are supposed to be served by governance'.[36]

The issues are thus concerned with whether the reform or realignment of the state will be achieved in time to facilitate democratisation, whether the changes will exacerbate or constrain corruption. Conversely, will democratisation affect the reform of the state and will it create new types or levels of corruption?

REBUILDING A STATE FIT FOR DEMOCRACY?

How the state may be developed to respond to the expectations of democratisation is relatively uncharted, given that neither history nor centralised authoritarianism were seen as repeatable templates for the future for multinational aid agencies or donor countries. Indeed, Leftwich warns of the obvious divergence of such templates from the recent experiences of the latter:

official theories of good governance eulogise the minimal state, a Weberian-type bureaucracy, rigorous respect for human rights, a rich and diverse civil society, political pluralism and a sharp separation of economic and political life. Uncomfortable as it may be to acknowledge it, the model of the developmental state, on the other hand, whether democratic or not, entails a strong and determined state which protects a powerful and competent bureaucracy that largely shapes and directs development policy, a dubious (and sometimes appalling) civil and human rights record, the suppression and control of civil society and fusion – at least at the top – of the political direction of economic power.[37]

Further, there is no certainty of the efficacy of developed countries' experiences in the developmental context. During the 1980s and into the 1990s they have promoted structural reforms directed at administrative reform, tax reform, organisational change and staff redeployment, decentralisation, deregulation and privatisation. While many of these reforms have followed overall needs assessment – such as an 'efficiency audit' (Ghana 1994–97), a 'management audit' (Malawi) or an 'organisational audit' (Senegal) – state reform predicated on the experiences of the developed countries to reduce the size, cost and roles of the state has, in its enthusiasm for deregulation, decentralisation and disaggregation, moved away from the notion of a public administration. The existence of a distinct public sector may thus be the consequence of a distinct development sequence for developed countries which are moving to a much more limited and mixed provision of public services. Much of the developed countries' public management agenda may have major implications if state strengthening is considered a key prerequisite of democratisation:

> the shrinking of the state sector, without any complementary strengthening of state institutions and skills, turns a bloated weak state into a small weak state, further reducing its capacity to check corruption. Worse, the *combination* of a weak "civil society" and weak state allows small, predatory political machines the more easily to dominate an unorganised electorate ... and take control of the institutions of the state.[38]

Thus reforms should not be predicated on theories of the minimalist state drawn from public choice theory when what may be required is 'an "activist" state which sets prices, is engaged with civil society and intervenes more effectively than in the past to facilitate an improvement in living for the poor'.[39]

Second, the blanket imposition of structural adjustment programmes during the 1980s could not occur 'without destabilising some *status quo*, without decoupling some coalition and building another, without challenging some interest and promoting others',[40] leaving entrenched interests reluctant to embrace state reform and no certainty that the reforms would achieve their stated purpose, given the varied social, economic and political contexts within which they have been implemented. In Latin America, it would be surprising

> to expect serious reform to come from the class which profits from this state of affairs. Presidents may fulminate and Congress may pass laws but unless and until revenue investigators, public prosecutors, and financial regulators are fully professionalised nothing will be done. The fact that the law is so tolerant of abuse and that those agencies responsible for protecting state patrimony are so chronically underpowered and ill-organised is not accidental. It is not a question of what to do (merit, good pay and conditions, punishment for infraction) so much as a matter of political will.[41]

In Africa, the

> development of political machines and the consolidation of clientelistic networks within the formal political apparatus has been immensely advantageous. It has allowed them to respond to the demands for protection, assistance and aid made by the members of their constituency communities in exchange for the recognition of the political prominence and social status which, as patrons, they crave. The instrumentalisation of the prevailing political (dis)order is thus a disincentive to the establishment of a more properly institutionalised state on the Weberian model. Why should African political elites dismantle a political system which serves them so well?[42]

In India, regional, caste and religious politics work through the democratic system to constrain administrative decisions and reforms; in East Asia, administrative reform is hampered by the bureaucracy's previous success in fuelling economic development.

Even where the need for reform is accepted in principle, the pace and nature may be affected by the perceptions of leaders who may have 'a genuine belief that democratisation and either some or all aspects of good government would not serve the country well in its present circumstances, for example because of fears about the consequences for social, economic, or political stability'.[43] Partial or uneven patterns of reform may thus lead to dysfunctional consequences; in

> Latin America, although geographic and constitutional legitimacy of states has in general been more secure than in Africa, the conditions for democratic politics are not well established. While the coercive

capacity of states has become stronger and civil society has grown more robust, regime legitimacy has commonly been low and political polarisation high. Social inequalities are often grotesque and the military has also played a significant political and coercive role in defence of dominant interests.[44]

For many of the entrenched interests, the agenda for reform thus may have inherent risks. One, for example, concerns the opportunity for financial gain where the release of market forces has disaggregated the 'pursuit of collective self-interest' that typified entrenched political interests in some countries. That is, the interests have competed for and secured, as in the case of eastern Europe, economic assets at the expense of their political control, leaving a vacuum which has distorted or delayed the development of the political sphere;[45] privatised state industries, as in Latin America, to secure personal or party gains rather than the more economical and efficient services to the public;[46] or sought, as have state officials in China, to 'convert their power into control over economic assets, transforming political power into economic capital'.[47] Another example concerned the ability of existing elites and vested interests to reconstitute themselves within a democratic context – reflecting 'the element of continuity between old and new regimes in both their social and political complexions'[48] – in order to maintain their hold on power, and they have adversely affected the development of the political competition arena:

> as part of the strategy employed by incumbent regimes to weaken the opposition, public sector patronage was withdrawn from private sector business organisations that were sympathetic to or identified with the opposition. This acted to weaken the financial base of opposition parties and, in so doing, limited their organisational capacity even as incumbents freely availed themselves of state resources to finance their bids for remaining in power.[49]

In perpetuating existing inequalities and denying 'the need for significant, structured political competition', the democratisation process becomes further hijacked by prevailing interests because their control of the forms of democratisation – party, majority party in the legislature and so on – allows them to avoid implementing the other conditions necessary to competition: 'a free flow of information (and thus upon civil liberties and a relatively free press), a lack of pervasive violence in everyday life, a viable civil society, and political will and determination among opposition leaders'.[50] Further, it underlines the potential to negate another key element of democratisation – participation – if both dysfunctional institutional reform and the hijacking of the democratisation process take place at the same time: in the case of Nigeria, for example, the vast majority of the people are not only apathetic to and alienated from the state, but have also been brutalised by its enormous coercive and extractive capacities. This alienation of the people, particularly in the rural areas, has been extended to the democratisation and development processes that have from time to time been introduced in Nigeria. The creation of a large number of new local governments since 1986, and a series of local government reforms undertaken since 1976, have failed to resolve the problem of popular alienation from politics and development.[51]

INTRODUCING THE PEOPLE TO DEMOCRACY

Proponents of democratisation have a clear consensus about what democratisation is for and the context necessary to achieve its purpose, including: a 'secure and broad-based consensus about the rules of the political game'; 'governmental restraint on the extent of policy change undertaken by the winning party or parties' with an emphasis on a 'consensual, conservative and incrementalist' approach; a rich and pluralistic civil society that acts as a brake on the state but also underlines the capabilities for 'democratic self-management'; the absence of a serious threat to the state from, for example, private armies; the absence of significant regional and ethnic tensions.[52] They also have a clear view of embedding the process:

> deep and widespread legitimation at the elite and mass levels, and the behavioural consensus on the rules and constraints of democracy, that denote democratic consolidation ... deepening democratic structures to make them more liberal, accessible, accountable, and representative; strengthening the formal institutions of democracy, including parties, legislatures, and the judicial system; and improving regime performance, both economically and politically (by maintaining order, safeguarding liberty, and combating corruption).[53]

The way there – the move from form to practice, the linear nature of the democratisation process as well as the sequencing and complementarity of reform – is less clear. Gordon White makes an important point about this in terms of the political arena – where the 'range of institutions and actors ... mediate and channel the relationships between civil society and the state' – when he says that the 'two crucial elements of political society are political parties and political leaders, both of which can act to strengthen or weaken the democratic or authoritarian potential of a given configuration of civil society'.[54] If the state is to be persuaded to refocus on the people, and if the forms of democracy are not to be hijacked by existing elites, then the political society must have an aggregated and articulated civil society as constituency and resource, both to balance the power currently residing with the state and entrenched interests, and to provide leaders, party members and issues for the political arena.

One crucial step towards the democratisation process, if its purpose is to be achieved, is thus to ensure that the state and the existing elites – who have the power and the motivation to interfere with the process of democratisation – accept what democratisation is all about:

> the assumption that political power is crucial and potentially repressive in its own right has led to the further assumption that democracy is worth promoting because it serves as the most effective restraint on such power. In this context, it is a widely shared assumption that elections and the consequent threat of replacement as well as the codes of ethics or "rules of the game" which elites in a democracy must be seen to adhere to in order to gain and maintain power ... are crucial in restraining power and power struggles ... It has less frequently been pointed out, however, that the democratic rules are fragile, that they are easily circumvented when interests are at stake, and that they are not always clear-cut and definitive.[55]

A second is to ensure that they accept that the process begins, rather than ends, with electoral participation to avoid a situation in which:

> political elites cannot or will not respect the rule of law, encourage institutions of civil society or act accountably – democracy cannot be completed, even if free elections are held. Such a regime is called a broken-backed democracy, because it is incapable of dealing with the burdens and responsibilities that it faces ... In a broken-backed democracy, free competitive elections continue, and they do make a difference. But constant use of Schumpeter's democratic right to throw the rascals out does not produce good government; it only ensures the "circulation of rascals".[56]

Third, there is the need to ensure that institutional mechanisms for accountability and scrutiny are firmly in place to monitor the process, from the vote through to the performance of the victors. Thus, electoral monitoring is an important tool since it not only targets electoral fraud, but also provides a basis to incorporate citizen participation and can offer a platform from which to address general anti-corruption concerns such as political violence, party corruption or money politics. However, not only is it important to determine whether that monitoring is provided externally or internally, but also whether too much attention may be devoted to the polling day itself rather than the run-up to the election, its aftermath or the general context of the political process: 'in many cases the mechanical aspect of the voting is reasonably fair but the pre-election period is plagued by numerous problems', including voter registration, preparation of voter lists, campaign financing, adjudication of complaints, media bias, government use of resources and so on.[57] Equally importantly, the scrutinised party also becomes the scrutinised government: accountability requires that governors are continuously under pressure to justify their actions in parliament, in the media and to the public. Without accountability, 'electoralism' flourishes:

> the election winner regards victory as giving a free hand to pluck fruits of office to his or her taste. Instead of being responsive to institutions of civil society, the government can claim that popular endorsement justifies doing anything that it wants, not only in terms of public policy but also in the private enrichment of themselves and their supporters. as long as free and fair elections continue, the electorate can periodically reject a klepocratic government. Yet Latin America illustrates that the replacement of one set of politicians by another need not heal the faults of a broken-backed democracy'.[58]

All such steps have to inform and be informed by those on whose behalf they are acting, however. The purpose of democratisation includes bringing the public into the political arena in ways and numbers which make it meaningful and which aggregate that participation as an effective counterbalance to the state, protect it from capture by the party political process or by political elites and, even if the majority are not continually involved in active political activity, give it an independent strength that demands recognition, reciprocity and consultation. Here the issue is two-fold; first, it requires that information, and access to information, is widespread, and secondly, but more importantly, providing ownership over those issues or activities which affect their daily lives, to remove arbitrary and unilateral exercise of state power and encourage a negotiated or consultative relationship. This may be assisted through autonomous newspapers or radio stations, or with service delivery surveys, which combine 'social and economic data with information on the experience, expectations and perceptions of citizens about service delivery'. It can involve citizens in specific activities, such as town planning in eastern Europe or food distribution projects in Africa, where it was noted that 'if citizens involved in (participatory) programmes are provided information and training regarding their roles as participants, many failures might be avoided'.[59] It can be developed through a self-balancing dynamic with locally appointed staff and effective scrutiny communities, with the role of the state to raise 'the communities' hopes about what to expect from the government, and then educate them precisely about what workers, supervisors, and mayors should be doing'.[60] It is interesting that in his article on canal irrigation in South India Wade sets out two proposals to deal with demands for bribes by officials that take this perspective. Firstly he suggests strengthening

> the user side of the irrigator-official relation, both by the familiar device of a user organisation ... *and* by monitoring of the performance of each canal system by an independent monitoring organisation whose reports would be made public ... Opportunities for the exercise of "voice", if coupled with a non-partisan source of information, could be much more effective in curbing the arbitrary exercise of authority.[61]

He also goes on to suggest a technical means of 'designing-out' the potential for corruption by opening up availability of, and access to, water at crucial times with more storage reservoirs, 'filled according to a pre-determined, well-advertised schedule, and irrigators would themselves have more responsibility for allocating the water to the fields'.[62] A similar approach has been tested by Mazdoor Kisan Shakti Sangathan (MKSS), a people's movement in Rajasthan, which regularly calls village elites to account for their behaviour, especially in relation to funds allocated for village projects. A significant gain for the MKSS was to persuade the Government of Rajasthan to recognise the people's legal right of access to official documents at the panchayat (village) level.[63]

Developing social capital – the civil society – has, however, to be as systematic and planned as any institutional reform programme. It is as prone as any part of the democratisation process to be hijacked. In a country like Nigeria there is a thriving level of local civil society,[64] albeit lacking in resources and often working outside formal structures, but promoting them as part of the democratisation process may force to the fore sectional rather than national or public interest perspectives: 'minority spokespersons ... believed that the national question could only be resolved with justice through the creation of largely autonomous ethnic states, and a restructuring of the revenue allocation system to reverse the unacceptable situation where those whose areas provided the bulk of national revenue but were politically marginalised and the least developed.'[65] One of the

> primary consequences of "democratisation" in Thailand and the Philippines since the 1980s has been the re-flowering of "bossism" in numerous localities in these two countries. The common manifestations of bossism in Thailand and the Philippines – the electoral and economic entrenchment of powerbrokers with virtually

monopolistic control over entire localities – reflect a decisive change ... bossism in contemporary Thailand and the Philippines reflects the *decentring* of "rent-seeking opportunities away from the national capital and the central state apparatus and towards province, district, and town".[66]

Reform therefore has to be targeted at the means for institutionalising participation within the political arena – developing 'integrative institutions ... able to group together disparate or conflictual elements of civil society into broad and stable political coalitions'[67] and identifying the change agents by shifting support away 'from the inconclusive promotion of civil society and social capital to the specific support of genuine actors in real processes of democratisation'.[68] This is because community and other grass-roots groups require the technical and *political* skills to grow in what may be a competitive and potentially hostile environment. As Schonwalder argues in the local context in Latin America, by developing 'fairly sophisticated negotiation skills' groups may be able to consolidate

> to the point at which they can handle such pressures and even take advantage of the potentially conflicting interests of their various allies. For instance, some urban popular movements in El Agustino, a low-income neighbourhood of the Peruvian capital, Lima, have demonstrated an astonishing ability to develop coalitions with like-minded movements, and they have proved quite adept at defending their interests in their dealings with local government, political parties, and NGOs.[69]

CONCLUSION

Above all, however, it must be argued that here, as elsewhere,

> social capital, in so far as it refers to social networks and habits of association in civil society, is not sufficient on its own to determine the prospects of a democratic decentralisation reform, even in the most promising environment. A culture of accountability springs up from an interaction between civil society and appropriate institutions, which generally have to be created by a strong central political force.[70]

Manor and Crook conclude that, 'even at the local level, our research did reveal that, where people at the grassroots were offered the opportunity to participate in decentralised institutions they did so on the whole with enthusiasm and felt (on the evidence of our surveys) that the experiments were valuable and worth continuing. Governments would be wise not to ignore or disappoint these kinds of popular expectations'.[71]

For this to be achieved, there has to be a sequenced and co-ordinated approach to reform, not simply between donors, but also between different projects, and across different sectors, in terms of how far they support or threaten the process of democratisation. All this requires the underlying commitment and engagement both of donors and of existing political and administrative elites. The donor community, for example, may promote the role of NGOs in recognition 'of the constraints on resource distribution, given their own limited capacity for direct distribution and their increasing disappointment with weak and corrupt state bureaucracies and programs'.[72] Developing countries' governments may accept the demands of structural reform, such as decentralisation which may bring the state closer to the people, but 'a programme of decentralisation and power-sharing which is not preceded by a systematic effort at democratising power by disciplining it to the popular prescriptions specified by the populace could easily amount to an exercise in nullity'.[73] The

> bottom-up approach obviously relies on supportive measures by government authorities ... better access of marginalised groups to the formal economic and legal system requires a change in political and bureaucratic attitudes by definition. Hence, the bottom-up approach does not provide an alternative to top-down attempts at greater participation and better governance. Rather, both approaches may supplement each other in countries revealing at least a minimum of domestic reform-mindedness.[74]

The process of democratisation is complex, lengthy and risky; it requires sequence, focus, co-ordination and long-term support, but democratisation is a goal that both developed and developing countries must continue to pursue, for themselves and for each other. It is, as Georges Nzongola-Ntalaja concludes:

> the ultimate prize won by a determined people who are committed to improving their lives economically and socially. Democracy is above all a moral imperative for any people who care about their dignity as human beings ... it is a political practice that empowers people to rise up against a decadent or oppressive political order to replace it with one likely to improve their material conditions of life and ensure a better future for their children.[75]

NOTES

1. R. Sandbrook and J. Oelbaum, 'Reforming Dysfunctional Institutions through Democratisation? Reflections on Ghana', *Journal of Modern African Studies*, 35, 4 (1997), 608.
2. A bibliography published by USAID in June 1996 on democracy in Africa noted that nearly 40 articles and 14 books had been published on the topic since 1994.
3. D. Held, *Democracy and the Global Order* (Cambridge: Polity, 1995), 36.
4. F.W. Bealey, *Democracy in the Contemporary State* (Oxford: Clarendon Press, 1988), 6.
5. O. Tornquist, *Politics and Development* (London: Sage, 1999), 98.
6. K.F. Dyson, *The State Tradition in Western Europe* (Oxford: Martin Robertson, 1980), 208, 275.
7. Bealey, *Democracy*, 1.
8. M. Burch and B. Wood, *Public Policy in Britain* (Oxford: Blackwell, 1995), 34.
9. G. White, 'Civil Society, Democratisation and Development', in R. Luckham and G. White, *Democratisation in the South* (Manchester: Manchester University Press, 1996), 184.
10. Held, *Democracy*, 207.
11. I. Serageldon and P. Landell-Mills, 'Governance and the External Factor', *Annual Conference on Development Economics, World Bank, Washington DC* (1991), 4.
12. World Bank, *Managing Development: The Governance Dimension* (Washington, DC: World Bank, 1991), 5–6.
13. F.F. Ridley (ed.), *Policies and Politics in Western Europe* (London: Croom Helm, 1984), 8.
14. 1 I am indebted to Robin Theobald for furthering the themes on development.
15. See T.H. Marshall, *Class, Citizenship and Social Development* (Westport, CT: Greenwood Press, 1973).
16. Held, *Democracy*, 82.
17. See, for example, J. Moran, 'Corruption and NIC Development: A Case Study of South Korea', *Crime, Law and Social Change*, 29, 2–3 (1998), 161–77.
18. A. Leftwich, 'Governance, the State and the Politics of Development', *Development and Change*, 25, 2 (1994), 377.
19. Ibid., 378–80 (emphasis original).
20. G. Nzongola-Ntalaja, 'The State and Democracy in Africa', in G. Nzongola-Ntalaja and M.C. Lee (eds.), *The State and Democracy in Africa* (Trenton, NJ/Asmara, Eritrea: Africa World Press, Inc, 1997), 19.
21. M. Glasman, 'The Great Deformation: Polyani, Poland and the Terrors of Planned Spontaneity', in C.G.A. Bryant and E. Mokrzycki (eds.), *The New Great Transformation? Change and Continuity in East-Central Europe* (London: Routledge, 1994), 212.
22. M. Galeotti, 'The Mafya and the New Russia', *Australian Journal of Politics and History*, 44, 3 (1998), 421.
23. J.S. Migdal, 'Why Do So Many States Stay Intact?', in P. Dauvergne (ed.), *Weak and Strong States in Asia-Pacific States* (Australia: Allen and Unwin, 1998), 36.
24. M. Turner and D. Hulme, *Governance, Administration and Development* (London: Macmillan, 1997), 241.
25. Held, *Democracy*, 173–4.
26. Ibid., 214.
27. A.D. Smith, *National Identity* (Harmondsworth: Penguin, 1991), 107.
28. J. Painter, *Politics, Geography and 'Political Geography'* (London: Arnold, 1995), 37.
29. Ibid., 37.
30. M. Szeftel, 'Misunderstanding African Politics: Corruption and the Governance Agenda', *Review of African Political Economy*, 76 (1998), 236.
31. Drawn from D. Sanders, *Losing an Empire, Finding a Role* (Basingstoke: Macmillan, 1990), 107.
32. L. Cockcroft, *Africa's Way* (London: I.B. Taurus, 1990), 95.
33. P. Chabal and J.-P. Daloz, *Africa Works: Disorder as Political Instrument* (Trenton, NJ/Asmara, Eritrea: International African Institute/James Currey/Indiana University Press, 1999), 15.

34. 'Corruption in Government', Report of an Interregional Seminar, United Nations Department of Technical Cooperation for Development and Centre for Social Development and Humanitarian Affairs, 1989, 17.
35. 'Crime Prevention and Criminal Justice in the Context of Development: Realities and Perspectives of International Cooperation; Practical Measures Against Corruption', 8th United Nations Congress on the Prevention of Crime and the Treatment of Offenders, Cuba, 1990, 4.
36. See National Research Council, 'Assessing Progress Toward Democracy'; Summary Report of a Workshop: Panel on Issues in Democratisation, National Academy Press (US), 1991, 7.
37. Leftwich, 'Governance, the State and the Politics of Development', 381–2.
38. Szeftel, 'Misunderstanding African Politics', 233, 235.
39. Turner and Hulme, *Governance, Administration and Development*, 184.
40. A. Leftwich, 'Governance, Democracy and Development in the Third World', *Third World Quarterly*, 14, 3 (1993), 607.
41. W. Little, 'Political Corruption in Latin America', *Corruption and Reform*, 7, 1 (1992), 64.
42. Chabal and Daloz, *Africa Works*, 14.
43. P. Burnell, 'Good Government and Democratisation: A Sideways Look at Aid and Political Conditionality', *Democratization*, 1, 3 (1994), 486.
44. Leftwich, 'Governance, Democracy and Development', 618.
45. See Q. Reed, 'Transition, Dysfunctionality and Change in the Czech and Slovak Republics', *Crime, Law and Social Change*, 22, 4 (1994/95), 332–3.
46. R.P. Saba and L. Manzetti, 'Privatisation in Argentina: The Implications for Corruption', *Crime, Law and Social Change*, 25, 4 (1996/97), pp.353–69.
47. G. White, 'Corruption and Market Reform in China', in B. Harriss-White and G. White (eds.), *Liberalisation and the New Corruption* (IDS Bulletin, 27, 2, 1996), 45.
48. J.-F. Bayart, S. Ellis and B. Hbou, *The Criminalisation of the State in Africa* (Oxford/Bloomington, IN/Indianapolis, IN: International African Institute/James Currey/Indiana University Press, 1997), 5.
49. A.O. Olukoshi, *The Politics of Opposition in Contemporary Africa* (Uppsala: Nordiska Afrikainstitutet, 1998), 29.
50. M. Johnston, '"Frontier Corruption": Points of Vulnerability and Challenges for Reform', UNDP-PACT and OECD Development Centre Workshop on Corruption and Integrity Improvement Initiatives in the Context of Developing Countries (Paris, 1997), 14.
51. A. Adedeji, 'Looking Back to the Journey Forward: Renewal from the Roots?', in A. Adedeji and O. Otite (eds.), *Nigeria: Renewal from the Roots?* (London/New Jersey: Zed, 1997), 196.
52. Leftwich, 'Governance, Democracy and Development', 615–17.
53. L. Diamond, 'Consolidating Democracy in the Americas', *Annals of the American Association of Political Science*, 550 (1997), 12.
54. G. White, 'Civil Society, Democratisation and Development', in R. Luckham and G. White, *Democratisation in the South* (Manchester: Manchester University Press, 1996), 184.
55. E. Etzioni-Halevy, *Bureaucracy and Democracy* (London: Routledge and Kegan Paul, 1983), 226.
56. R. Rose, W. Mishler and C. Haerpfer, *Democracy and its Alternatives* (Cambridge: Polity Press, 1998), 218, 220.
57. T. Carothers, 'The Rise of Election Monitoring: The Observers Observed', *Journal of Democracy*, 8, 3 (1997), 22.
58. Rose *et al.*, *Democracy*, 220–21.
59. N.A. Braithwaite and W.A. Hodge, 'Citizen Participation in Food Aid Planning and Implementation: A Successful Strategy in Ghana', *Community Development Journal*, 22 (1987), 46–51.
60. J. Tendler and S. Freedheim, 'Trust in a Rent-Seeking World: Health and Government Transformed in Northeast Brazil', *World Development*, 22, 12 (1994), 1784.
61. R. Wade, 'The System of Administrative and Political Corruption: Canal Irrigation in South India', *Journal of Development Studies*, 18, 3 (1984), 321.
62. Ibid.
63. Transparency International, *Newsletter* (Sept. 1998).

64. See Adedeji and Otite, *Nigeria*.
65. E.E. Osaghae, *Crippled Giant: Nigeria since Independence* (London: Hurst, 1998), 247.
66. J.T. Sidel, 'Siam and Its Twin?', in Harriss-White and White (eds.), *Liberalisation and the New Corruption*, 57, 63 (emphasis original).
67. White, 'Civil Society, Democratisation and Development', 184.
68. Tornquist, *Politics and Development*, 168.
69. G. Schonwalder, 'Participation in Latin American Local Government', *Development and Change*, 28, 4 (1997), 768.
70. R.C. Crook and J. Manor, *Democracy and Deecntralisation in South Asia and West Africa* (Cambridge: Cambridge University Press, 1998), 304.
71. Ibid., 304.
72. S. Feldman, 'NGOs and Civil Society: (Un)stated Contradictions', *Annals of the American Association of Political Science*, 554 (1997), 59.
73. Olukoshi, *Politics of Opposition*, 34.
74. P. Nunnenkamp, 'What Donors Mean By Good Governance', in M. Robinson (ed.), *Towards Democratic Governance* (IDS Bulletin, 26, 2, 1995), 15.
75. G. Nzongola-Ntalaja, 'The State and Democracy in Africa', in G. Nzongola-Ntalaja and M.C. Lee (eds.), *The State and Democracy in Africa* (Trenton, NJ/Asmara, Eritrea: Africa World Press, Inc, 1997), 22.

Democratisation or the Democratisation of Corruption? The Case of Uganda

DAVID WATT, RACHEL FLANARY AND ROBIN THEOBALD

THE PAST AS A PROPHET OF THE FUTURE?

A World Bank Mission to Uganda in November 1998 concluded that Uganda was experiencing 'significant corruption' at a level which was constraining economic growth and poverty alleviation. The mission identified a range of systemic problems in the government's revenue and expenditure management, public procurement systems, the civil service reform programme, the deregulation of the economy and the privatisation and reform of state enterprises. Its findings included the estimate of Uganda's Auditor General that between ten and 20 per cent of public funds are being misused or diverted from their intended use.[1] The Mission's report was presented to the Consultative Group meeting of donors in December 1998, when it was held for the first time in Uganda's capital Kampala. Donors expressed their collective unease, which was received and reciprocated by President Museveni prior to the pledging of $750m aid for the following year.

Four years previously a joint mission from the World Bank's Economic Development Institute and Transparency International visited Uganda to evaluate the success of the government in curbing corruption. The mission 'expressed serious concern about the pervasiveness of corruption' and concluded that the scope and scale of corruption in Uganda was influenced by a range of factors rooted in the country's troubled past including: very low levels of public service pay; lax enforcement of auditing requirements within the government and parastatal sector; an under-resourced and under-developed judicial system; the inability to monitor assets and income of political leaders and senior public servants.[2]

David Watt, LIPAM, University of Liverpool; Rachel Flanary, Liverpool Business School, Liverpool John Moores University; Robin Theobald, Westminster Business School, University of Westminster

FROM COLONY TO INDEPENDENCE

Any examination of the current causes and effects of corruption in Uganda must be placed within the context of the country's cultural and political development to understand both the nature of the country's development and the origins of a number of current issues. Uganda is a fertile and diverse country with a complex history based around indigenous kingdoms, which have existed since the fourteenth century. Although Uganda experienced intrusion from a number of outsider groups, including Protestant missionaries from Britain in 1877 and Catholic missionaries from France in 1879, it was only when Frederick Lugard entered Buganda in 1890 that British imperialism ushered in significant changes. Buganda and the neighbouring kingdoms of Toro, Ankole and Bunyoro were brought under British control, leading to the creation of the state of Uganda in 1900. The imposition of colonial dominance inaugurated Lugard's characteristic system of indirect rule under which native chiefs were used as mediators between the resident authorities and the indigenous population.

As was the case elsewhere – most notably in Northern Nigeria – this system served to reinforce the separation of the various ethnic groups as well as exacerbate the inequalities between them. Such tendencies were particularly evident in the British propensity to favour the southern Baganda who were disproportionately recruited into the civil service and whose chiefs benefited from lucrative land grants. Northern ethnic groups – especially Lango and Achole – by contrast, in the absence of alternatives, tended to gravitate towards the army. Overall, in creating stark regional disparities, colonial practice laid the foundations for the serious north/south divide that continues to threaten stability in Uganda today.

Despite these recurrent problems, the economic situation at independence in 1962 was reasonably strong, with an annual real GNP growth rate of six per cent,[3] and the future outlook was promising. This was helped by the existence of legislative and parliamentary institutions and sound electoral procedures. Furthermore, the country displayed a relatively high level of accountability at the centre, which was aided in part by a lively and free press and an efficient civil service. This facilitated a relatively painless transition in 1962, when the Kabaka (King) of Buganda became president, with Milton Obote of the Uganda People's Congress (UPC) as Prime Minister. The alliance between the UPC and Kabaka Yekka was an attempt to sideline the Democratic Party (DP) and capture the majority of votes in the pre-independence elections. It was regarded as an 'unholy alliance' given the inherent ethnic and ideological contradictions between the two parties. Soon after independence Uganda started to experience difficulties caused primarily by ethnic tensions. The attempt at federalism came to an abrupt end in 1966, when Obote abolished Buganda and the other kingdoms and forced the Kabaka into exile. Obote proceeded to lead the country under the rubric of unitary presidential rule and tentatively held power with the aid of a fragile coalition government and a weak support base. Having dismantled all the traditional bases of authority, undermined the authority of the chiefs and abolished the local government system inherited at independence, Obote had achieved his aim of creating a centralised system which reduced independent organisation and limited pluralist activities. Such actions failed to take into account the various ethnic and regional fissures in Ugandan society, and Obote's rule ended in 1971 with a *coup d'état* led by Idi Amin, a senior army officer from the north.

Amin's take-over was initially celebrated by the population and the international community. This soon gave way to concern as Amin proved himself to be even more brutal and repressive than the previous regime. As with Obote, Amin failed to foster a significant political base, which would allow for consensual rule. He therefore relied heavily on force in order to secure compliance and proceeded to suspend all political activity and most civil rights. The National Assembly was effectively dissolved and Amin ruled Uganda by capricious decree. In addition to the political turmoil created by Amin's actions, he also succeeded in bringing the economy to a situation of almost total collapse. In 1972, Amin waged an 'economic war' and expelled Uganda's Asian community of around 80,000 in order to 'Africanise' the private sector. Given that the Asians provided the mainstay of Uganda's industry and business, this drastically undermined the economic base of the country through the sudden loss of technical skills and enterprise. A quickly deteriorating economic situation soon led to poverty, shortages and increased levels of corruption. Furthermore, the government became increasingly arbitrary in its use of force, with widespread killings becoming the norm.

Following an ill-conceived attack on Tanzania in 1979, Amin's regime was overthrown by the combined forces of the Tanzanian regular army fighting alongside 26 anti-Amin groups 'united' in the Ugandan National Liberation Front (UNLF). After a series of transitional governments, Obote came to power for a second time as a result of elections, which were widely believed to have been rigged. Significantly, it was at this point that seasoned guerrilla fighter and former Minister of Defence, Yoweri Kaguta Museveni, took to the bush with 27 supporters, forming the nucleus of the National Resistance Army (NRA). High hopes that the overthrow of Amin in 1979 would bring the trials of the long-suffering Ugandans to an end proved unfounded. Obote inherited a shattered economy that had shrunk by 20 per cent since independence onto which was clamped a bloated and corrupt administration. In the belief that anything had to be better than Amin, Western donors ignored the appalling human rights abuses perpetrated by out of-control northern soldiers. It will never be known precisely how many Ugandans perished under Obote's regime, but it is now generally accepted to have exceeded those slaughtered under Amin. Overall, in the 'living hell' that was Uganda during the 1970s and 1980s, probably one and a half million people were murdered with a similar number imprisoned, tortured or forced into exile.[4]

MUSEVENI AND THE NRA IN POWER

In the wake of this avalanche of violence, a guerrilla army that did not loot or rape, whose soldiers would be severely disciplined if not executed for such offences, was virtually certain to win the support of the Ugandan peasantry. Thus the NRA seized power in January 1986 with the capture of Kampala, followed by the installation of the NRA leader Yoweri Museveni as President and the formation of a National Resistance Council, an administration made up of civilian and military representatives. Having succeeded in attaining power, Museveni and his National Resistance Movement (NRM – the NRA's metamorphosis into a peacetime organisation) faced two major challenges. Firstly, control of the national government needed to be established across the country, particularly in the north and north-east. Secondly, the Ugandan economy had to be revived and people brought back into the formal economy.

One major challenge facing the NRA was to try and overcome the zero-sum character of political competition. The pattern of behaviour since independence lay in the recognition of the ephemeral nature of political power, which turned the plunder of the state into the quickest and most rational means of acquiring wealth. The overall effect of this was an emergence of uncertainty in the political system, a loss of commitment to the common good and a general decline in the level of public behaviour. The need to change this environment and foster a legitimate political system, which operated for the good of the population, provided a significant challenge to the NRA.

At an early stage of his war from the bush Museveni had welded the NRA's philosophy into a Ten-Point Programme which was to form the basis of the government's manifesto. It contended that, post-independence, Uganda's political rulers who had promoted individual ethnic and religious interests rather than the country's genuine development had then compounded the economic distortions created by British colonial rule. Its proposed solutions constituted a radical political and economic strategy based upon the creation of a complete democratic infrastructure from village level upwards;

the restoration of individual and community security via these local democratic structures, supported by an army and police under political control and maintained by uncorrupted political leaders and public servants; the removal of ethnic factionalism and the consolidation of national identity; the provision of basic social services; and, most importantly, the building of an independent and sustainable national economy.[5]

The elimination of corruption and the abuse of power was specified as a discrete objective within the programme, but it also represented a pre-condition for all the other elements of the programme in order to increase actual tax and customs revenue, reduce the losses associated with procurement, remove constraints on business development create the revenues necessary for the provision of public services and ensure that available services reached their intended recipients, thus alleviating social inequality and poverty.

Thus, after over two decades of civil strife and economic decline, the NRM embarked on a reform programme to construct a democratic political system, restore the rule of law and respect for human rights and rebuild the social infrastructure and the economy. This has involved constitutional change, the reorganisation of public services, the privatisation of state enterprises, the decentralisation of power and putting in place institutions to combat corruption.

INSTRUMENTS OF CHANGE

The British government's Department for International Development (DFID), when defining programme initiatives and objectives, makes the distinction between 'direct instruments' and 'indirect instruments'. Direct instruments being those policies and initiatives designed to impact immediately on corruption – for example, anti-corruption strategies and campaigns, establishing or strengthening anti-corruption agencies, improving judicial processes and so on – while indirect instruments are those policies and activities that impact less directly and less immediately on corruption – including political and economic development, administrative and regulatory changes, electoral reform and improving the role and status of parliamentary and civil society monitoring of the executive.[6] Using these two general distinctions, this article seeks to evaluate the direct and indirect instruments of the NRM's reform programme in relation to its efficacy in fighting corruption and also to use the scope and scale of corruption in Uganda as a yardstick for measuring the impact of the democratisation programme.

The NRM was unequivocal in its stated aim to combat the problem of corruption, viewing it as an evil inheritance from colonialism and from post-independence regimes. Museveni's oft-repeated message was that continuing corruption was a constant threat to Uganda's political and economic stability and a constraint on the establishment of a full democracy. The indirect instruments used in Uganda have included constitutional reform; the restoration of an active parliamentary culture; the restoration of a parliamentary Public Accounts Committee; the reactivation of government audit; the strengthening of the role of the Director of Public Prosecutions; the reorganisation of the public services; the decentralisation of decision making and service delivery and the implementation of a radical privatisation programme. The Ugandan government has introduced a range of direct instruments to combat corruption, including the establishment of an anti-corruption agency, the strengthening of the legislative framework including wealth declaration legislation, the creation of a Human Rights Commission and the development of a National Fraud Squad in the Ugandan Police Force and, arguably most significantly, the creation of a government Department of Ethics and Integrity.

DRAFTING A NEW CONSTITUTION

The early years of NRM rule were dominated by the need to consolidate its control of the country, which meant dealing with armed dissidents, particularly in the north and north-east. By 1989, however, Museveni was ready to address the issue of the type of political system that could embody 'popular democracy' without the multi-party systems that he ardently believed had brought so much misery in the past. Accordingly, he authorised the setting up of a Constitutional Commission, chaired by a Supreme Court Judge, whose task was to embark upon an extensive, country-wide consultation process to seek views from every parish on the political arrangements they would like to see established. The Commission was to report back after two years. However, such was the scale of the task, the sheer volume of submissions, petitions and the like, that the process went on for four years. The draft constitution that finally emerged was then debated by a specially elected Constituent Assembly. The debates were protracted and covered a range of issues. But two of the most significant decisions taken related to what for many had been the locus of acute political instability in the past: a multi-party system and a federal structure. The multi-party system was voted out by 199 to 68 and federalism rejected without a vote. The decision to reject parties led opponents of the movement system to charge Museveni with using the whole elaborate process of consultation to provide a cloak of legitimacy for the system he had long been fixed upon. Monarchists, who would have supported a federalist structure, were somewhat appeased by the Assembly's decision to accord legitimacy to the 'parliament' of the Kingdom of Buganda for the first time since it was abolished by Obote in 1966. In an astute move – not insignificantly on the eve of the elections for the Constituent Assembly – Museveni had restored Uganda's monarchies in 1993, albeit without giving them a formal political role.

Having established appropriate constitutional frameworks, Museveni moved to consolidate his legitimacy in 1996 by holding a presidential election in which other candidates could stand, but only on a no-party basis. Despite this proscription, the election was to a significant degree determined by past party affiliations. This was because Museveni's principal opponent, former cabinet minister and leader of the Democratic Party, Paul Ssemogerere, not only forged an injudicious alliance with the UPC but stated that, if elected, he would not prevent Obote's return from exile. For obvious reasons Ssemogerere's links with Obote and the UPC lost him much support, particularly in his native south, where Museveni polled twice as many votes. Only in the north, where the NRA had been conducting counter-insurgency operations against the Lord's Resistance Army and other dissident groups, did Museveni lose significantly. Overall, in an election that was generally judged to be free and fair and with a high turnout, Museveni secured 72.45 per cent of the vote to Ssemogerere's 24 per cent. Such a result was held to confer a high degree of legitimacy on Museveni and the NRM not only within Uganda but also in the eyes of the international community, especially donors who had partly funded the election and who seemed untroubled by the ban on political parties.

It has been suggested that this apparent vote of confidence in Museveni partly explains the low turnout – 50 per cent overall and only 30 per cent in Kampala – in the June parliamentary elections which followed: the bulk of Ugandans had registered their support for the regime, why turn out to repeat the exercise?[7] Other factors might explain the low rates of participation: the complicated nature of the electoral process, with separate elections for certain special interest groups such as women, youth, the army and the disabled, who were each guaranteed a certain number of seats (62 in total). The more informed of Uganda's citizens might have decided that since the Electoral Commission which presided over the process was dominated by NRM supporters, the result was a foregone conclusion. Whether victory for the NRM was indeed ever inevitable, it was made much more likely by the injudicious decision of opposition 'parties' to boycott the elections. As Oliver Furley has pointed out, this left the field clear for NRM candidates, who were not short of funds, and who could 'treat and bribe the voters'. Furley quotes Professor George Kanyeihamba, at the time senior adviser to the President and now Judge of the Supreme Court, that the election was 'undemocratic and corrupt'. Under the circumstances, it is not surprising that 'opposition' candidates, in the sense of those known to be 'anti-movement', secured only five of the 276 seats in the House.[8]

REFORMING THE PUBLIC SERVICE

The NRM government was fully aware from the outset that the future economic success, internal political stability and external political acceptability of Uganda would be dependent upon the creation of new political institutions administered by officials motivated by a public service ethos rather than personal greed. The main concern was to foster an environment that would improve democratic accountability and service delivery. The civil strife and economic deterioration that characterised Uganda in the 1970s and early 1980s had undoubtedly taken their toll on the Ugandan public service,[9] as on many other national institutions, with provision of public services virtually non-existent and rife with corruption. Reform of the public service was also closely linked to donor recommendations and structural adjustment.[10] The government recognised that in order to carry out its objectives of macroeconomic stability and democratisation, it was important to build a public service that was capable of meeting these challenges.

It was against this backdrop that the Ugandan government developed a Public Service Reform Programme (PSRP) which was designed to develop a service which could operate as a facilitator rather than a bureaucratic hindrance.[11] The first step towards reform involved a thorough diagnosis of the problem, which was undertaken by the Public Service Review and Reorganisation Commission set up in 1989. The Commission blamed a poorly performing and inefficient service on a number of key problems, including inadequate pay and benefits, dysfunctional organisation and inadequate personnel management and training.[12] The Commission's recommendations were subsequently accepted by government and endorsed by the National Resistance Council.[13]

These recommendations formed the basis of the PSRP, which began in 1992. The principal elements of this reform programme included: reduction and reorganisation of the public service; clearer demarcation of staff roles and responsibilities; pay improvements and the introduction of a performance management system. The main objective of the PSRP was to create a service that would be smaller, well remunerated, and therefore more efficient, effective and accountable in its actions. The longer term aim was to establish an organisational culture that would support and enhance efficient operation, which was based on the belief that 'the public service will not change until the people within it change first'. This was to be achieved by instituting a 'value system which enhances effective and prompt service delivery and moral integrity'.[14]

Considerable progress has been made, particularly in terms of staff numbers and wage levels. Retrenchment has meant that the public service staff establishment has been reduced from over 320,000 in 1990 to less than 134,000 in 1997. This has been achieved mainly through the computerisation of the payroll system that has made possible the removal of large numbers of 'ghost' workers. Pay levels have also been significantly increased, with a primary teacher's pay increasing by 930 per cent, a nurse's by 1,175 per cent, a policeman's by 1,004 per cent, and a permanent secretary's by 42,464 per cent over a four-year period from 1993 to 1997. However, despite these gains, the programme seemed to lose momentum in the mid-1990s. In order to re-invigorate the process the Ministry of Public Service has drawn up a new strategy for the period 1997–2002 (PS2002), which has attracted significant support from a number of donor agencies, including UNDP, DFID and IDA. PS2002 aims to deepen the reform process by focusing on 'results oriented management', with the linking of pay to performance and improving budgeting and financial management systems.

Whilst it is clear that public service reform has led to an increase in wage levels, it is also clear that pay levels are still abysmally low and cannot be classed as a 'living wage'. Whilst this situation remains, it would be difficult to foster an efficient and professional service. Wage levels are not sufficient to entice people to operate wholly in the formal system. This is exacerbated by the significant gap between public and private sector wages. Salary reform has attempted to overcome this to a certain degree by creating higher paid enclaves in principal public services such as the Uganda Revenue Authority and judiciary. This policy, although justifiable on the grounds that it will increase the efficiency of key areas, has overall served to undermine the morale of those outside 'preferred status' organisations.[15]

In addition to inadequate levels of pay, attempts at reforming the public services have run up against the essentially patrimonial character of the Ugandan state, where recruitment and promotion within the public service have less to do with meritocracy than with personal ties and patronage networks. This has clear implications for the efficiency, competence and professionalism of the service, as family and friends are likely to be employed in preference to someone qualified for a post. Such an opaque and nepotistic system, which is inherently based on complex informal arrangements, provides a problematic environment in which to foster meaningful reform efforts. Virtually every proposal for reforming the public sector in Africa and other developing states has emphasised the primacy of institutionalising meritocratic principles in recruitment and rewards. Yet so far none has been specific as to how this is to be achieved in states where patrimonial relationships are deeply embedded in the social structure.[16]

This has meant that there has been little success in terms of reduced levels of corruption and improved service delivery. In fact, there is little evidence that any reduction in the level of corruption has been achieved at all. Data from a recent National Integrity Survey undertaken by CIET international indicate that corruption is still systemic within the Ugandan public service, particularly the police and judiciary.[17] Out of over 18,000 households surveyed, two-thirds of users were said to have paid bribes to the police and half were paying bribes to the judiciary.[18] On both counts, only one-third of users were happy with the service they received.[19] These factors point to a failure in the reform effort's stated aim to foster a service which is more transparent, accountable and public service-minded. Corruption still remains a serious problem in all segments of the public service, illustrated through the reports of the Auditor General, the Public Accounts Committee and the Inspectorate of Government, as well as reports by the press.

DECENTRALISATION AND LOCAL ACCOUNTABILITY

Decentralisation has been a core theme in the NRM's programme, as a 'means to make the state more responsive and adaptable to the local needs than it could be with concentration of administrative powers and responsibility of the state'.[20] This process typically involves a transfer of responsibility for planning, management and the raising of revenue and resources to lower levels of government. Decentralisation is seen as an important factor in improving communication between central government and the population, thereby improving the responsiveness of the civil service to the needs of the people.[21] Decentralisation of decision making and public service delivery is conventionally regarded as an important element of combating corruption in countering the potential lack of transparency and accountability in centralised systems of government.

The NRM established a political-administrative framework of resistance committees and councils which operated at five levels from the village upwards.[22] Resistance committees and councils were originally organised to enlist sympathetic civilians to help in the war effort, but they are now regarded as the NRA's attempt to draw on popular support in order to counter and survive state repression and broaden its support base. This system, now known as local committees and councils, should be understood as part of a more general move to decentralise decision making and authority and provides the basis for the Decentralisation Statute which was formalised in 1993 and entrenched in the new Constitution of 1995. The aim of these moves was to establish unity along party, ethnic and regional lines, and to strengthen local autonomy and accountability.

In Uganda, the 1995 Constitution makes provision for a number of key principles, including the establishment of a sound financial base with a reliable source of revenue for each local government unit; people's participation and democratic control in decision making; appropriate measures to enable local government units to plan, initiate and execute policies in respect of all matters affecting the people within their jurisdiction; and local government units to have the power to levy, charge, collect and appropriate fees and taxes.[23] In addition to these new functions, local governments are required to be financially accountable by providing a comprehensive list of all internal revenue sources and initiating regular audit procedures.

This is clearly an ambitious programme which, unsurprisingly, has encountered a number of problems, although opinions regarding the success of decentralisation in Uganda vary widely. Some observers regard it as a system which has 'created a politically accountable institutional structure that could, with some modification, manage local services and serve as a basis for local autonomy'.[24] Others are more sceptical and feel that there are fundamental weaknesses in the system.[25] Indeed, the benefits of decentralisation have not been as clear-cut as would at first appear.

Many areas have been plagued by a lack of resources, skills and experience, although there is a great deal of variation among districts. Whilst decentralisation effectively devolves greater financial and managerial control to the districts, in many cases these districts do not have the expertise or experience to carry out many of their functions. In a series of district profiles carried out by the New Vision in 1998, it was discovered that many districts were experiencing difficulties in carrying out their roles effectively. In Iganga, it was highlighted that 'councillors did not know their roles' and whilst 'the decentralisation of powers and personnel was good ... the pace ... was too fast for most local governments who had no knowledge of financial accounting'.[26] In the case of Kiboga, there is clearly a need to sensitise local councillors, particularly at LC1 level, about the proper use and management of funds and the law, as at present many councillors 'act outside of [the law]' in their handling of various issues.[27] These problems, according to the World Bank, are evidence that the decentralisation policy is 'running ahead of implementational capacity with large amounts of cash and attendant delivery responsibilities being channelled to district administrations which lack the capacity and systems to manage them'.[28]

Systems for financial control and management are poorly developed in the majority of districts, and are an area which requires significant strengthening if the record of decentralisation is to be improved. A recent study tracking public expenditure between 1991 and 1995 clearly highlights the weaknesses of decentralisation in respect of primary health and education. It notes that, although more resources are now available at the district level than before decentralisation, 'diversions and other financial abuses are not only rampant in districts, but seriously appear to be negating government efforts to provide essential services'. Furthermore, 'audit functions at district level and school inspection are poor and irregular' and 'capacity of local government to provide their own funds for health and education is low'.[29]

Whilst Uganda's decentralisation programme clearly represents a radical attempt at building capacity at the lower levels and improving democratic accountability and service delivery, it has to date been plagued by inefficiency, scarcity and poor performance. Deficiencies in political accountability are clearly evident in the districts, as outlined in the examples described above. This is hampered by the fact that the majority of councillors have a limited level of education and resources, and often lack an understanding of what their new role entails. This has generally led to an increase in corruption as many have been found to use their positions to 'divert' and embezzle money and take advantage of lucrative tenders. The lack of institutional capacity has meant that in many cases districts have been incapable of enforcing accountability checks to monitor the use of funds and resources. These weaknesses have hampered the possible success of the decentralisation programme as local councils have proved unable to rise to the challenge of local autonomy. The limited taxing capacity of a large number of district councils has meant that they still rely heavily on resources from central government.[30]

The lack of capacity at the district level, and the attendant corruption which has thrived as a result, could lead one to argue that, instead of reducing the incidence of corruption by devolving state functions to the district level, it has effectively led to a 'decentralisation of corruption'. A recent study tracking public expenditure clearly illustrates that corruption resulting from the transfer of funds from the centre has actually been reduced since decentralisation, whereas corruption by means of 'diversions' and other financial abuses have increased at the district level.[31] Therefore, rather than reduce the levels of corruption, decentralisation has simply dispersed it, redefining the character of corrupt relationships from those controlled by the centre to those controlled by district-level officials. In this sense, decentralisation has simply multiplied the possible sites for corruption to take place, complicated the lines of accountability and diluted enforcement capacity.

In so far as the decentralisation of corruption is taking place, it can be related to the analytical framework discussed earlier. This is to say, the notion that the political arena is thoroughly penetrated by informal clientelistic type relationships and that those in office are expected to further the ends of their kith and kin. In a situation where access to the state is the principal means of acquiring wealth, the dispersal of the state's functions through decentralisation may be expected to open up political resources to a wider constituency. In fact, there is a good deal of evidence from a range of contexts which points out that decentralisation programmes frequently result in an upsurge of corruption.[32] Decentralisation therefore does not significantly alter the relationship between enrichment and political legitimacy.

PRIVATISATION AND PERSONAL PROFIT

Privatisation has also played a central role in the reform of the Ugandan state and has been pushed strongly by the donor community, especially the World Bank. In 1993 a Public Enterprise Reform and Divestiture Statute inaugurated a process which has run into serious difficulties. The institution which was initially set up to handle the technicalities of the process, the Public Enterprises Reform and Divestiture Secretariat (PERDS), was abolished, amidst controversy, a mere two years after it had been formed. The primary responsibility for privatisation was then passed to a Minister of State in the Ministry of Finance.[33] Serious undervaluation of public assets seems to have been the principal reason behind PERDS' early demise. However, whether inappropriate valuations were the result of incompetence, the intractability of assigning a realistic value to public enterprises which are often in a serious state of decline, or to conflict of interest and corruption, is very difficult to establish. Certainly there is a widespread belief in Uganda, as evidenced by frequent stories in the press, that the whole process has been compromised by malpractices such as deliberately low valuations, conflict of interest, and enterprises failing to be awarded to the highest bidder. For example, in a high-profile case in 1998, it was widely reported that the President's half brother and former commander of military operations in the north, Major-General Salim Saleh, had secretly bought the country's largest bank, the state-owned Uganda Commercial Bank, allegedly to stop it falling into the hands of the Malaysians. Shortly after taking over the bank General Saleh arranged for substantial loans to be made to companies he owned without reporting the transactions, as required by banking regulations, to the Bank of Uganda. Under these circumstances it is not surprising that the 1998 World Bank Mission drew particular attention to a number of unsuccessful sales and bemoaned the general lack of transparency in the process. Uganda's privatisation process is currently under suspension while a Parliamentary Select Committee subjects it to investigation.

A further problem has been that, in some cases, bidders have failed to follow through with the purchase, or fail to pay following completion of the sale. According to the World Bank, as of mid-1998 some one-third of total sales value was outstanding in deferred payments and two-thirds of that amount was in arrears.[34] One example is the sale of Uganda Fisheries Enterprises Limited, which was sold in 1995 to the Nordic African Fisheries Company Ltd. The buyers agreed to make a down-payment of 30 per cent on execution of the agreement. However, out of the 30 per cent, which is equivalent to US$ 330,000, only US$ 110,000 was paid. By the time of the audit in 1997, although all the instalments were due, no payment had been received from the buyers.[35]

Despite initial support and enthusiasm for privatisation, the process has been judged, on the whole, to be seriously flawed, leading to an erosion of both public and political support. The primary problem seems to be that the process is too opaque, which has led to allegations of insider dealing and corruption. Furthermore, sales have been plagued by conflicts of interest where enterprises have been sold at an undervalued level to ministers, public officials or their relatives. It is thus clear that the privatisation process has so far not only failed to reduce the opportunities for corruption, but may indeed have increased the potential sites of corruption by spreading it to the private sector. In other words, the supply of corrupt opportunities from state officials remains high because 'the regulatory responsibilities of the state in the new economic system remains substantial while political controls over the behaviour of state officials remains weak'.[36]

ADVANCING POLITICAL SOCIETY

The heavy preponderance of NRM supporters in parliament has not meant that MPs uncritically support the government. The absence of a party whip system has meant that MPs may have more room for manoeuvre than under a disciplined party system. Accordingly, over the past two years parliament has taken an increasingly high-profile role in targeting inefficiency and abuse by ministers and public employees. As a consequence, ministers have been forced to explain and in some cases amend departmental practice, particularly in relation to financial procedures. In a few cases ministers have been forced to resign, or at least have been subsequently dropped from office as a result of censure by the House.[37] Parliament has recently been pressing the case against Salim Saleh, going beyond his secret purchase of Uganda Commercial Bank (UCB) to allegations he may have benefited from a deal involving the acquisition by the armed forces of a fleet of military helicopters from Belarus, all of which subsequently turned out to be defective. Further, towards the end of 1998 censure papers against the Minister of Finance, Planning and Investment were sent to the President. This minister was allegedly involved in the deliberate undervaluation of

Uganda Airways prior to privatisation. He also had an interest in one of the companies bidding for the airline. These charges arise out of comprehensive investigation by a parliamentary committee into the whole process of privatisation.

On the other hand, and despite their apparently increasing vigilance, MPs have been criticised by the current Inspector General of Government, Jotham Tumwesigye, for being too soft on corruption. Speaking at a regional seminar on governance in February 1999, he accused MPs of 'making a lot of noise' about corruption but then doing nothing about it – 'until Parliament punishes some people, others won't know that corruption is bad and must be stopped' – and argued that parliament had more power than it realised but lacked the will to exercise it.[38]

Ironically, Tumwesigye's predecessor at the Inspectorate, Augustine Ruzindana, is currently chair of the potentially powerful Public Accounts Committee. Ruzindana has been proactive in spearheading an increasingly rigorous approach to scrutinising the reports of the Auditor General. But since the Auditor General is required to audit and report on the accounts of all public offices in the country, the task of subjecting them to any form of meaningful inspection is truly gargantuan. In this respect, the Public Accounts Committee is severely hampered by shortage of resources in the form of researchers, other support staff and even basic office equipment.[39] Given that MPs have numerous other commitments if they take their responsibilities at all seriously, the scarcity of such resources places serious limitations on their investigative capability. These limits are intensified by the pervasive secrecy that surrounds the conduct of government business and by the ascendance of a culture which places a premium upon retaining rather than sharing information.

STRENGTHENING CIVIL SOCIETY

Over the last decade the notion of civil society has played an increasingly central role in the study of political change generally, and specifically in discussions of the phenomenon of corruption. It is now widely accepted that in the absence of a vigorous civil society, administrative measures aimed at combating corruption will achieve little. However, less developed economies, by definition, are unlikely to manifest strong civil societies. With a significant proportion of the population, often a majority, locked into an inward looking peasant economy, with poor communications and high levels of poverty and illiteracy, the fundamental ingredients of meaningful association are in extremely short supply. In addition to these factors, the absence of consensus that is encountered in states fragmented by ethnic, regional, linguistic and other differences, forms a serious impediment to the emergence of the basic trust that is a *sine qua non* for effective associational behaviour. Accordingly, the citizens of such states find it difficult to invest much confidence in relationships which transcend the orbit of kin, clan and region.

Uganda is no exception to these conditions. On the contrary, having endured more than two decades of political turmoil and often murderous internecine conflict, the foundations of trust are, to say the least, unstable. With 80 per cent of the population living in rural areas, many of them in dire poverty, the basic task of even communicating with others and of being able to pay the subscription dues necessary to support a rudimentary administration, is fraught with extreme difficulties.

Having made these points, it is important not to underestimate the scope of civil society in Uganda. It has been estimated, for example, that since 1986 over 1,700 NGOs and civil associations have come into existence. These include a wide range of business and professional associations, human rights and women's groups, and religious, recreational and cultural organisations. But especially noticeable are the number of NGOs dedicated to the provision of basic services, particularly in the areas of health and education, and to overall development and poverty eradication goals. Most of these have been brought into existence because of the inability of the state to provide these services, and possibly a majority of them could not survive without some kind of external donor support. Since many of these NGOs are primarily engaged in emergency 'fire-fighting', they tend to take on an essentially reactive character leaving little room for the development of advocacy skills. The fact that NGOs in Uganda are required to register with the NGO Registration Board – significantly overseen by the Ministry of Internal Affairs rather than Planning and Economic Development – also seems to inhibit the range of activities. On the basis of research among indigenous NGOs during the early 1990s, Susan Dicklich identifies a distinct unwillingness to stray too far into 'political' activities. This, together with their over-dependence upon donors, conspires to emasculate their civic influence.[40]

Just as the Museveni era has seen a marked expansion in the number of civic associations, so also has there been a proliferation of newspapers and journals and other mass media. According to one estimate, there are now 40 publications, including four dailies, 13 weeklies, as well as five private radio stations and three private television stations operating alongside government-owned radio and television.[41] Freedom of speech is not enshrined in the Constitution, neither do journalists have right of access – or ease of access – to information. Because of a combination of poor record keeping and the predominance of a culture of secrecy around government departments, access to crucial information is often limited. The media are also hampered by a shortage of experienced and suitably trained journalists. But despite these limitations there is no doubt that the media play an important watchdog role in general and have been particularly effective in exposing cases of corruption. Even the government-owned *New Vision* took the lead in running the story of Salim Saleh's clandestine take-over of the UCB, apparently without official interference. However, there is the view that NRM tolerance of media criticism is deliberately calculated to promote the idea that it is possible to operate a democracy without resort to political parties. There are, however, subtle ways in which the government can exert pressure upon the media, especially newspapers. The fact that the latter are heavily dependent upon government advertising is one obvious source. Harassment by the Uganda Revenue Authority is another.

Overall, then, despite the proliferation of civic groups and mass media, the political effectiveness of civil society in Uganda is extremely limited. One of the most obvious indicators of a strong civil society is the effectiveness of trade unions in protecting working conditions. In Uganda this is minimal. The NRM's desperation to attract foreign investment has led it to turn a blind eye to abuses in the form of poor working conditions and below subsistence wages among Ugandans employed by transnational corporations.[42]

COMBATING CORRUPTION

The elimination of corruption and the abuse of power have been primary goals for the NRM since coming to power in 1986. In addition to revitalising existing institutions directed at curbing corruption, such as the Office of the Auditor General and the Public Accounts Committee, 1987 saw the creation of a new body, the Office of the Inspector General of Government (OIGG). According to the statute, the Inspector General was charged with the duty of protecting human rights, promoting the rule of law in Uganda and working to eliminate corruption and the abuse of public office. However, the 1995 Constitution transferred the responsibility for human rights to the Uganda Human Rights Commission (UHRC), while the renamed Inspectorate of Government (IG) was given wider powers of investigation, arrest and prosecution.

From its inauguration in 1987 the organisation of the OIGG/IG was somewhat inchoate, with an absence of clear lines of authority and division of labour. Furthermore, its stretched resources were pushed even further as a result of organisational changes following a visit in April 1996 by a former director of the Hong Kong Independent Commission Against Corruption brought in as a consultant. Unsurprisingly, the arrangements recommended and adopted follow the Hong Kong model, with its three-pronged division between investigation, prosecution, and education and prevention. A public relations and intelligence section and a complaints follow-up office completed the organisational alterations.

The IG receives complaints of alleged abuse from members of the public, or is asked to investigate suspect areas by members of parliament or government departments, especially the Auditor General's office or the Ministry of Ethics and Integrity. It may also choose to act on the basis of press reports, or because it has unearthed an arena of abuse during routine operations. Between July 1997 and April 1998 the IG received 1,428 complaints, of which 98 were investigated and completed whilst 420 were referred to other government departments or dealt with through correspondence. Nearly one-quarter of these complaints involved the non-payment of salaries and other benefits. Property disputes (13.5 per cent) constituted the next largest category, followed by forgery and issuing false documents (12.6 per cent). In terms of department or area against which these complaints were lodged, significantly, in the light of the previous discussion of decentralisation, district administrations accounted for the largest category (22.6 per cent). The districts were followed by the police and the private sector (each 8.5 per cent), with the Ministry of Education – source of the bulk of the complaints about the non-payment of salaries – coming next.[43] As decentralisation continues, and as the IG extends its work through the media, presentations and workshops to enlist public support in the fight against corruption, so it is expected that such sources will continue to produce significant numbers of cases.

The IG is also responsible for implementing Uganda's Leadership Code. Enacted in 1992, the Code was initially supposed to be enforced by a parliamentary Leadership Code Committee. But as this Committee was never appointed the Code was brought under the jurisdiction of the 1995 Constitution and responsibility for its operation handed over to the IG. Enforcement began in January 1997, when designated 'leaders' were required to declare their assets on a standard official form that had to be returned to the IG by a certain date. To date the whole procedure has been dogged by a combination of problems, not least a high rate of non-return. More serious are the limitations of the form, which turned out to be too imprecise in terms of the information required. As a consequence, what has been an elaborate and costly exercise yielded little in the form of useful information. Accordingly, in August 1997 the Inspector General submitted proposals to amend the Code to the Ministry of Justice. These proposals include extending the range of 'leaders' required to make a declaration, as well as amending the form to demand more specific information as to the assets not only of the declarant but also those of the spouse and children. The Inspector General has also proposed that because of the cost of the process in terms of resources and time, it should henceforth be conducted every two years rather than annually. As of the beginning of 1999 these proposals had not been ratified.

On the question of the IG's resources, this will be of little surprise given that Uganda is one of the world's poorest countries. Consequently, the work of the Inspectorate is seriously constrained by a shortage of overall funding and an acknowledged over-reliance upon donor assistance. Despite this assistance, the IG labours under the burden of inadequate staffing – with less than 50 investigators in 1998, whereas over 100 are needed to cover the volume of existing work – and an all-round insufficiency of logistical support in the form of vehicles, computers, photocopiers and so on.[44] In the face of these constraints and the scale of the problem, the IG has had limited success so far in combating the problem of corruption. In fact, the general consensus in the country at large, particularly as reflected in the media, seems to be that it is getting worse.

The Inspector General of Government acknowledged at the beginning of 1999 that the various institutions in Uganda had not had 'a big impact' on the fight against corruption.[45] These include the Office of the Auditor General, the Director of Public Prosecutions, the Judiciary, the Uganda Police Force's National Fraud Squad, the Human Rights Commission, the inspectorates in various ministries and the Anti-Corruption Unit in the President's Office. To these should be added the role played by political society in the form of parliament, especially the Public Accounts Committee, and of course civil society as manifested in the media and NGOs. One reason for this has been the difficulty in implementing an effective strategy. The Anti-Corruption Unit in the Office of the President was established during the election year of 1996, which President Museveni declared the year of fighting corruption and poverty. The responsibility for overseeing the crusade against corruption was initially assigned to the Office of the Vice-President. However, in July 1998, after the Vice-President had herself been the subject of press and political speculation about mismanagement of funds in her office as Minister of Agriculture, the 'corruption portfolio' was re-assigned to a newly created Minister for Ethics and Integrity.

The ministerial post, afforded Cabinet status, is located in the Office of the President. The first and current minister is a Member of Parliament with a reputation for outspoken criticism of government policies. The functions and activities of this unit embrace a somewhat ambitious amalgam of policy development, the supervision of policy implementation, lobbying, advocacy and the promotion of social change or – as the current minister has expressed it – 'the mainstreaming of anti-corruption activities and enhancement of the operations of the various anti-corruption agencies in fighting corruption and the inculcation of transparency and integrity in government, public and private sectors and the general public'.[46] In practice, this appears to comprise formulating anti-corruption policy and strategies; monitoring the implementation of the recommendations of the Public Accounts Committee and the Auditor General; conducting public awareness campaigns; introducing courses on ethics and integrity into the school curriculum and community education; and promoting co-operation and collaboration between elements of civil society.

However, in the absence of a separate budget and with a staff establishment of three (including the minister), it is debatable what policy initiatives will add to those that already exist. It appears likely that the emergence of this minister (without a ministry), rather than having been the outcome of a carefully thought out strategy, had more to do with anti-corruption rhetoric in what was an election year. In theory, the minister has assumed responsibility for supervising and co-ordinating the anti-corruption activities of the entire range of Uganda's various institutions with individual responsibilities for monitoring the allocation and usage of public expenditure, collecting public revenues, investigating public complaints of abuse of office and mismanagement of state finance and the criminal investigation, and prosecution of alleged fraud and corruption. In practice, however, the delivery of any strategy may flounder on lack of resources and past experiences: each of these bodies, while willing to communicate and co-operate with one another, may be reluctant, given the country's chaotic past, to accept the overt supervision and co-ordination of government.

APPROACHING DEMOCRATISATION?

All the above issues have also to be seen within the wider context of the process of Ugandan democratisation. Whilst political parties have not always been at the centre of the conditionalities imposed by creditors, their absence, even more their proscription, must set limits on the ability of individual citizens to exert meaningful influence over the political process. In this respect, President Museveni's refusal to countenance parties until at least after the referendum now scheduled for 2000, would seem to fall short of the usual requirements. Museveni's rejection of parties is of course based upon the familiar grounds that their operation in Uganda would simply provide a vehicle for the assertion of the ethnic/regional rivalries that have had such a devastating impact in the past. The movement system is, for the time being, the only means of not only containing such tendencies but also, under appropriate conditions, drawing them into some kind of national system of participation and involvement. Museveni insists that democracy without parties is possible as long as there are five key elements:

1. participation of people at all levels of governance; 2. the rule of law; 3. observance of human rights; 5. transparency and accountability; and 5. periodic and democratic elections.[47] In effect, these five can be treated under three headings: participation and elections; transparency and accountability; and rule of law and human rights.

So far as participation and elections are concerned there is no question that the massive process of consultation leading to the debates in the Constituent Assembly and eventually to the 1995 Constitution involved levels of participation not previously seen on the continent of Africa and rarely elsewhere. Such levels of involvement have undoubtedly invested the NRM with a degree of legitimacy enjoyed by no previous regime in Uganda. However, the extent to which what emerged was really a people's constitution is open to question. For Furley and Katalikawe, the outcome was almost inevitably a product of the country's elites, hence they refer to the process as 'a noble lie'.[48] There is also a view that the whole consultation procedure was an elaborate ritual exercise which finally delivered the constitutional arrangements which Museveni and the proconsuls of the NRM always intended. In other words, the prospect of a return to multi-party politics was never on the agenda. Whether or not this was the case, there is no evidence that the desire to return to a multi-party system is widespread among the Ugandan people. On the contrary, there are reasonable grounds for believing that the ban on political organisation does not provoke general resentment so long as there is freedom of speech and, more important, its corollary, freedom from harassment, as well as continued opportunities for political participation within the single movement framework.[49] This suggests that the bulk of the pressure for a shift to multi-partyism comes from certain members of the political class whose interests are to no small degree driven by ethnic regional preoccupations.

The issue of mass participation is being pursued by the system of local councils, which, according to some commentators, has facilitated rates of participation which are probably unprecedented in Third World states. Anthony J. Regan has estimated that, with around 45,000 village councils in Uganda, as many as 400,000 people may be serving in elected offices in the local council system. Out of a population of 18 million, such levels of participation are deemed impressive. This leads Regan to conclude that the village-level regional councils, in giving people the power to participate in decisions which affect their daily lives, have promoted 'a remarkable degree of democratisation in Uganda'.[50] Others writers have been less sanguine. We have already noted an apparent upsurge of corruption at the local level, an upsurge which has led some commentators to talk of the 'democratisation of corruption'. Such a situation suggests that the structures of accountability are not particularly effective and that decentralisation may be in the process of replacing 'one unresponsive elite [in this case the chiefs] with another'.[51] Further, Regan's observation does not distinguish between rates of male and female participation. On this point there is evidence that regional councils are overwhelmingly male-dominated. Since, as Mary Mugenyi points out, women comprise 53 per cent of the population, 80 per cent of agricultural labour and 90 per cent of domestic labour, their overall marginality to decision-making processes raises a number of fundamental questions about the nature of democratisation.[52]

However, to what extent the high level of abuse in the area of local administration is the result of deliberate malfeasance or the inevitable outcome of an overall scarcity of resources is impossible to determine. It is widely recognised that decentralisation, whether administrative or political or both, even in developed economies, is at the same time fraught with difficulties and cost.[53] In a society where both material and human capital are in extremely short supply; where public servants are generally poorly trained and poorly paid; where scrutiny of the administrative process is dependent upon citizens most of whom have had very little formal education; where this process is subject to an escalating and ultimately limitless level of demand, the scale of maladministration is inevitably high. But in addition there is no doubt that the lack of transparency which these pathologies engender provides ample opportunity for misappropriation. In fact, a growing body of evidence attests to the fact that decentralisation in a variety of contexts is associated with significant increases in abuse.[54]

If public servants at the local level are able to exploit weak accountability and lack of transparency, this has as a counterpart – and is in some sense a reflection of – fairly pervasive elite or grand corruption.[55] We have already noted the irregularities in the process of privatisation, irregularities that betoken serious potential or actual conflicts of interest among ministers and no doubt some MPs. Symptomatic of such conflicts of interest is the foot-dragging over the Leadership Code manifested both in the high level of non-return of questionnaires and in government inertia over its amendment and reinforcement. Serious concern has been raised about 'classified accounts' and the military by the outspoken MP for Mbarara, Mrs Winnie Byanyima.[56] Even the President has fulminated against the level of corruption in the army, but since the accounts of State House are also classified, thereby permitting unknown levels of patronage within the political elite, such criticisms could appear to represent mere hand-wringing.[57] Also, since in addition to the antics of Salim Saleh, other members of Museveni's family are held to be profiting from opportunities arising from current military operations in eastern Congo, such protests may be expected to encounter some cynicism.[58]

There are two further elements to non-party democracy in Uganda: the rule of law and the observance of human rights. For almost two decades the citizens of Uganda endured a situation in which there were effectively no limits on the exercise of power.[59] Accordingly, compared with the early 1980s, the situation in Uganda embodies a degree of improvement that could scarcely have been imaginable during the dark days of Amin and Obote II. The Uganda Human Rights Commission was created in 1995 with a solid legal base that is embedded in the Constitution. The President, with the approval of parliament, appoints its chairperson. The Constitution also endows the UHRC with a secure financial base in the form of its own budget, which means that, in theory, all administrative expenses including salaries, allowances and pensions are guaranteed. This does not, of course, mean the UHRC has abundant resources, as evidenced by the fact that it has recently solicited donor aid for the purchase of a new HQ. The UHRC investigates human rights abuses either on its own initiative or in response to complaints. UHRC staff also visit prisons to monitor conditions. In 1997, 406 complaints were received, the figure rising to 982 the following year. This 140 per cent rise probably reflects an increasing awareness of human rights issues partly as a consequence of the educational work of the Commission itself. A large proportion, probably 70 per cent, of the complaints originate in the Kampala area – a figure which probably indicates the relative ignorance of rights in the country at large or the perceived inability to do anything about abuses.

In this respect, the progress in the area of human rights and respect for the rule of law is unquestionably an achievement for the NRM and is likely to preserve Museveni's credibility for many years to come. Despite this, there are still areas of concern mainly in the north, where the army is conducting operations against the Lord's Resistance Army and other factionalised dissident groups.[60] Overall, there is increasing apprehension about arbitrary acts of violence against citizens, whether this springs from members of the armed forces, the police, local defence forces, rebels or bandits, and, as the 1998 CIET survey revealed, a significant number of the public are subject to demands for bribes for the delivery of basic public services and, as such, are unlikely to develop trust and confidence in the state's ability to protect and serve their interests.

CONCLUSION

Considerable resources have been and are being dedicated to the task of combating corruption in Uganda. Despite this, it is generally accepted that the panoply of reforms, strategies, institutions and legal instruments have to date made little impression on the problem, with Uganda considered to be the thirteenth most corrupt country in the world in the 1998 Transparency International Corruption Perception Index. The index, a 'poll of polls' based upon surveys of business people, risk analysts and the general public, ranked Uganda as more corrupt than over 70 countries, including Pakistan, Ukraine, Turkey, and many other African countries such as the Ivory Coast, Senegal, Malawi and Zimbabwe.[61] Even the Inspector General of Government conceded that Uganda's fight against corruption has been ineffective.[62] What are the principal reasons for this lack of success?

First, as is the case with most developing countries, Uganda is chronically short of all resources, both material and human, required for economic development and efficient public administration. The continuing AIDS epidemic serves to compound these constraints and regrettably may yet confound even the most persistent supporters of Uganda's continuing social and economic development.[63] Those resources that do exist are spread thinly over a wide range of institutional areas, leaving often poorly trained, inadequately equipped and invariably badly paid public servants to deal with problems whose volume and complexity would be likely to defeat administrators anywhere. Such difficulties have been exacerbated by the retrenchments and hiring freeze imposed by the exigencies of the Public Service Reform programme and the government's stringent maintenance of cash budgets. The consequences for public service provision and public service management morale are obvious.

Secondly, and in relation to the last point, a culture of professional public service, allegedly of pivotal significance in the development of the West, is not well entrenched in Uganda.[64] This is due to two factors: the continued social and political predominance of personal kinship and clanship; and clientelistic relations that militate against the development of neutral and universalistic principles which underpin effective modern public administration. These powerful relationships have been invested with additional potency by the acute instability that afflicted Uganda for two decades. As the state increasingly became synonymous with violence, oppression and plunder, its 'citizens' came to be dependent upon the only relationships they could trust.

The third major reason underlying the limited impact of Uganda's anti-corruption arrangements is the example presented by the country's ruling elite. This factor is so fundamental to the understanding of why corruption in Uganda is not being remedied by its political and economic reforms that it needs fuller considerations. Virtually every commentator on the design and delivery of effective anti-corruption strategies has highlighted the centrality of political will and commitment from the top. In terms of rhetoric, anti-corruption themes are certainly at the forefront of the movement's public pronouncements, but there is less evidence of widespread commitment in practice. The President has not been accused of personal gain, but press coverage of the business activities of his brother, his wife and his son, as well as some of his senior ministers, contrasts with the high moral tone of the movement and may yet provide a challenge to Museveni as symbol and statesman.

Thus, in the face of what appears to be extensive cronyism within the government elite, Museveni continues to confront the dilemma he faced upon gaining power in 1986, that of welding the disparate factions thrown up by Uganda's ethnic, regional and economic diversity first into a workable coalition and then into a unified state. The 1986 solution, which took the form of distribution of the spoils, seems likely to remain the only viable option for the foreseeable future. Museveni's Marxist-inspired analysis that in a decade Uganda will have developed into a society where classes have superseded ethnic and regional divisions appears unlikely to be realised. On the contrary, Uganda's embroilment in wider regional conflicts, particularly in southern Sudan and the Democratic Republic of the Congo, may work to perpetuate or even intensify those divisions.

The 1990s solution has to date involved the President maintaining a balance between providing sufficient political and social reforms to satisfy the demands of the donor community and continuing to maintain the support of the country's power elite while stopping short of democratic reforms that may well bring in forces of genuine opposition. The increased stringency of the donor community and the increasing political volatility of the region may yet serve to undermine the current political approach of balancing the maintenance of reform with the continuance of corruption and thus render Uganda's ecology of corruption ultimately unsustainable. In just over 25 years Uganda has been transformed from an international pariah and a byword for state terrorism into an apparent exemplar of political, economic and social rectitude. Many commentators await irrefutable evidence of whether this transformation has a genuine and sustainable foundation. Others fear they are witnessing an illusion achieved through either purely cosmetic change applied within Uganda or via the wishful thinking of those observers outside the country who look for signs of any positive change in any part of Africa. In 1988 Mahmood Mamdani expressed concerns about obstacles to the continuing political development of the country, which at the time was half-way through a four-year 'transitional' period, decreed by the NRA when it came to power on 26 January 1986, leading towards 'the blooming of a fully flowered democracy in Uganda'. His concerns focused on the question of what form Uganda's democracy would take.[65] Now, more than a decade later, despite presidential and parliamentary elections, a programme of decentralisation and a period of sustained internal stability, the question remains largely unanswered, awaiting a referendum on support for a multi-party system promised for next year. In the interim, questions focus now on the equally fundamental question of whether corruption, if allowed to continue unchecked, will undermine all further attempts at maintaining political stability and promoting sustainable economic development in Uganda.

NOTES

1. World Bank, 'Report of a World Bank Mission to Support the Program of the Republic of Uganda to Improve Economic Governance and to Combat Corruption', Poverty Reduction and Social Development Unit, 1998.
2. Augustine Ruzindana, 'The Part Played by Structural Reforms of the State in Fighting Corruption: The Case in Uganda', International Anti-Corruption Conference, 1997.
3. Petter Langseth, 'Civil Service Reform in Uganda: Lessons Learned', *Public Administration and Development,* 17 (1995), 366.
4. Oliver Furley and James Katalikawe, 'Constitutional Reform in Uganda: The New Approach', *African Affairs* 5, 383 (April 1997), 243–60. See also George Kanyeihamba, 'Power that Rode Naked through Uganda under the Muzzle of a Gun', in Holger Bernt Hansen and Michael Twaddle (eds.), *Uganda Now: Between Decay and Development* (London: James Currey, 1995), 70–82.
5. Library of Congress (1990) http://lcweb2.loc.gov/frd/cs/ugtoc/htm#ug0073.
6. Andrew Goudie, 'United Kingdom Department for International Development', Organisation for Economic Co-operation and Development Conference on Corruption and Integrity Initiatives, 1997.
7. Oliver Furley, 'Democratisation in Uganda', African Studies Association of the United Kingdom Biennial Conference, School of Oriental and African Studies, University of London, 14–16 Sept. 1998.
8. Ibid.
9. The government has recently adopted the term 'public service' in place of 'civil service', which is consistent with the use of the term in the 1995 Constitution.
10. Structural adjustment policies often emphasise the need to redefine the role of government and its relationship to the population. Public service reform plays an integral part in this process given that it undertakes such functions as economic policy making, revenue collection, infrastructural provision and the delivery of services, all of which are fundamental in defining the links between the government and the public.
11. Ministry of Public Service, 'Public Service 2002: Public Service Reform Programme 1997–2002', Republic of Uganda, 1997, iii.
12. Langseth, 'Civil Service Reform in Uganda', 366.
13. Ministry of Public Service, 'Public Service 2002', 2.
14. Ibid., 4.
15. World Bank, 'Report of a World Bank Mission', 50.
16. See especially the World Bank which, in its 1997 Report, although unequivocal as to the pivotal importance of meritocratic principles in administrative reform, remains vague about their establishment. World Bank, *The State in a Changing World* (New York: Oxford University Press, 1998), 7, 9, 104, 105.
17. CIET International, 'National Integrity Survey: 1998 Baseline Uganda' Report to the Inspectorate of Government, Kampala, Uganda, 1998.
18. Ibid., 13.
19. Ibid., 12.
20. Dubey, 'Decentralisation: Some Afro-Asian Reflections', *Indian Journal of Public Administration,* 44, 1 (1998), 50.
21. K.G. Enid, 'Customer Service as an Element of the Civil Service Reform Programme in Uganda', *Development and Socio-Economic Progress,* 20, 66 (1996), 47.

22. The lowest level of the RC system is RC1, which is composed of all adult residents of a village. RC1 then elects nine representatives to the RC2 (parish) level. RC2 go on to elect nine representatives to the RC3 level (sub-county) and so on to RC4 (county) level and RC5 (district) level. The parliament is partially elected through this system. See C. Cannon-Lorgen, 'NGOs in Transition: The Changing Context of the Health Sector in Uganda' (unpublished Ph.D. thesis, Oxford University, 1998), 4.
23. The Constitution of Uganda (1995) Chapter 11. http://www.uganda.co.ug/Content.htm, version current at 02.04.99.
24. E.A. Brett, 'Rebuilding Survival Structures for the Poor: Organizational Options for Development in the 1990s', in Holger Bernt Hansen and Michael Twaddle (eds.), *Changing Uganda* (London: James Currey Ltd, 1991), 307.
25. Susan Dicklich, 'The Democratization of Uganda Under the NRM Regime' (International Political Science Association, 1994).
26. Erich Ogoso Opolot, 'Iganga is not all about Corruption', *New Vision*, 23 Feb. 1998, 18.
27. Joyce Namutebi, 'Kiboga can only Boast of its Hospital', *New Vision*, 11 Feb. 1998, 16.
28. World Bank, *The State in a Changing World*, 10.
29. Economic Policy Research Centre (EPRC), 'Tracking of Public Expenditure on Primary Education and Primary Health Care' (Makerere University, 1996), xiii.
30. Extreme cases of this are Adjumani, where government grants make up 74 per cent of projected revenue (*New Vision*, 16 Feb. 1998), and Hoima, where they make up 82 per cent of the budget (*New Vision*, 28 Jan. 1998).
31. EPRC, 'Tracking of Public Expenditure, xiii.
32. See, for example, Ting Gong, 'Forms and Characteristics of China's Corruption in the 1990s: Change with Continuity', *Communist and Post-Communist Studies*, 30, 3 (1997), 277–88; and Lydia Segal, 'The Pitfalls of Political Decentralisation and Proposals for Reform: The Case of New York City Public Schools', *Public Administration Review*, 57, 2 (1997), 141–9. Even the World Bank, whilst enthusiastic about decentralisation, warns of the potential danger of 'local capture'. World Bank, *The State in a Changing World*, 11.
33. Geoffrey Tukahebwa, 'Privatization as a Development Policy', in Holger Bernt Hansen and Michael Twaddle (eds.), *Developing Uganda* (Oxford: James Currey, 1998), 59–72.
34. World Bank, *The State in a Changing World*, 22.
35. Auditor General, 'The Public Accounts of the Republic of Uganda for the Year Ended 30th June 1997', Republic of Uganda, 1998, 171
36. Barbara Harriss-White and Gordon White, 'Corruption, Liberalisation and Democracy', *IDS Bulletin*, 27, 2 (1996), 3.
37. Furley, 'Democratisation in Uganda'.
38. *New Vision*, 3 Feb. 1999.
39. See Furley, 'Democratisation in Uganda', 8, 9.
40. Susan Dicklich, 'Indigenous NGOs and Political Participation', in Hansen and Twaddle (eds.), *Developing Uganda*, 145–58.
41. Ogoso Opolot, 'The Media: A Pillar in Fighting Corruption', in Petter Langseth and Augustine Ruzindana (eds.), *Fighting Corruption in Uganda: The Process of Building a National Integrity System* (Kampala, Uganda: Fountain Publishers, 1998).
42. See J. Oloka-Onyango, 'Uganda's Benevolent Dictatorship', *Current History*, 96, 610 (1997), 212–16.
43. Inspectorate of Government Report to Parliament, July 1997–April 1998, Chapter 4. Republic of Uganda.
44. Ibid., 19–22. Also Inspectorate of Government Corporate and Development Plans for the Period January 1999–December 2001, Government of Uganda.
45. *New Vision*, 3 Feb. 1999, 3.
46. M. Matembe, 'Government Policy and Action Plan to Fight Corruption', Statement to the December 1998 Consultative Group Meeting.
47. Y. Museveni, 'Democracy and Good Governance in Africa: An African Perspective', *Mediterrean Quarterly*, 5, 4 (1994), 1–8.
48. Furley and Katalikawe, 'Constitutional Reform in Uganda', 252–3.

49. Goran Hyden, 'The Challenges of Constitutionalizing Politics in Uganda', in Hansen and Twaddle (eds.), *Developing Uganda*, 117.
50. Anthony J. Regan, 'Decentralisation Policy: Reshaping State and Society', in Hansen and Twaddle (eds.), *Developing Uganda*, 171.
51. Segal, 'The Pitfalls of Political Decentralisation', 147.
52. Mary R. Mugenyi, 'Towards the Empowerment of Women: A Critique of NRM Policies and Programmes', in Hansen and Twaddle (eds.), *Developing Uganda*, 133–44. See also Aili Mari Tripp, 'Local Women's Associations and Politics in Contemporary Uganda', in ibid., 120–32.
53. Edward A. Brett, 'Rebuilding Organisational Capacity in Uganda under the National Resistance Movement', *Journal of Modern African Studies*, 32, 1 (1994), 71.
54. See Segal, 'The Pitfalls of Political Decentralisation'; Mark Turner and David Hulme, *Governance, Administration and Development: Making the State Work* (London: Macmillan, 1997).
55. For example, the accounts of State House being classified afford ample opportunities for cronyism as evidenced by the extraordinary number of ministers (60) when there are only 21 ministries.
56. *New Vision*, 10 Feb. 1999.
57. *Sunday Vision*, 7 Feb. 1999.
58. The Tanzanian *Daily Mail* of 14 Jan. 1999 mentioned six companies operating in eastern Congo in which Museveni's wife, his brother, Vice-President Paul Kagame and James Kagame are alleged to have shares. Cited by Filip Reyntjens, 'Briefing: The Second Congo War, more than a Remake', *African Affairs*, 98, 391 (April 1999), 249.
59. Goran Hyden, 'The Challenges of Constitutionalizing Politics in Uganda', 112.
60. Sandrine Perrot, 'Rebellions in Northern Uganda: The Paradox of Instability', African Studies Association of the United Kingdom Biennial Conference, School of Oriental and African Studies, University of London, 14–16 Sept. 1998.
61. Transparency International and Gottingen University (1998), http://www.transparency.de/documents/cpi/index.html.
62. *New Vision*, 3 Feb. 1999.
63. We note, but for obvious reasons are unable to deal with here, the likely devastating consequences of AIDS for the development of Uganda's human resources. See Maryinez Lyons, 'AIDS and Development in Uganda', in Hansen and Twaddle (eds.), *Developing Uganda*, 194–206.
64. Brett 'Rebuilding'.
65. Mahmood Mamdani, 'Uganda in Transition: Two Years of the NRA/NRM', *Third World Quarterly*, 10, 3 (1988), 1155–81.

Causes and Consequences of Corruption: Mozambique in Transition

DAVID STASAVAGE

Corruption in Mozambique in recent years has been prevalent in a number of different areas of government activity, and there are indications that it is more prevalent than was the case ten years ago, when the FRELIMO government launched an ambitious economic reform programme. It is puzzling that corruption has increased during this period of reform, since one of the principal goals of reform in structural adjustment programmes is to reduce opportunities for corruption and rent-seeking (by unifying exchange rates, for example). This article considers what factors are responsible for the increase in corruption in Mozambique, and what effect increased corruption has had on the Mozambican economy. The study on which this article is based will hopefully help complement the growing number of cross-country studies on corruption, bureaucratic efficiency, and growth.[1] While the incidence of corruption has changed somewhat in Mozambique since the research for the study was completed in 1996 (and often for the better), corruption remains a serious problem, making the study relevant both for comparison with other countries and for those interested in developing strategies for a further reduction in corruption in Mozambique.

The apparent increase in corruption in Mozambique in the last ten years can, to a great extent, be explained by a change in the basic conditions for deterrence of corruption as expressed in principal-agent models. Bureaucrats in Mozambique retain extensive control rights over economic activity, with individuals (or individual agencies) often holding monopoly and discretionary power over provision of a particular government-supplied service. At the same time, structures for monitoring bureaucrats and holding them accountable for their actions have been dramatically weakened during a transition from enforcement centred around the FRELIMO party to one based on the rule of law and an independent judiciary and police force. A decrease in real wages for civil servants and increasing inequalities in pay between the public and private sectors have also contributed to the increase in corruption. Finally, while changes in material factors may explain much of the increase in corruption of recent years, any study on this subject would

David Stasavage, Centre for the Study of African Economies, Oxford University be amiss in not mentioning the significance of a decline in the public service ethic as a source of corruption.

In addition to being more and more widespread, corruption in Mozambique today has an organisational form which is particularly detrimental to economic growth. Government officials or agencies engaged in corruption operate largely independently. They do not participate in centralised bribe-taking arrangements, nor are there commonly enforced 'rules of the game', either of which might keep bribe prices within reason. There is also little evidence of the sort of networks between businesses and government officials which, through repeated interaction, could reduce the uncertainties inevitably involved with corrupt transactions that are unprotected by formal property rights. In Mozambique, the absence of these forms of organisation means that private sector operators often have little idea when a bribe will be required for a certain service, what the bribe price will be, and whether an initial payment will lead to the service being delivered or simply to further demands for illicit payments.

Corruption appears to have had two major effects on the Mozambican economy. First, there is a distorting effect on government trade and tax policies. Widespread corruption in customs has resulted in high, negative effective rates of protection for import-substituting firms, since informal sector traders have been able to pay bribes to import goods without paying duties, while manufacturing firms in the formal sector have more commonly been obliged to pay duties on imports and taxes on their outputs. Second, there has been both a disincentive and a distortionary effect on investment. Without an idea of what flows of foreign direct investment in Mozambique might be if corruption were absent, it is impossible actually to measure this effect. Nonetheless, there are indications that a number of potential investors have been deterred by fear of corruption, while others have chosen to invest in activities which promise a high rate of return in the short term in order to hedge against perceived risks from corruption. These effects may be most pronounced for smaller firms.

The article proceeds by first briefly reviewing hypotheses about the causes of corruption and its effect on economic growth, as derived from theoretical work on the subject. It then provides evidence on the level of corruption in Mozambique and the organisation of corruption. This is followed by a look at the sources of corruption, and finally at the effects of corruption on the economy

REVIEW OF HYPOTHESES ON CORRUPTION AND GROWTH

Most economists and many political scientists who have written about the causes of corruption have done so using arguments derived from principal-agent models. Three general causes of corruption appear in this literature.[2] For one, corruption will be more of a problem when government bureaucrats have extensive control rights over economic activity and when individual bureaucrats or individual bureaucratic agencies have monopoly and discretionary power over the provision of licences, registrations and other government-supplied goods and services.[3] Second, the level of corruption will also depend upon whether officials receive sufficient rewards for service to reduce the relative returns for engaging in corruption. The most important aspect here is the level of public sector pay.[4] For lower-level employees one might suggest that the principal question is whether compensation is so low that they are obliged either to engage in corruption or moonlight in order to make a subsistence income. For upper-level civil servants in African countries the major consideration will be whether public sector pay is substantially less than that available for performing similar duties in the private sector. Another incentive involves the way in which opportunities for advancement within a bureaucracy can be turned into a constraint on current behaviour in the expectation of future rewards.[5] A third principal cause of corruption is the failure of institutions to monitor bureaucrats and hold them accountable for their actions. These include internal services, such as customs inspectors, as well as external services like the police and judiciary.

There are important reasons to believe that the effects of corruption depend not just on how much of it there is, but also on how corrupt activity is organised. For one, once corruption occurs through collusive arrangements, bribe prices will be lower. Shleifer and Vishny[6] suggest that when officials engaged in corruption are able to collude to set bribe prices at a certain level or share corruption proceeds (rather than acting as independent monopolists), the distorting effect of corruption on growth will be less marked, because aggregate bribe revenues will be maximised at a lower average bribe price than that which would prevail if officials were acting independently. This sort of arrangement could presumably involve either centralised bribe taking and sharing, or well-enforced rules of the game limiting the price of bribes for certain services. Shleifer and Vishny argue that corruption in the Soviet Union was of the collusive type, and co-ordination between different bureaucrats and agencies was enforced by the Communist Party and the KGB. In Russia today, however, the party no longer plays the same role, collusive arrangements have been broken up and corruption has a much more anarchic, and therefore more damaging, character.

In addition to lowering bribe prices, the fact that corrupt activity occurs through collusive arrangements should also minimise uncertainty. Corrupt transactions by definition are not protected by formal property rights, and so in the absence of such collusion they are likely to involve greater uncertainty for businesses than would payment of a tax or legal fee in exchange for the same service.[7] The existence of networks in which business representatives and government officials regularly associate might help improve flows of information and reduce incentives for bureaucrats to renege on a promise to provide a particular service for a bribe, as their reputation within the group might be damaged. Because such corruption networks would need to remain secretive, however, they would still hinder innovation to the extent that new firms are excluded from such arrangements. Recent work on East Asian economies has emphasised the importance of contacts of this sort between business and government.[8]

THE PATTERN OF CORRUPTION IN MOZAMBIQUE

The Level of Corruption

It is a fundamental problem in this area of research that there is no convincing method for measuring the level of corruption in Mozambique as a whole, or even within individual areas of government activity. The one exception here is with the customs administration, where one can provide a quantitative estimate of how much revenue has been lost, and from this one can make judgements about the level of corruption.[9] Given the difficulty in saying anything about how much corruption there is at the national level, what the article attempts to do is to provide as much partial evidence as possible, on the basis of 30 interviews conducted in Mozambique with private sector and donor representatives and based on recent reports which have looked at the more general issue of the business environment. These sources suggest that corruption is prevalent today in Mozambique, and that its level has increased dramatically over the last ten years.

One indication of the extent of corruption is the degree to which businesses in Mozambique see it as a problem, and how they rank this problem compared to other potential sources of uncertainty for their operations. Fifteen private sector representatives were asked which of the following would be a greater potential deterrent for someone considering investing in Mozambique today: 1. fear of political instability; 2. fear of a reversal in economic policy; or 3. fear of administrative problems related to corruption. Ten out of the 15 respondents suggested that administrative delays related to corruption were a major problem, and that they were the biggest deterrent among the potential problems cited. Three respondents suggested that political instability, instability of economic policy and administrative problems with corruption were each an equal source of uncertainty, given Mozambique's recent history. Only two respondents placed political instability ahead of corruption on the list of concerns, even though Mozambique had just recently emerged from a lengthy civil war at the time these interviews were conducted.[10] While 15 respondents is obviously quite a small sample size, this provides at least some indication of the degree to which corruption is seen as a problem.

Further indication of a high level of corruption in Mozambique can be found in the priority given to the subject in statements by donors, by the Mozambican government itself, and in reports on the business environment. A number of bilateral donors in the two most recent consultative group meetings on Mozambique have focused their statements on the issue of corruption. Likewise, the Mozambican Prime Minister and President each referred at length to problems of corruption in their 1996 May Day statements.[11] Certainly, the rhetoric of donors and government officials does not always reflect reality, but recent reports on the business environment in Mozambique provide further confirmation of the degree to which corruption is perceived as a problem by the business community and by those who work with the business community. A working group at Mozambique's first 'Private Sector Conference' in 1995 described the 'interrelated issues' of excessive bureaucracy and corruption as Mozambique's 'main obstacle to the development of the private sector'. A study commissioned by the International Finance Corporation placed a similar emphasis on corruption.[12]

There is also partial evidence of an increase in the level of corruption since the beginning of the reform programme. While they often differed in their assessment of whether there was a significant level of corruption in Mozambique in 1986, none of the 15 interviewees from the private sector was willing to claim that corruption had not increased substantially in Mozambique since that time, and the interviewees from government and the donor community had similar opinions. Reports by a variety of different agencies provide further backing for this assertion. The Mozambican government's presentation to the consultative group meeting in Paris in the spring of 1995 commented that, 'while increased emphasis has been given to regular auditing of projects and credit accounts, the government is aware that the increase in corruption is undermining progress'.[13] Similarly, a report prepared for the International Finance Corporation in May 1994 suggests that 'corruption in Mozambique is nowhere near as widespread as in many other African countries, however, it is a growing problem made easier by the excessive regulations that offer ample opportunities to underpaid officials and bureaucrats'.[14]

While most people would accept the proposition that there has been a substantial increase in the level of corruption, people interviewed for the study gave widely divergent opinions on how much corruption there was in Mozambique between independence (in 1975) and the beginning of economic reform in the mid-1980s. For some, the first decade of independence was marked by a strong ideological commitment to the FRELIMO cause and by an absence of corruption at either high levels or low levels of government. For others, some corruption has always existed in Mozambique; during the colonial period, during the early years of FRELIMO rule, and during the period of economic reform.

Unfortunately, there is little published material to draw upon in order to judge these two points of view, but it does seem significant that as early as 1980 the President of Mozambique, Samora Machel, launched a public campaign against corruption.[15] This campaign involved well-publicised tours of public institutions like hospitals, ports and railways by the President, followed up by a number of actions to dismiss officials that had been caught embezzling funds or demanding bribes. Machel launched a second campaign in 1981, this time directed against corruption in the security forces. One might suggest that, like many similar campaigns in African countries, Machel's efforts were primarily a pretext to root out opposition to his rule, and that, as a result, they cannot be taken as an accurate indication of the existence of corruption at the time. This seems unlikely, though, because there was no major faction fighting within FRELIMO at the time.[16]

The Level of Corruption in Specific Areas of Government Activity

In addition to considering corruption as a general phenomenon, it also makes sense to consider and compare the level and sources of corruption in individual areas of government activity. This is all the more important in that it seems difficult to obtain concrete conclusions about the level of corruption for an entire country. The study considered corruption in customs, in the regulation of business (particularly with regard to foreign investment), and in the management of foreign aid. This choice was dictated by the fact that corruption in one or more of these areas is likely to have a particularly dramatic effect on economic growth.

Corruption in customs. Unlike other areas of government activity, it is possible to establish a rough quantitative estimate of the level of corruption in customs by looking at evasion of import taxes and by assuming that the principal cause of the evasion is customs officials accepting bribes by importers seeking to avoid duties. There are several different ways in which one might estimate the amount of import tax evasion that occurs as a result of corruption, none of which is wholly satisfactory.

The most straightforward method is to take the figure for imports reported by customs and calculate the value of import taxes that should have been collected. Looking at the difference between what should have been collected and what was actually collected will then provide a figure for revenue lost as a result of exemptions (legitimate and illegitimate) and revenue lost from cases of corruption where importers declare the value of their goods correctly but do not pay the full duty (other factors can also explain part of the difference, in Francophone African countries, in particular, practices involving establishing minimum duties. These differences may also be due to funds lost in transit between the customs administration and the Treasury). The difference between the value of import taxes that should have been collected and what was actually collected might be calculated either in the aggregate or for individual products, but for Mozambique only aggregate data are available.[17] Using this method one finds that as a result of legitimate granting of exemptions, illegitimate granting of exemptions, and other types of corruption, for the years 1993 and 1995, the Mozambican customs collected only 46 per cent of the revenues it should have in 1993 and only 49 per cent in 1995.[18]

The true figure for the revenue shortfall in Mozambique is undoubtedly larger than the first method indicates, because it does not capture the sort of corruption where importers bribe customs officials in exchange for accepting a false declaration on the value of their goods. Information provided by pre-shipment inspection companies, like SGS, can help measure this additional effect, but this sort of data is generally only available when a government gives the inspection company a mandate to conduct an 'ex-post reconciliation', which involves investigating how frequently customs officials acted on its recommendations. This was not the case in Mozambique for the period in question. While these measures should be interpreted only as approximates, data from a sample of six other countries which had such reconciliation programmes on at least a trial basis show a maximum revenue shortfall of around 50 per cent in three African countries – Zambia, Tanzania and Mali.[19] The estimated revenue shortfall for Mozambique quoted above exceeds 50 per cent even without taking into account false declarations, but this shortfall estimate also includes legitimate exemptions. If, for purposes of comparison, one takes the figure for revenues missing in Mozambique for reasons other than exemptions (both legitimate and illegitimate), there was a shortfall of 45 per cent in 1993. Provided that false declaration of goods accounts for at least a further five per cent shortfall, then it can be suggested that corruption in the Mozambican customs is at least as serious as in the other countries above.

A third way to measure the level of corruption in customs might be to estimate unrecorded imports by comparing the figure for imports reported by customs – $599 million for Mozambique in 1993 – and a figure for total imports calculated as a residual from other items in the balance of payments

– \$878 million for Mozambique in 1993.[20] The problem is that measures of other items on the current and capital account might very likely be either significantly overestimated or significantly underestimated. As a result, estimating unrecorded imports by this method is likely to produce a very unreliable figure.

Interview evidence provides further support for the idea that corruption in customs is a major problem in Mozambique. Each of the private sector representatives reported experiencing substantial problems involving corruption in customs, either directly or with their clients (in the case of consulting firms). Customs officials regularly add extra delays to the process of clearing goods in an effort to ask for money in exchange for then speeding things up. They also frequently overestimate the value of goods or apply a higher tariff rate and then suggest that the fee could be reduced in exchange for a bribe. These problems do not only affect businesses, as one importer of humanitarian aid reported experiencing similar demands. In some cases customs officials succeed in pushing the official cost on a shipment so high that the importer can no longer afford to pay. When this occurs, the goods are sold at auction, often to the original owner, and it is not clear what happens to the proceeds. Importers reported that the price for goods obtained by auction varied considerably.

Corruption in business regulation. It is more difficult to assess the level of corruption in the area of business regulation. There are no figures with which to measure expected performance versus actual performance of state agencies, and interviewees preferred to discuss the subject only indirectly, rather than respond to a standardised set of questions from which systematic measures might be drawn. This has produced much anecdotal evidence but little possibility of providing a systematic assessment. All interviewed agreed that corruption existed in this area, and that it had increased substantially in the last ten years, but some claimed that it was still less widespread than in many other African and non-African countries. Others subscribed to the viewpoint that 'you have to pay to get anything done'. One alternative strategy for future research might be to attempt to assess corruption indirectly by measuring transaction costs in terms of time and/or money needed to undertake certain activities, like obtain a building permit.[21] Using this to measure corruption would, of course, depend upon the assumption that all delays or excess fees are the result of corruption, not other sources of inefficiency, like a shortage of personnel with the appropriate skills.

Because government regulation of business activity is such a broad area to cover, a somewhat narrower focus of corruption in the regulation of foreign investment was chosen for the study. The first institution with which foreign investors have to deal in Mozambique is the Centre for the Promotion of Investment (CPI), which, despite its name, has been more of a hindrance than a help to potential investors (since 1996 the CPI has improved its performance in this regard). That an organisation charged with facilitating investment should function in this manner is a pattern that has been observed for many other developing countries.[22] The CPI was originally set up to regulate and screen investment, but not necessarily to encourage it, and only recently has the Mozambican government attempted to make facilitation of investment the top priority.[23] The CPI's procedures for approval of projects are especially time-consuming because of the need to submit a 'feasibility study'. Interestingly, while they generally bemoaned it as a source of delays and uncertainty, none of the interviewees, either from the private sector or from donor agencies, cited direct examples of corruption at the CPI.

There were many examples cited of corruption involving other government agencies, although it is important to distinguish between delays which investors suffer purely because of bureaucratic inefficiency, and delays that they may suffer as a result of bureaucrats stalling in order to force bribe payments. Once past the CPI, businesses encounter substantial problems in setting up operations, and they also reported frequently experiencing demands for bribes in exchange for provision of import licences, operating licences, and other forms of approval which a business needs to renew periodically. Access to utilities like water and electricity has also at times been made difficult in order to attempt to extract bribes. Problems of this sort have occurred even in the case of major industrial clients with known political connections, like the SOSUN company, which has a licence to produce Coca-Cola.

Once operating, the most common problem cited by companies in the sample was difficulty in procuring an import registration bulletin from the Ministry of Commerce, although when pressed they refrained from directly acknowledging that it took a bribe to procure one (since 1996 this system has been changed). An indirect form of corruption in this area was reported by one factory manager who found that when he did not work through a well-connected import–export broker, he encountered major problems with the Ministry of Commerce. In addition to encountering difficulties of this sort, businesses also reported encountering difficulties in gaining access to hard currency. A final regulatory aspect which can cause delays for foreign investors is the system for granting visas. Fines for overstaying one's visa date have actually been increased recently from $100 per day to $350 per day. There are a number of different potential motivations behind this development, one of which is a desire to restrict immigration to Mozambique from South Asia. Another is that money from visa fines reportedly is frequently diverted to private uses rather than being transferred to the State Treasury.

Corruption in foreign aid. As with business regulation, evidence of corruption in this area remains anecdotal in nature. The secrecy inevitably involved in corruption in aid projects makes it difficult to gather useful information, but it also seems true that donor countries have often been ineffective in collecting data on the extent of corruption in their own projects. Evaluation reports prepared by donors frequently steer around the issue of corruption, and audit reports identify that improper accounting procedures have been used but often reserve judgement on whether corruption has taken place. That corruption in the management of foreign aid is a problem was disputed by none of the interviewees for this study, and they also agreed that the problem has increased in recent years, but there was no agreement on the percentage of aid projects which suffered diversion of funds.

Given these constraints, there are several conclusions one can draw from a limited number of cases that have received public attention. Diversion of emergency food aid shipments appears to be the major example of corruption in aid administration, and there is evidence that it has been occurring at least since the late 1980s. One auditor from a major donor calculated that anywhere between a third and a half of emergency food aid to Mozambique in the late 1980s and early 1990s (from this particular donor), disappeared as a result of corruption. Several different agencies within the Mozambican government bear responsibility for such disappearances. According to a Netherlands Development Co-operation evaluation report, there have been substantial losses of food aid at Mozambique's two main ports of Beira and Maputo (presumably due to corrupt port and customs authorities). The report also observes that 'the DPCCN, the government organisation in Mozambique responsible for emergency operations, is a body that several international NGOs try to avoid as much as possible'.[24] More recently, in a very high profile example of corruption in food aid, 92 truckloads of emergency food aid donated by USAID simply disappeared.

In addition to disappearing emergency food aid shipments, corruption has been apparent with other types of aid. What is more difficult to conclude is whether a series of recent scandals point to an actual increase in corruption, or just an increase in publicity. The recent incident that has received the most attention involved diversion of funds from a programme called the PESU, which was set up by the Swedish and Norwegian governments to distribute emergency shipments of seed and tools to Mozambican farmers. An audit of the programme showed that $2.3 million dollars in funds was unaccounted for, and as a result the Swedish and Norwegian governments have asked the Mozambican government to reimburse the money.

The Organisation of Corruption

Recent theoretical work on corruption suggests that the effect of corruption on economic growth will depend not only on how widespread corruption is but also on how it is organised. When bribe taking is centralised, or when there are well established 'rules of the game' governing bribery contracts, corruption will still have a negative impact on the economy, but much less so than in cases where bribe taking is uncoordinated and unpredictable. The two key aspects of organisation on which the study focused involved whether there is collusion between agents demanding a bribe and what forms of association exist between government and business. Neither of these two forms of organisation exist today in Mozambique.

A lack of co-ordination between those taking bribes. There is little reason to believe that there is any centralised system in Mozambique for collusion on the part of those taking bribes. This observation is supported by looking at how different parts of the Mozambican government communicate with each other (or fail to communicate) with regard to more mundane affairs and with observations from businesses about how they deal with corruption.

The best evidence for the anarchic nature of corruption in the Mozambican customs is the substantial delays which companies suffer in getting goods cleared. If corruption in customs was organised in a centralised manner, or if certain 'rules of the game' were evident, businesses would probably have a good idea what payments were required for what kind of shipments, regardless of which customs official was being dealt with, and as a consequence might not expect substantial delays. In fact, two companies reported having to keep three months' worth of inputs on hand at all times in order to provide a cushion against the uncertainty involved in clearing shipments. A further indication of the anarchic nature of corruption in customs is that even companies that are very well connected politically have continued to experience major delays in clearing goods without having to pay bribes. Two of the firms interviewed have current or former top FRELIMO officials in management positions or on their governing board, but both reported having considerable problems with customs.

In the area of regulation of foreign investment, the anarchic nature of corruption stems from the fact that potential investors have to deal with a series of different government agencies which do not co-ordinate their actions. The CPI, while not accused of corruption itself, has little authority to see that once it clears a project other agencies are also co-operative. Further indication of the anarchic nature of corruption in Mozambique is given by the lapses in communication between officials in different ministries and by the inability of ministers to exert authority over their subordinates. Recent examples where communication failed at the formal level involve an inter-ministerial tourism promotion committee, where the ministers involved reportedly could not even get subordinates from different ministries to meet with each other. The committee that has been created to oversee development of the Pretoria–Maputo transport corridor has experienced similar problems.

Ministers also reportedly have a difficult time exerting authority over their subordinates. Interviewees were unanimous in agreeing that a potential investor deals with ministers and other high-level officials, but once an investment is agreed upon the investor has to deal with lower level officials from a number of different agencies over whom ministers have no effective control. Some businesses reported being able to make complaints at the ministerial level when a lower level official delayed in processing an application and demanded a bribe, but they also emphasised that this could not be done every time a lower level official caused trouble, and in some cases ministerial intervention did not solve the problem.

Finally, no one suggested that there were commonly known bribe prices for certain licences or permits, something which has been reported for several Asian countries and which would be a good indicator that a well-ordered form of corruption exists.

Forms of association between government and business. Corruption in Mozambique does not seem to take place within networks between business and government which might reduce uncertainty for private sector operators. This absence of such networks for government–business dialogue is arguably a characteristic of many African states.[25] One indication comes from a recent private sector conference report, which highlighted the 'lack of involvement of the private sector and businessmen in decision-making'. In addition to a lack of co-ordination on the government side, the absence of a business–government dialogue can also be blamed on the many divisions within the private sector itself. A recent meeting in the port city of Beira, which was designed to assemble all the elements of the private sector, attracted over 150 different groups. Mozambique does have two main private sector associations, the AIM and AIPM, which have received government support, but by all accounts they are quite weak (this problem has to some extent been tackled since 1996 thanks to the creation of a more cohesive business confederation). As far as informal contacts between business and government are concerned, none of the 15 private sector representatives interviewed made reference to any informal, regularised associations between businesses and government officials, as instead when businesses mentioned their contacts with government they always involved relationships with individual officials.

Other indications of a lack of interaction between business and government in the organisation of corruption come from observations by interviewees about the environment in which payments are made. If there was some form of organisation to reduce uncertainty about bribery payments, one might expect businesses to treat such payments as they would treat a regular fee for a service. Instead, a number of different businesses reported trying to avoid having to make bribery payments as much as possible because 'once you start paying you have to keep paying'. A first payment to an official rarely guarantees that the same official will not come back and ask for more, or that other officials in the agency will not then assume that because the company has made an illicit payment it will be willing to make others in exchange for the same service.

Why is corruption in Mozambique so anarchic? Shleifer and Vishny[26] claim that collusion in bribe taking among a government's officials will be more likely to occur when, first, a country's political elite is small; second, when there are no major ethnic cleavages within the elite; and, third, when there is an effective policing machine for monitoring those who participate in such an arrangement and for punishing those who defect. Similar factors should also favour the formation of business–government associations. It has generally been observed that East Asian states might be more likely to fulfil these criteria than would most African countries.

Mozambique does have quite a small ruling elite, although for a different reason than East Asian states. The lack of highly educated people in Mozambique has meant that those who do have a university education (less than 3,000 out of a population of 16 million[27]) form a fairly compact ruling elite. The problem is that this ruling elite has become increasingly fragmented as a result of the reform process. While a well-disciplined FRELIMO party once controlled almost all resources in the Mozambican economy, today liberalisation and privatisation have offered a number of opportunities for different elite groups to gain substantial incomes on assets that are no longer directly controlled by the party. An increase in faction fighting has taken place as different groups vie for control of assets that are being privatised.[28]

Mozambique also does not fulfil the second factor of social homogeneity. For one, there are a number of different ethno-regional groups throughout Mozambique's vast territory, but the FRELIMO party has always been based primarily in the south of the country. Lack of homogeneity is also a problem in the area of business–government relations. As in other African countries, relations between the private sector and government often suffer from the fact that the government perceives a danger in a private sector whose largest firms may well be controlled by businessmen from the former colonising country. This is further complicated by the presence of many South Africans in the formal sector and many people of South Asian ancestry in commerce. Tensions between a government fearful of control by foreign capital and a private sector that feels unwelcome would probably be a major hindrance to the development of business–government networks. This seems plausible, but it ignores the fact that the business elite in several Southeast Asian countries has often had a large, and even dominant, participation from ethnic (or 'overseas') Chinese. Government officials in countries like Thailand and Indonesia may have been able to establish close associations with 'foreign' capital of this sort by establishing partnerships with foreign investors.

Summary

Among the different areas of government activity, customs has received the worst reputation for corruption in Mozambique, and it is possible to confirm the existence of a high level of corruption in customs through estimates on revenue losses. Corruption is also commonplace in business regulation and in the management of foreign aid, but the exact level of corruption in these two areas of government activity remains harder to assess. Business representatives cited numerous examples of corruption in the bureaucracy and donor representatives did the same, and both groups agreed that the level of corruption has increased substantially in the last ten years. There is no obvious way to corroborate these statements, however, nor is there any indication of how one might assess the level of corruption in Mozambique in these areas today compared to other African countries. Finally, one characteristic common to corruption in all three areas considered here is its anarchic nature.

SOURCES OF CORRUPTION

General Evidence

While it proved difficult to measure the level of corruption, the sources of corruption in Mozambique often involve more readily observable factors like the design of state institutions and levels of pay for civil servants. The Mozambican government has been relatively successful with a number of macroeconomic reforms that have reduced opportunities for corruption, as when it reduced the gap between the official and black market exchange rate for the metical, to virtually zero, from 150 per cent in 1990. It also, according to the World Bank's data, narrowed the scope of price controls quite dramatically, from 69 per cent of total production before reform to less than five per cent of production by 1993. It has made much less progress with a number of additional reforms necessary to reduce opportunities for corruption. In the area of trade liberalisation, a simplified, but still overly complex, tariff structure continues to fuel corruption. Efforts to simplify the functioning of the bureaucracy have also been limited. The result is that government officials continue to enjoy monopoly and discretionary activities over a wide range of activities where their having this privilege seems to serve no real purpose in either efficiency or equity. At the same time that opportunities to engage in corruption remain, the incentive for individual civil servants to exploit these opportunities has increased as wages have fallen in real terms and as a large gap has emerged between wages available for similar skilled tasks in the private and public sectors. Finally, in terms of monitoring its officials and holding them accountable for wrong-doing, the Mozambican government can no longer rely on the same tools which were used to fight corruption during the first ten years of independence, and it is only beginning to strengthen alternative institutions for monitoring and accountability, mainly an independent and effective judiciary and police force.

Monopoly and discretionary power for bureaucrats. Mozambican civil servants retain a bewildering variety of rights to regulate and control economic activity. The design of the Mozambican administration most often gives individual agencies a monopoly over allocation of particular permits, licences or registrations, and there are a large number of permits necessary for setting up and operating a business. One recent report notes that 'even when compared to other developing countries, the legalities and costs of setting up and operating a company in Mozambique are high'.[29] This system is in part a colonial inheritance from the Salazar regime in Portugal, which sought to create institutions to exert firm bureaucratic control over the private sector both at home and in the colonies. It is also an inheritance of regulations put in place in the first decade after independence, often inspired by examples of government regulation in eastern Europe and the Soviet Union.[30] Monopoly power provides opportunities for corruption in the area of business regulation, where the fact that only one agency (or sometimes only one individual) has the right to allocate a specific good provides an opportunity to extract bribes even when this raises costs for the person giving the bribe.

Substantial discretionary power exists for civil servants both because many regulations are quite vague, and because there are so many regulations left over from both the colonial period and the socialist period that officials have a large amount of *de facto* discretion in deciding what to enforce. One bank manager claimed: 'if the civil servants actually applied every single regulation that remains on the books no company would be able to do business in Mozambique.' One example involves accounting procedures, where the government added a host of new procedures and requirements to accounting that were designed to improve the management of public enterprises. The problem has been, as one report cites, that 'it is virtually impossible even for the best run company to comply 100 per cent with all requirements'.[31]

In the end, what is most striking about the extent of monopoly and discretionary power is that despite its clear commitment to economic reform in many areas, the Mozambican government has not undertaken the sort of bureaucratic simplification necessary to minimise opportunities for corruption. One major reason for this is that bureaucratic simplification would make certain departments within ministries superfluous, and, as a result, the personnel in these departments become fervent advocates of the *status quo*.

The incentive structure for civil servants. At the same time that government institutions provide opportunities for Mozambican civil servants to engage in corruption, trends in public sector pay have increased incentives to exploit these opportunities. In terms of pay, at the lower levels of the Mozambican civil service there is evidence of a drop in real wages since the commencement of economic reforms. As shown in Figure 1, real wages

FIGURE 1
MONTHLY WAGES OF LOWER-LEVEL CIVIL SERVICE WORKERS
(IN 1987 METICAI)

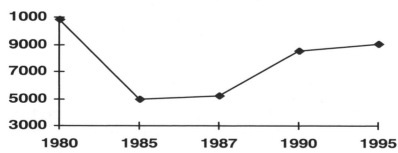

Sources: Nominal wages from World Bank 1991 and AIM News Service for June 1995, GDP deflator from World Bank, *World Tables*, Jan–June 1995 computed based on Mozambican CPI, World Bank mission, Maputo.

appear to have suffered a sharp decline between 1980 and 1985, but this was followed by a gradual improvement between 1987 and 1995.

However, due to the phasing out in the early 1990s of additional benefits provided to civil servants in the form of food coupons, the actual decline in purchasing power for lower level civil servants is undoubtedly understated here. In 1990 these coupons for a household of five were equivalent to a 36 per cent bonus on a lower level civil servant's salary.[32] Because there was extensive rationing of consumer goods during the early 1980s, and public sector employees had priority access to a number of items, it also seems likely that much of the adjustment provoked by the initial drop in real wages between 1980 and 1985 may actually have been delayed until after the beginning of economic reform.

A decline in real wages at the lower levels of the public sector has also occurred in a number of other African countries, although there has been substantial variation between states.[33] Governments needing to cut total wage expenditures face the choice of either firing people or cutting average salaries. The latter option has proven more politically palatable in most cases. The problem is that when real wages descend to a certain point, lower level civil servants either begin moonlighting in order to maintain a subsistence income or they resort increasingly to using their post as a means of generating bribe revenue. The Mozambican government has taken this route to fiscal stabilisation and it has suffered similar consequences. Health workers in the province of Manica recently complained publicly to the provincial governor that they were forced to demand bribes because their monthly salaries alone could not sustain even small families for more than a week. Where Mozambique differs from the same story played out in some African countries is that the number of civil servants per inhabitant is low by African standards: only seven per 1,000 inhabitants in 1990 as compared with an average of 15 per 1,000 in a collection of nine other sub-Saharan African countries. One study thus concluded that, if anything, the number of civil servants in Mozambique is too low.[34] This would suggest that there is less room than may exist in some countries to reduce the total wage bill by reducing numbers of civil servants rather than reducing salaries.

At higher levels of the civil service a more important consideration for reducing corruption than absolute levels of pay is the differential between pay available for performing similar tasks in the public and private sectors. Accurate comparison between these two sectors is complicated by the fact that public sector employment often offers greater job security, and other benefits for which the value is hard to quantify, but in the case of Mozambique the difference between wages in the public and private sectors for skilled professionals is so large that it undoubtedly outweighs these other considerations. At the beginning of the reform programme, the issue

TABLE 1
PAY STRUCTURE ACROSS SECTORS IN MOZAMBIQUE (1990)
(MONTHLY SALARY IN $US)

	Civil Service	Parastatal	Private Sector	International Organisations
senior admin.	243	171	na	na
professional staff	272	76	1,111	1,355
lower level tech	48	42	42	489
clerical staff	32	23	38	325
drivers	25	48	48	315
unskilled manual	20	14	14	220

Source: World Bank (1991)

TABLE 2
RATIO OF PUBLIC SECTOR TO PRIVATE SECTOR SALARIES:
A COMPARISON WITH EAST ASIA

	Senior Level	Mid-Level	Entry Level
Singapore	114	115	107
South Korea	99	82	84
Taiwan	63	65	60
Malaysia	37	42	–
Thailand	38	38	79
Philippines	26	29	63
Mozambique	24*		84**

Source: for Asian countries, World Bank, *The East Asian Miracle*, 1993 [* for professional staff; ** for clerical staff]

of relative pay between the private and public sectors was not a serious problem, because there were so few opportunities for employment in the private sector. By 1990, however, a huge gap had emerged in pay levels for professional staff between the public and private sectors (see Table 1).

For the period since 1990, there is every indication that the gap between public and private sector wages for skilled personnel has persisted, and there has been a continued trend of skilled people leaving the public sector either to work in the private sector or for international organisations.[35] Data on wages in the public and private sectors for several East Asian states show that Singapore, South Korea and Taiwan offered public sector salaries that were highly competitive with those available for similar work in the private sector, while Malaysia, Thailand and the Philippines chose not to offer competitive salaries for senior staff in particular. It is interesting to note that Thailand rates as one of the most corrupt countries on the index produced by

Business International.[36] In any case, for senior level officials Mozambique compares unfavourably with all of the countries listed in Table 2.

In addition to wage incentives, another major source of corruption in Mozambique derives from the fact that current civil service regulations do not provide sufficient opportunity for internal promotion (this problem has been addressed to some extent by a new civil service recruitment and promotion scheme introduced in 1998). Systems for internal promotion based on merit, combined with punishment for those that abuse public office, have proven to be an effective means of improving bureaucratic efficiency in a number of East Asian and other countries.[37] One reason for the dearth of opportunities for internal promotion in the Mozambican civil service involves the lack of interaction between the central administration in Maputo and provincial administrations. Provincial officials have opportunities to rise within the ranks of the service in their own province, but they have little hope of ever being promoted to a higher position in Maputo once they reach the top of the provincial ladder. A second reason for the lack of possibilities for internal promotion is an overemphasis on formal educational requirements, as promotion rules fail to consider that, to a certain extent, work experience can substitute for schooling. A lack of possibilities for rising within the ranks of the Mozambican bureaucracy can only add to the other incentives for officials to abuse public office for private material gain. If possibilities for internal promotion did exist, then officials might be more inclined to refrain from corrupt acts today, lest it end up preventing them from exercising authority at a higher level in the future. Improvement in this area is stalled by the fact that macroeconomic reforms in Mozambique have not been accompanied by a fundamental reform of the civil service.

Institutions for monitoring and accountability. Decreased effectiveness in monitoring officials has been a major factor behind the expansion of corruption in Mozambique. At the higher levels of the civil service, the problem seems to be not that the government is devoting fewer resources than it used to in monitoring its officials, but that the transition to a market economy has inevitably made it more difficult to detect corruption. Previous to the undertaking of the economic reform programme, there was a rule forbidding FRELIMO party members to own a stake in a private enterprise or to employ more than a few individuals. This regulation, which was seen as a way of preventing some of the injustices suffered during the colonial period, also had an effect of making it much more difficult for officials to portray the purchase of an expensive new car or a new house as a product of legitimate private enterprise. Clearly, the possibility for holding corruption proceeds abroad must still have existed, but there was at least some sort of limitation. This constraint on private sector activity made it much easier to detect corruption indirectly and in a low-cost way. It was all the more effective in that FRELIMO membership was fairly large (two per cent of the adult population according to a 1985 World Bank report). Several interviewees insisted that this formal rule was reinforced by a strong set of norms opposing self-enrichment within the FRELIMO government at the time. Mozambique's first president after independence, Samora Machel, made considerable efforts to set a personal example in this domain. Adherence to these principles was also strengthened by the low rate of turnover among top FRELIMO personnel at the time, as the only change made to the Political Bureau in the first 15 years of independence was to add one official.[38] Today, self-enrichment is seen in a different light, and senior government officials have many business dealings in addition to their regular jobs, making it much more difficult to distinguish between income from corruption and that from legitimate business.[39] Given the necessary abandonment of the old rule banning public officials from engaging in private business, new means of monitoring officials need to be developed. This could include mandatory declarations of personal assets on the part of officials upon assuming and leaving office (this sort of requirement was introduced in 1996 in Mozambique, but it was subsequently decided not to make the declarations public, nullifying the potential benefit of this measure).

In addition to increased difficulty in monitoring officials, there has also been a significant change in the extent to which officials who are discovered to have engaged in corruption are held accountable for their actions. Today, even when those involved in major affairs of corruption are discovered, the punishments appear to be minimal. The PESU scandal involving misuse of aid funds destined for seeds and tools for agriculture provides a good example. After a lengthy investigation, several of the main officials involved were identified, but the only penalty they received was to be demoted by several civil service grades for a year, after which they would be fully reinstated. Robert Klitgaard has suggested that one of the most effective initial steps for a government willing to control corruption is to set an example by 'frying big fish', but in Mozambique no big fish have been fried (the only such instance was the firing of the former Interior Minister who subsequently remained unprosecuted despite numerous abuses of office). The lack of clear examples of punishment for engaging in corruption today contrasts sharply with the example set during the anti-corruption campaign that Samora Machel inaugurated in Mozambique in 1980, when a number of officials were summarily dismissed or arrested.

With the transition away from socialism, the institutions of the judiciary and the police and the practice of holding free elections have taken on increased importance for monitoring and holding both civil servants and politicians accountable for their actions. The effectiveness of the judicial system in this task has been very limited. Interviewees referred unanimously to a system pervaded by corruption. Mozambique's critical shortage of skilled people is also a major source of inefficiency in the judiciary. There were only 90 fully qualified lawyers in 1992 in a country of 16 million people, and although constitutional reforms adopted in 1990 provide a strong basis for the independence of the judiciary, it will be a number of years before the judicial system is effective enough to be a practical recourse for those seeking to challenge public officials who demand bribes in exchange for government services.[40] It is also a major problem to attract lawyers to low-paid jobs in the judiciary when there are much more lucrative possibilities in the private sector. All of the companies interviewed for the study suggested that they currently sought at all costs to avoid settling disputes through the judicial system, because it was ineffective, and there was in fact a substantial risk of having to pay even more bribes. One bank manager reported having sent over 20 cases of employee theft to the courts, and not a single case was actually heard in court. Similarly, in the case of the police, it can be argued that low pay has the same effect as in other areas of the civil service, as the police have acquired more of a reputation for robbing people than protecting them.

Regular open elections and a free press can, in theory, also serve as important mechanisms for monitoring politicians and holding them accountable for their actions. Several recent episodes of corruption have received major attention in the Mozambican media, including the theft of the USAID food aid shipment and the misuse of funds involved in the PESU programme funded by the Nordic countries. The problem is that press reports involving scandals such as these have not generally been able (or wanted) to identify the major figures responsible. National elections have now taken place in Mozambique, but it would be overly simplistic to suggest that the mere fact of having free elections will increase accountability. Real possibilities for holding top officials in Mozambique accountable for their actions will probably not exist until there are groups in Mozambican society which are well organised enough to launch sustained demands that blatantly corrupt officials be replaced, either through elections or through other constitutional means.

Alternative explanations. There are at least two plausible alternative explanations to those detailed above for the rapid spread of corruption in Mozambique. One possibility would be a norm-based explanation. Several interviewees strongly emphasised the importance of the fact that corruption today has become morally acceptable in a way that it was not ten years ago.

The exact reason why this would be the case is not clear, however. One could suggest that this is the result of a lengthy civil war and all the trauma that it has brought to the population, but while the civil war began much earlier, corruption did not visibly increase until the late 1980s. Some have also argued that the arrival of a particularly unbridled form of capitalism has changed people's values by increasing their tolerance of corruption. Since one of the main characteristics of an unbridled form of capitalism would seem to be corruption, however, this explanation might suffer from problems of circularity.

A second alternative explanation might be one that drew inspiration from economic models of corruption with frequency-dependent equilibria, where the number of officials already engaged in corruption affects the perceived chance of getting caught for any additional actor considering whether to remain within the law or engage in corruption.[41] In Mozambique's case a temporary shock (of which there have been many) may have had a long-lasting effect in increasing the level of corruption in the economy. It is true that interviewees frequently spoke of corruption in Mozambique today as 'feeding itself', as people increasingly sense that they can engage in corruption with impunity. However, the basic conditions structuring the principal-agent relationship between government and civil servant have also changed radically in the last ten years. This makes it difficult to judge whether the frequency-dependent model or the standard principal-agent more closely fits the pattern of corruption in Mozambique.

Sources of Corruption in Specific Areas of Activity

Customs. Since most corruption in customs probably is corruption with theft, monopoly power is not a prerequisite for being able to engage in corruption. Instead, importers eager to lower the amount of duty they pay can be expected actively to seek opportunities for paying bribes. One of the most important determinants of corruption in customs in developing countries is the existence of high tariffs which encourage tax evasion. In Mozambique, while tariffs have not been lowered to East Asian levels, the current system of five different rates with a minimum of five per cent and a maximum of 35 per cent represents a relatively successful reform by the standards of a number of African countries. As a consequence, the tariff structure may be partially at fault, but one also needs to look further to understand why corruption in the Mozambican customs is such a problem.

Excess discretionary power for customs officials derives from legislation on customs exemptions that provides few guidelines for determining what objects fall within the five categories to which exemptions are granted. These include exemptions for foreign aid, diplomatic exemptions, industrial inputs, authorised investments under the investment code, imports of essential goods like medical supplies and personal effects of returning miners. This last category was, apparently, defined in extremely vague terms in the statutes. In many cases, exemptions are granted to ineligible goods in exchange for bribes, although it is impossible to make any judgement about the extent to which these are abused because there has been no system of *ex-post* reconciliation in place to see how inspection reports match with what was actually declared by the importer to customs and how the good was classified by the customs officer. The same story of excess complexity creating room for discretion is true for the paperwork required to transit through customs. A recent report on modernising customs in Mozambique found that 'customs procedures, documentation and information requirements, work/paper flows, etc. have been found to be highly bureaucratic, administratively cumbersome and not in conformity with internationally accepted customs norms. Customs procedures are contributing to unacceptable cargo delay times and high costs of transacting trade in Mozambique'.[42] Businesses interviewed in Maputo were quick to note that the extreme complexity of customs procedures provides customs officials with substantial room for discretion in deciding what to enforce strictly and what not to enforce strictly.

The existence of substantial *de facto* discretionary power for customs officials is a convincing explanation for the existence of corruption in customs, but it does not provide a full explanation for the apparent increase in corruption in customs in recent years, since many of the bureaucratic features listed above have been in place since well before the beginning of the economic reform period. To account for the change one needs to refer to the same evolution in real wages and monitoring that has led to increased corruption elsewhere. In addition, one could suggest that the decision to extend the legal right to import goods to companies other than state-run trading monopolies has led to increased corruption. Shleifer and Vishny[43] argue that in cases of corruption with theft, competition among businesses will lead to an increase in corruption. In the pre-reform period in Mozambique a large share of international trade was conducted through state-run companies which often had very close ties to top members of FRELIMO and to officials in the security-oriented ministries. Once trading operations were opened increasingly to competition, corruption inevitably became more of a problem.

Like many other governments in similar situations, the Mozambican government in 1991 contracted the services of a pre-shipment inspection firm (SGS in this case) to help verify the value of shipments to Mozambique before they actually leave the country from which they are exported (SGS has since been replaced by Inchcape, another pre-shipment inspection firm). Once an import licence is issued for a particular good, an SGS affiliate office in the exporting country inspects the cargo to verify its contents, either issuing a Clean Report of Findings or recommending a change in the valuation of the good. Customs officials in Mozambique are then supposed to ask the importer to show the report from SGS.

This level of involvement for SGS may have helped reduce the incidence of cases where people mislead customs with false declarations, but it has not cut down on corruption of customs officials, who in many cases simply agree not to ask for the SGS document in exchange for payment. Some indication of the Mozambican government's reluctance to use pre-shipment inspection vigorously is given by the fact that the initial fine for not presenting the Clean Report of Findings certificate was only $12. Pre-shipment inspection can help address the problem of individuals smuggling goods through customs without knowledge of customs officials, but it clearly does not automatically solve the monitoring problem. In order for pre-shipment inspection to be effective as a check on corrupt officials in customs departments, the system must include a mandate for the PSI company to perform an *ex-post* reconciliation.[44] This involves comparing information from pre-shipment inspection forms with customs documents, shipment by shipment. There also exists the possibility of giving the PSI company an even wider mandate by obliging importers to demonstrate to an official of the company that they have deposited the recommended duty in a bank account held by the government. This system, known as 'securitisation', was first adopted with substantial success in Indonesia during the 1980s, and more recently has been implemented in Cameroon. Today, the Mozambican government is undertaking a privatisation of customs operations which should work on similar principles. Even systems involving securitisation are still open to abuse, however, if top politicians are unwilling to push for reform, since discretionary exemptions can be granted on certain imports that are judged to be 'essential for national security', and so on.

Given the obvious importance of *ex-post* reconciliation as part of a pre-shipment inspection programme, it is worth asking why the contract awarded by the Mozambican government to SGS from 1991 to 1995 did not include such a mandate. One official involved in the discussions that led to the signature of the first pre-shipment inspection contract in 1991 indicated that the merits of *ex-post* reconciliation were well understood at the time, but the donors simply did not choose to exert pressure on the Mozambican government to give the PSI company a mandate to perform this important service. Nor was there any serious consideration of adopting securitisation. For a government interested in cutting down on the smuggling of goods through customs but not necessarily interested in removing the rent-seeking opportunities for customs officials themselves, pre-shipment inspection without either *ex-post* reconciliation or securitisation seems the politically safe solution. The recent change in Mozambique towards advocating a more effective PSI system seems attributable primarily to donor pressure and to a new Finance Minister who seems determined to improve revenue collection in customs. It is unclear, however, to what extent the broader political conditions necessary to make this measure effective are present.

Business regulation. Bureaucratic control of businesses in Mozambique includes a large number of regulations that are an inheritance from both Portuguese colonialism and the attempts to construct a command economy after independence. Existing regulations involve a lengthy process for company registration, including items like the need to prove that no other company has registered with exactly the same name.[45] Once licensed, industrial and other firms need to procure operating licences, for which there are a number of different potential obstacles (including apparently the possibility for competitors to complain that a new entrant into the market will lead to unhealthy competition). After obtaining an operating licence, industrial and other firms face a number of cumbersome labour regulations, many of which seem to serve no purpose other than to provide civil servants with an opportunity to engage in corruption, since minor infractions (like not informing the Ministry of Labour about when employees take holidays) can be punished with heavy fines.

The basis for many of the regulations from the colonial era is the Commercial Code, which dates back to 1888. In many cases, there are overlapping regulations from the colonial period and the post-independence period, leading to substantial confusion for private sector operators and providing government employees with a large amount of *de facto* discretion. In addition to the existence of substantial discretion, what makes the above controls such an opportunity for corruption is the monopoly aspect, that in many cases only one agency, or only one individual, can provide the needed service. For the various licences, stamps and authorisations necessary to do business, interviewees could not cite any examples of 'overlapping jurisdictions', where if one branch of one agency caused them problems they could get the service elsewhere.[46] In some cases, like delivery of papers for car registrations, there is only one person in the entire Mozambican civil service that is authorised to deliver the necessary document. According to several interviewees, such positions are often jealously guarded by those who hold them because of the opportunity to make a second income out of illicit payments.

With regard to foreign investment regulation, substantial opportunities for corruption are provided because 'not only is documentation extensive but often neither the investors nor the government officials know what the documents should be with certainty'.[47] According to another study, for foreign investors attempting to implement a proposed investment, under current regulations there are *seven* different processes that have to be gone through even after approval is granted by the Centre for the Promotion of Investment.[48]

1. Registering the company with the Public Notary.
2. Registering the company with the Commercial Register.
3. Publication of the company's articles in the *Boletima da Republica.*
4. Registering with the relevant tax authority.
5. Obtaining a land concession title.
6. Presenting a detailed technical study and environmental impact study to the relevant sectoral ministry for approval.
7. Obtaining an operating licence following inspection of the premises.

Incentives for any one of these seven agencies to put a freeze on a particular application and demand a bribe are increased by the fact that a company is required to complete each of the seven above steps within 120 days. Even when investors do get past this stage, separate procedures are necessary to acquire trading licences, to operate bank accounts, to negotiate loan agreements, to hire foreign staff and to register with tax authorities and customs.

In the end, while corruption in the investment process is clearly a problem, there are many sources of inefficiency in this area that do not necessarily involve corruption, the chief of which is a lack of skilled people. The best example of this is the CPI itself, whose actions have prompted much criticism but (as noted above) few direct accusations of corruption. Numerous interviewees suggested that a major problem at CPI is that the current staff do not have the necessary training to fulfil effectively the desired goal of making CPI an institution that actually assists investors in their dealings with other government agencies. This points to the potential risk in using transaction costs (such as length of time to get an investment approved) as proxies for measuring the level of corruption.

Foreign aid. Mozambique has an extremely high dependence on foreign aid, and increased foreign aid flows in recent years may have provided new opportunities for corruption. Aid funds in Mozambique have been especially prone to corruption, because the mechanisms for monitoring aid funds suffer from a number of problems. While the Mozambican government includes aid projects in its budget calculations, there is no central accounting system for aid projects as there is for the rest of the government budget. The Mozambican government's lack of skilled personnel is of critical importance here. Faced with a government that is not currently in a position to monitor effectively the use of aid funds on its own, individual donors have tended each to set up their own system for monitoring use of aid. Several representatives from donor agencies reported that the problem with this solution is that donors often lack the knowledge of local conditions necessary to monitor use of funds effectively, and by bypassing the government they undermine any possibility of strengthening the capacity of the Mozambican administration so that it might participate in monitoring aid funds in the future .

A degree of laxity in donor supervision of funds has, in some cases, clearly played a role in the emergence of corruption in foreign aid. Representatives of several different accounting firms suggested that the Nordic donors had been lax in not performing a sufficient number of audits and not demanding that recipients adhere to certain accounting standards. This argument should not be overdone, however, because certain aspects of the Nordic country aid programmes made them particularly vulnerable to misuse of funds. The Nordic countries have focused on 'high-risk' donor activities which involve giving emergency aid to groups and areas that have been particularly damaged by Mozambique's lengthy civil war. One could argue that these are precisely the areas in which state institutions are likely to be the least effective in controlling corruption. Increased corruption for them may be an inevitable price to pay given the area of aid in which they specialise.

In addition to the question of monitoring, there may be a greater risk of corruption involving foreign aid depending on who makes the initial choice of how aid funds are to be spent. Unlike foreign direct investment, the granting of aid is a bilateral decision where both the recipient and the donor play a role in choosing how aid will be distributed. Does a particular agricultural project really need an extra car, or is it being requested purely for personal use? The desire to avoid corruption in the recipient country might imply that donors should restrict participation by recipients in the decision-making process, but this will come at the price of leaving the allocation process to those who know less about local conditions. This seems similar to the trade-off with regard to decentralisation and corruption. Decentralisation will bring clear benefits by giving people with better knowledge of local conditions increased decision-making power, but it also may hinder attempts to maintain arms-length relationships between decision-makers and those who might corrupt them.

THE EFFECTS OF CORRUPTION ON ECONOMIC GROWTH

Even if it is impossible to measure the overall effect of corruption on growth in Mozambique, this does not preclude a discussion of certain probable effects of corruption on the economy. The article looks first at the distorting effect corruption in the customs service has had on Mozambican industry and on government finances. It then considers the likely disincentive and distorting effects on foreign direct investment.

The Distorting Effects of Corruption in Customs

A first major distorting effect of corruption in customs has been to contribute to a recent decline in government revenues collected on import taxes. The result has been a need to offset revenue losses with cuts in expenditure. This effect should be kept in proper perspective, however. Between 1991 and 1994 total revenues dropped slightly from 21.8 per cent to 19.2 per cent, while collections on import taxes remained stable between 5.1 per cent and 5.4 per cent of GDP, with the exception of a poor performance in 1994 (3.9 per cent of GDP). This was generally attributed to poor performance by customs. Increased illegal imports of beer in particular also had an effect of reducing demand for beer produced in Mozambique, leading to a decline in revenue from the consumption tax on beer.[49]

Customs corruption has also had a distorting effect on tax rates across firms, weakening the competitiveness of Mozambican industry (this factor should not, of course, be seen as the sole cause of the poor performance of industrial firms). Import-competing industrial firms in Mozambique have been penalised by the fact that no taxes are paid on a large percentage of imports, because they are smuggled by informal sector firms that are difficult to track. Managers from firms producing cigarettes and batteries both described having difficulties competing with products that are imported illegally, while as major firms in the formal sector they noted that they themselves are the easiest targets for tax assessors. The firms which are immune to this problem are those selling products for which transport makes up a substantial portion of total costs. The best example of this is the Coca-Cola bottling plant whose manager reported being able to remain competitive despite the ease with which soft drinks can be imported without paying full duties. For firms trying to export, a number reported that while duty drawback schemes exist on paper (to enable exporters to gain access to imported inputs at world prices) these have not functioned well in practice, and corruption is a factor in this failure. For inputs not imported under one of these schemes, exporting firms have had the same difficulties with customs as anyone else. A well-ordered form of corruption should actually reduce costs for exporters if they were able to pay bribes in order not to pay duties, but the substantial uncertainty that many businesses reported in dealing with the different customs agents who can hold up a shipment has reportedly outweighed this benefit.

The Distorting and Disincentive Effects of Corruption on Investment

It is difficult to judge the degree to which the uncertainty created by the presence of corruption is affecting foreign investment flows to Mozambique. It may create a disincentive effect that prompts potential investors either to invest elsewhere, or temporarily place their money in more secure markets, adopting a 'wait and see' attitude until the Mozambican government takes further steps to improve the climate for investment. The same trend could also occur for domestic investment. Corruption may also have a distorting effect by biasing those foreign investments which are made towards sectors where there are assured returns in the short-term. This would suggest increased investment in natural resource exploitation and less investment in manufacturing activities. There might be a tendency for new firms (which would be more likely to bring new technologies to Mozambique) and for small firms to be especially nervous about problems related to corruption.

It is not possible to assess these effects fully without an idea of what type of investments would be occurring in Mozambique if no corruption existed. Companies today may be deterred from investing in Mozambique because of perceptions specific to Mozambique, or they could be deterred by perceptions of investing in African countries in general, which would imply that reducing corruption in Mozambique might actually have little effect on investment. Figure 2 shows that net flows of foreign direct investment have increased substantially in the 1990s, albeit from a very low base.

FIGURE 2
NET FOREIGN DIRECT INVESTMENT FLOWS TO MOZAMBIQUE

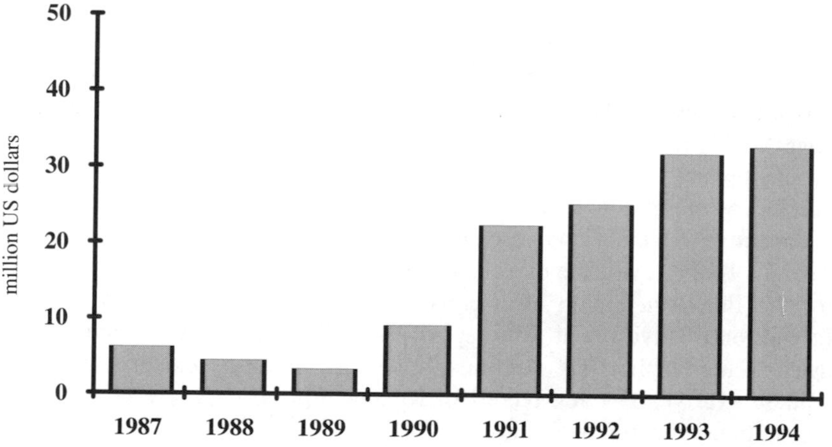

Source: World Bank, *World Tables*.

FIGURE 3
MOZAMBICAN SHARE OF NET FOREIGN DIRECT INVESTMENT FLOWS TO NON-
OIL PRODUCING SUB-SAHARAN AFRICAN COUNTRIES

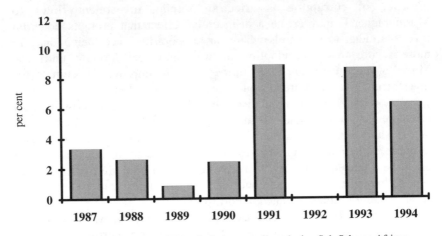

Source: World Bank, *World Debt Tables,* includes non-oil producing Sub-Saharan African
countries for which data was available (Benin, Burkina Faso, Burundi, Central African
Republic, Chad, Côte d'Ivoire, Eq. Guinea, Gambia, Ghana, Guinea, Guinea-Bissau, Kenya,
Madagascar, Mali, Mauritania, Mozambique, Rwanda, Senegal, Zaire, Zambia, Zimbabwe). No
figure is included for 1992 because net FDI to the above countries was negative, notably due to
massive divestment out of Côte d'Ivoire in anticipation of the devaluation of the CFA franc.

Mozambique has also increased its share of total FDI to non-oil producing
Sub-Saharan African countries – see Figure 3. Since 1994 this figure has
increased further due to the commencement of several large projects.

Despite this increase in foreign direct investment, there are indications
that corruption is still having a disincentive effect. A number of businesses
interviewed for this project stated that they had considered making new
investments but had been dissuaded from doing so because of the degree of
uncertainty in dealing with the Mozambican bureaucracy. Several
businesses not currently present in Mozambique but who had studied the
possibility of investing also suggested that corruption has had a major
disincentive on their own decisions whether to invest in Mozambique.
There is further evidence of a disincentive effect in a draft report prepared
for the European Union by a consultant working at the Centre for the
Promotion of Investment. The report notes that most new investments to
date, even after the 1994 elections, have been either by existing investors
with several years' track record in Mozambique or by new investors in
resource-based extractive industries.

CONCLUSION

While Mozambique's programme of macroeconomic reforms has been relatively successful in a number of different areas, reforms to date have not addressed the major problem of increased corruption. There has not been a major civil service reform, there has not been a reform in the commercial code, and there has not been a major attempt to simplify an excessively complex system of regulations. This absence of institutional reform has provided opportunities for civil servants to engage in corruption, opportunities which have been increased by a dramatic weakening in structures for monitoring civil servants and in holding them accountable for their actions. Pay incentives have provided increased incentives to exploit the many opportunities for corruption. The economic impact of increased corruption has been most evident in the distorting effect on tax and trade policies and in the disincentive and distorting effects on investment, prompted by increased uncertainty. These effects have been all the more pronounced, because corruption in Mozambique is anarchic in nature.

NOTES

1. See Philip Keefer and Stephen Knack, 'Why Don't Poor Countries Catch Up?: A Cross-National Test of an Institutional Explanation', IRIS Working Paper Series no.60, 1993; and Philip Keefer and Stephen Knack, 'Institutions and Economic Performance: Cross-Country Tests Using Alternative Institutional Measures', 1994; Aymo Brunetti, 'Political Variables in Cross-Country Growth Analysis' (manuscript, 1995); Paolo Mauro, 'Corruption and Growth', *Quarterly Journal of Economics* (Aug. 1995), 681–712.
2. See Susan Rose-Ackerman, *Corruption: A Study in Political Economy* (New York: Academic Press, 1978); J.-C. Andvig, 'The Economics of Corruption: A Survey', *Studi Economici*, 46, 43 (1991), 57–94; Gary Becker, 'Crime and Punishment', *Journal of Political Economy* (1968); Timothy Besley and John Mclaren, 'Taxes and Bribery: the Role of Wage Incentives', *The Economic Journal*, 103 (Jan. 1993), 119–41; Robert Klitgaard, 'Incentive Myopia', *World Development*, 17 (April 1989), 447–59; Robert Klitgaard, *Controlling Corruption* (Berkeley, CA: University of California Press, 1988).
3. Monopoly is crucial in providing an opportunity for corruption where the costs for the person giving the bribe actually increase. This occurs when a bureaucrat demands a bribe in exchange for provision of a government permit but then passes on the regular permit fee to the state treasury. Andrei Shleifer and Robert Vishny, 'Corruption', *Quarterly Journal of Economics* (1993), 599–617; call this 'corruption without theft'. Monopoly is not crucial as a source of corruption in cases where corruption actually involves a reduction in costs for the bribe-giver. An example here is payment of a bribe in exchange for underpayment of a customs duty. Shleifer and Vishny call this 'corruption with theft', because the government never receives the required tax, fee, or payment.
4. Timothy Besley and John Mclaren, 'Taxes and Bribery: The Role of Wage Incentives', *The Economic Journal*, 103 (Jan. 1993), pp.119–41; and Deborah Brautigam, 'State Capacity and Effective Governance', in Benno Ndulu and Nicolas van de Walle (eds.), *Agenda for Africa's Economic Renewal* (Washington, DC: Overseas Development Council, Transaction Publishers, 1996).
5. When there are procedures for internal promotion within a particular agency, lower-level bureaucrats may have more of a tendency to refrain from engaging in corrupt behaviour which, if detected, might spoil their chances for rising in the ranks. For a formalisation of

this argument see David Soskice, Robert Bates and David Epstein, 'Ambition and Constraint: The Stabilizing Role of Institutions', *Journal of Law, Economics, and Organization*, 8, 3 (1992). For an empirical investigation of the effect of rules governing internal promotion on the level of corruption in different countries, see Peter B. Evans and James Rauch, 'Bureaucratic Structures and Economic Performance in Less Developed Countries' (IRIS Working Paper no.175, August 1995).

6. Shleifer and Vishny, 'Corruption'.
7. Andrei Shleifer, 'Establishing Property Rights', *Proceedings of the World Bank Annual Conference on Development Economics* (Washington, DC, 1994).
8. Jose Edgardo Campos and Hilton Root, 'Behind the Asian Miracle: Making the Promise of Shared Growth Credible' (manuscript, 1996).
9. Following Rose-Ackerman's approaches, there are several different ways to define the level of corruption. One would be the percentage of transactions with government that require a bribe payment. A second might be the total value of bribes in a given sector. Because theories exist which suggest that the frequency of bribes being demanded and the average value demanded for each bribe are two variables which are likely to vary independently, ideally one would be able to measure both. In practice, this is very difficult, and this article has been obliged to measure the level of corruption indirectly.
10. *Mozambique Inview,* 16 Oct. 1995; *Mozambique File, Mozambique News Agency Monthly,* December 1995.
11. AIM News Service, 1 May 1996. This resulted in a policy decision to set up an anti-corruption agency.
12. Giovanni Gnecchi-Ruscone, 'Mozambique Private Sector Review', prepared for the International Finance Corporation by Economisti Associati, 1994.
13. Republica de Mozambique, 'Establishing the Basis for Economic and Social Development: Key Policies', March 1995.
14. Gnecchi-Ruscone, 'Mozambique Private Sector Review'.
15. Catherine Scott, 'Socialism and the "Soft State" in Africa: An Analysis of Angola and Mozambique', *Journal of Modern African Studies,* 26, 1 (1988); Malvyn Newitt, *A History of Mozambique* (London: Hurst and Company, 1995); Tom Young, 'The Politics of Development in Angola and Mozambique', *African Affairs,* 87 (1988), 165–84.
16. There had been major disputes within FRELIMO during the late 1960s, but by the time of independence Samora Machel's faction had gained full control (see Scott, 'Socialism and the "Soft State" in Africa'; Marina Ottaway, 'Mozambique: From Symbolic Socialism to Symbolic Reform', *Journal of Modern African Studies*, 26, 2 (1988), and from this point on little change was to occur in the FRELIMO leadership.
17. For an analysis of corruption in customs based on revenue data by product, see Cécile Daubrée, 'Fraude Documentaire, Corruption et Contrabande: Modèle Théorique et Test Econométrique sur le cas du Senegal' (processed, 1996).
18. World Bank ('Mozambique: Impediments to Industrial Recovery', 1995), based on data provided by Mozambican customs, the Ministry of Finance, and the pre-shipment inspection firm SGS (World Bank data, 1996).
19. Patrick Low, 'Preshipment Inspection Services', *World Bank Discussion Papers,* no.278 (1995).
20. World Bank, 'Mozambique: Impediments to Industrial Recovery' (1995).
21. This is suggested by Susan Rose-Ackerman and Andrew Stone, 'The Costs of Corruption for Private Business: Evidence from World Bank Surveys' (processed, May 1996).
22. Louis T. Wells, Jr., 'Foreign Direct Investment', in David Lindauer and Michael Roemer (eds.), *Asia and Africa: Legacies and Opportunities in Development* (Cambridge, MA: Harvard Institute for International Development, 1991).
23. Centre for the Promotion of Investment, 'Summary of Main Investment Regulations' (1995).
24. Netherlands Development Cooperation, *Food Aid and Development: Evaluation of Dutch Food Aid with Special Reference to Sub-Saharan Africa; 1980–89* (1991), 69.
25. E. Gyimah-Boadi and Nicolas van de Walle, 'The Politics of Economic Renewal in Africa', in Ndulu and van de Walle (eds.), *Agenda for Africa's Economic Renewal.*
26. Shleifer and Vishny, 'Corruption'.

27. World Bank, 'Mozambique: Capacity Building Study' (1993).
28. M. Anne Pitcher, 'Faction Fights and Turf Wars among the New Capitalists of Mozambique' (processed, 1996). See also M. Anne Pitcher, 'Recreating Colonialism or Reconstructing the State? Privatisation and Politics in Mozambique', *Journal of Southern African Studies*, 22, 1 (1996).
29. FIAS, 'Mozambique: Draft Red Tape Analysis' (1996).
30. See Newitt, *A History of Mozambique*; Gnecchi-Ruscone, 'Mozambique Private Sector Review'; World Bank, 'Mozambique: Impediments to Industrial Recovery'; FIAS, 'Mozambique: Draft Red Tape Analysis'.
31. Gnecchi-Ruscone, 'Mozambique Private Sector Review', 33.
32. World Bank, 'Mozambique: Public Sector Pay and Employment Review' (1991).
33. David Lindauer, Oey Astra Meesook and Parita Suebsaeng, 'Government Wage Policy in Africa: Some Findings and Policy Issues', *The World Bank Research Observer*, 3, 1 (Jan. 1988), show that between 1975 and 1983 real starting salaries for those at the lower levels of the civil service declined by 60 per cent in Ghana, 15 per cent in Malawi, 36 per cent in Nigeria, 38 per cent in the Sudan, 84 per cent in Uganda, and they *rose* by 13 per cent in Senegal.
34. Angola, Ghana, Liberia, Malawi, Mali, Senegal, Sudan, Zambia, Nigeria. Most observations for these other countries are from the early 1980s. See World Bank, 'Mozambique: Public Sector Pay and Employment Review' (1991).
35. World Bank, *The East Asian Miracle* (1993).
36. Mauro, 'Corruption and Growth'.
37. Peter B. Evans and James Rauch, 'Bureaucratic Structures and Economic Performance in Less Developed Countries', IRIS Working Paper no.175, August 1995; Campos and Root, 'Behind the Asian Miracle'.
38. Newitt, *A History of Mozambique*; Ottaway, 'Mozambique'.
39. For one account of some of the business dealings of FRELIMO members, see *Africa Analysis,* 3 Sept. 1993.
40. World Bank, 'Mozambique: Capacity Building: Public Sector and Legal Institutions Development Project' (1992); Africa Watch, *Conspicuous Destruction: War, Famine, and the Reform Process in Mozambique* (New York: Human Rights Watch, 1993).
41. For reviews of these models, see Jens Andvig, 'The Economics of Corruption: A Survey', *Studi Economici*, 46, 43 (1991); and Pranab Bardhan, *The Economics of Corruption in Less Developed Countries: A Review of the Issues* (Paris: OECD Development Centre, 1996). See also Paul Collier, 'The Domain of African Government' (paper presented for the SAREC's colloquium on 'New Directions in Development Economics – Growth, Equity, and Sustainable Development', June 1994).
42. 'Action Plan for Reform of Mozambique Customs' (1995).
43. Shleifer and Vishny, 'Corruption'.
44. Low, 'Preshipment Inspection Services'.
45. FIAS, 'Mozambique: Draft Red Tape Analysis', 96.
46. Rose-Ackerman recommends creating overlapping jurisdictions as a mean of creating competition that should reduce corruption.
47. FIAS, 'Mozambique: Draft Red Tape Analysis'.
48. European Union, *Private Sector Development Report – Mozambique* (1996), chapter 9 'Investment Promotion Strategy in Mozambique'.
49. IMF, Mozambique article IV, April 1995.

The Changing Context of Corruption Control: The Hong Kong Special Administrative Region, 1997–99

JONATHAN MORAN

THE CONTEXT OF CORRUPTION CONTROL

Increasing attention has been focused on the analysis of corruption in its historical, social, political and economic context. While this is not a new development, recent studies have attempted to analyse corruption as a dynamic phenomenon, part of specific national and regional patterns of state–society relations, developmental trajectories, international linkages and political-economic structures.

This *political economy* approach has appeared in various studies.[1] Alan Block's work on organised crime situates the development of organised crime and corruption in the context of US economic development, urbanisation, federal political development and government intervention. Mike Davis' work on Los Angeles places corruption in the context of specific patterns of capitalist development and elite politics linking developers, planners, media and business interests in successive phases of urban expansion. Recent work on southern Europe has employed the concept of political opportunity structures not only to explain the development of corruption in Italy, France and Spain but also why scandals occur when they do. East Asian scholars have integrated corruption into historically specific accounts of the Philippines, for example, highlighting the role of corruption in state–society relations, rural–urban linkages, landowning structures and new development trajectories. In Thailand stress has been placed on urban–rural networks, financial development, state–business relations and the politics of counter-insurgency.

If these approaches can provide important explanations for the development of corruption, they can also apply to studies of anti-corruption policies. Existing approaches to the study of anti-corruption policies can be portrayed as too narrow. Some analyses of the success of anti-corruption policies in Hong Kong and Singapore provide important detail and policy

Jonathan Moran, Liverpool Business School, Liverpool John Moores University information but neglect the contextual variables which may actually explain their success.[2] Some valuable analyses have taken account of context, such as Lo's detailed account, in which he situates the development of corruption control and the ICAC in the relationships between the colonial government, powerful domestic business elites and the political position of the Hong Kong police. But his main argument, that anti-corruption campaigns are a manifestation of (hegemonic) class rule, leaves little room for the autonomy of politics or other variables.[3] A contextual analysis is as necessary for examining corruption control as it is to examining different criminal justice systems where, for example, the success of Japan and Singapore in producing high standards of public order cannot be abstracted from their political, social and historical context.[4]

The factors behind the success of corruption control in Hong Kong and the Independent Commission Against Corruption (ICAC) are structural, social, political, legal and economic, and an examination of the changes in them will provide pointers as to the current and future effectiveness of the ICAC. This article disaggregates *certain* important features of the Hong Kong political economy which are relevant to corruption control and examines how the handover has changed them or may change them. As such it is relevant to the debate as to the conditions for the success of an Anti-Corruption Agency (ACA) and whether ACAs can be transferred across borders. It can be argued that three structural variables have been important in the long term success of corruption control in Hong Kong and the performance of the ICAC. The capacity of the colonial state to institute an important change in political policy, linked to its relations with the metropolitan power; the effectiveness of the rule of law; and, finally, the balance of power within Hong Kong's political economy. All three are linked. This article discusses how these three have altered in the past two years, and then examines the major areas likely to be challenges for corruption control in the future. Before that the corruption control regime in Hong Kong will be briefly described.

OVERVIEW OF CORRUPTION CONTROL IN HONG KONG SAR

The corruption control regime in Hong Kong is composed of the relevant legislation and specific bodies charged with enforcing these laws. Anti-corruption work is identified with the ICAC but the impetus to reform had already begun in the early 1970s, fuelled by the expansion of the narcotics trade, increasing levels of drug addiction, extensive police corruption, and the political context of increasing anti-colonial/radical political sentiment.[5] The Prevention of Bribery Ordinance, which came into force in 1971 created a series of offences covering public servants soliciting or accepting widely defined 'advantages' or possessing assets disproportionate to their position. In the private sector it is also an offence for an agent to solicit or accept an advantage. Under the 1974 ICAC Ordinance responsibility for investigating offences under the 1971 Ordinance was transferred to the ICAC, which also enforces the Corrupt and Illegal Practices Ordinance. The ICAC has extensive powers of search, seizure, arrest and questioning, where the burden of proof lies with the suspect. The ICAC is structured around three main functions: operations, prevention and community relations. The ICAC is independent of the civil service and police, reporting only to the chief executive. ICAC accountability comes from two areas, through various oversight committees and judicial review. In practice, both have been co-operative with the ICAC but have overall reinforced the idea of operations adhering to the rule of law/due process. Other bodies also investigate corruption related offences in conjunction with the ICAC, for example the Commercial Crime Bureau of the Hong Kong Police. Other ordinances, which may involve the ICAC working with other police agencies, also cover offences connected with corruption, including the Theft Ordinance, Crimes Ordinance (which includes vice and forgery), Dangerous Drugs Ordinance and Gambling Ordinance.

STATE ANTI-CORRUPTION CAPACITY AND RELATIONS WITH THE MAJOR POWER

The ability to formulate and implement policy against the opposition of domestic interest groups has been held as an important variable in state effectiveness and thus corruption control. Under the colonial system the Governor was technically answerable to the UK Prime Minister alone and had authority over Hong Kong executive and legislative bodies. Nevertheless, the Governor could be subject to various pressures both in Hong Kong and in London. Foremost among the Hong Kong pressures was the structural corruption in the Hong Kong police which had largely neutered previous anti-corruption measures. The Godber scandal of the early 1970s provided the impetus for change. However it was the political space which existed between the colony and London which allowed the importation of British police officers and other officials to establish the ICAC and provided support for the policy. Thus the British government moved from tolerating corruption up to the 1960s (a variable in its expansion) to providing support for eradicating it in order to maintain political stability and confidence.

Following the handover another dual power structure exists, the 'one country, two systems' approach under which Hong Kong became a Special Administrative Region (HKSAR) of the People's Republic of China (PRC).

The HKSAR has its own mini constitution, the Basic Law based on the general principles laid down in the UK–PRC 1984 Framework Agreement. Hong Kong is to keep the political and economic features of the system currently in place for another 50 years, including its separate legal system. However, the PRC through its National People's Congress has supreme authority in certain matters including defence, foreign policy and state security. The latter area has yet to be legally clarified in Hong Kong law or interpreted in practice by the PRC.

How does this affect corruption? Hong Kong–mainland relations will function as an important variable governing the independence and capacity of the state, and the capability of the ICAC to control corruption. One could pose the question of whether, if another corruption explosion were to hit Hong Kong, even infecting the ICAC itself, the PRC would be able to assist the government in establishing corruption control again? There would be a constitutional issue of whether such a situation constituted an instance of state security. But in any case the chances of assistance would depend upon the prevailing conditions in the mainland, namely whether corruption was at that time a 'legitimate' political problem in the eyes of the PRC government. This of course was the case under British rule. However, one other difference is that the general environment in which the Hong Kong government and ICAC now operate is likely to remain more politicised and volatile as regards the major power, whereas under the British the relationship was stable from the 1970s. There are two main reasons for this.

First, although anti-corruption policies have become institutionalised in Hong Kong they have not in the mainland. The central question is the extent to which China's anti-corruption campaigns can be stabilised and regularised. The rapid development of the coastal growth zones since Deng Xiaoping's economic liberalisation policies commenced in the late 1970s has, for a number of reasons, led to an explosion of corruption and economic crime.[6]

The political economy of anti-corruption policy in mainland China is characterised by the influence of powerful elites at the central and local levels. Sections of the party, bureaucracy and People's Liberation Army have amassed substantial revenues through controlling the allocation of financial and administrative resources and/or participating directly in business ventures. In this environment, the lack of autonomy, and consequently professionalism, in the law enforcement establishment is evident. In anti-corruption work, 'in the 1980s and 1990s, for crimes involving the abuse of public office to pursue private gain, the Chinese criminal justice system appears to have regularly practised greater leniency than the rules permitted',[7] whilst anti-corruption campaigns have often been in effect purges aimed at resolving internal disputes such as factional struggles or centre–province relationships.

This links in with the second point. Following two decades of economic integration between Hong Kong and the mainland there are extensive links and, following 1997, the political structure now largely matches these economic relationships. Thus powerful political and economic interests could effectively place 'no-go' areas on ICAC investigations. Anti-corruption work in Hong Kong will increasingly become dependent upon the co-operation of the mainland authorities and the relevant Provincial Peoples Procuratorates, and this will continue to be a political issue. The situation is complex, as a 1995 scandal involving mainland party and Hong Kong interests only resulted in a prosecution because Beijing initiated it, highlighting 'how far Chinese family and factional networks had penetrated the Hong Kong economy, with the active collusion of local capitalists and complete impunity from local anti-corruption authorities'.[8] The question is, of course, what would happen if mainland political processes mitigate against a prosecution.

Mainland state elites have realised the problems inherent in endemic corruption in terms of its weakening political control through undermining party legitimacy and contributing to the rise of new elites, and in terms of its effects on foreign investment. President Jiang Zemin's oft-quoted statement about the battle against corruption being 'crucial to the very survival' of the party reflects this. The New Criminal Law of 1997 which contains a substantial section codifying and expanding criminal penalties for corruption will provide the framework for any new efforts to control corruption. However, the presence of influential elites who combine both legitimate and illegitimate business operations, and the absence of the rule of law in a politicised legal system (and the relative weakness of civil society), will place a limit on the mainland's anti-corruption drive. This in turn will obviously affect Hong Kong's corruption control system and individual investigations. Some of the implications of this relationship can be seen with reference to the rule of law.

THE RULE OF LAW

The rule of law has been central to the development of Hong Kong as a business and financial sector and to the institutionalisation of anti-corruption mechanisms. Hong Kong has displayed a specific form of the rule of law, different from the UK, Canada or Australia. The rule of law in Hong Kong has not on the whole been concerned with individual human rights. Rather, the stress has been on the sanctity of commercial contracts and established rules of political and bureaucratic administration which may be open to challenge in the courts or by the media. In fact, individual rights in the sense of those present in Western countries were absent in the presence of Hong Kong's strong anti-subversion laws, executive powers and *de facto* police authority.

The rule of law rested on a specific pattern of political and legal authority tempered by rules, procedures and debate within a relatively 'liberal' culture; in short, the reasonable exercise of power. This has been a vital variable as regards the success of the ICAC, since the Commission's powers are draconian. The ICAC has been subject to supervision and although the ICAC has generally held a co-operative relationship with the courts, it has been challenged and its operations have taken place within a legal culture inherited from Britain and with the Privy Council as a final court of appeal. This, along with oversight through various committees, has prevented the Commission from becoming a political police.[9]

In the two years since the handover the rule of law has remained intact but there are signs of weakening, largely for two linked reasons: first, the political strategy of the new Chief Executive, Tung Chee-hwa; and second, the apparent influence of the mainland in legal decisions and other administrative matters.

Even before the handover the PRC had declared the Patten-inspired 1995 Legislative Council elections illegitimate for allegedly violating the Basic Law, and this was followed by continuous mainland interference in Hong Kong up to the handover through various shadow bodies. After a quiet period, PRC interference has increased in 1999 during a series of important legal debates. A decision by the Hong Kong Court of Final Appeal effectively relaxed immigration to Hong Kong. More importantly this appeared to contain a judgment by the Court that it could declare mainland law invalid if it was inconsistent with the Basic Law. The Chinese authorities called for the ruling to be overturned. The Hong Kong government then asked the Court of Final Appeal for clarification of 'what legal commentators agreed was a perfectly clear and correct judgment'.[10] The Court restated its judgment with the proviso that the mainland has supreme authority over the interpretation of the Basic Law. Tung himself has recently asked China's parliament to 'interpret' the law differently from the court of Final Appeal, which, according to the Hong Kong Bar Council, sets 'a dangerous precedent for the government to use extra judicial means to overturn a decision it does not like'.[11]

The issue of Hong Kong SAR autonomy and the rule of law is also at issue in questions of criminal law concerning both organised crime and corruption. Following an ICAC investigation, three executives of the *Hong Kong Standard* newspaper were charged with conspiring to inflate circulation and thus defraud advertisers, but the paper's owner, Sally Aw Sian, was not charged. According to Justice Secretary Elsie Leung there was insufficient evidence. However, Aw's personal and business connections with both Tung Chee-hwa and the mainland are evident.[12] In another contemporaneous case, the Xinhua News agency, a mainland organisation based in Hong Kong, refused to hand over files on individuals within a legal time limit set by new personal data legislation. Xinhua was not prosecuted for an offence, described by Tung as 'technical breach'. Democratic Party leader Martin Lee linked this undermining of the rule of law directly with corruption, arguing: 'tax cheats and other offenders – who can now be expected to run the "technicality" line of defence – will certainly thank Mr. Tung.'[13]

In another case, Gang leader Cheung Tze-keung kidnapped the son of Hong Kong tycoon Li Ka-shing and tycoon Walter Kwok demanding huge ransoms. Allegedly Li did not inform the Hong Kong authorities, but instead asked 'the motherland' to deal with the problem in a meeting with CCP president Jiang Zemin. Jiang despatched PRC intelligence and security personnel to 'speed up' the investigation, and in fact Cheung was arrested smuggling arms and explosives between Hong Kong and the mainland. Despite the fact that most of the crimes Cheung was charged with (including the kidnappings) were committed in Hong Kong, he was tried and executed in the mainland. Apparently Hong Kong police authorities co-operated but did not request extradition and Tung Chee-hwa defended the decision, but debate centred on whether Cheung was being tried for crimes committed in Hong Kong, crimes committed on the mainland or crimes committed under Article 7 of the PRC Criminal Code which permits trial in PRC jurisdiction for crimes which have only been planned, or have consequences in, China.[14]

It appears that in these and other cases the balance of legal autonomy between the mainland and Hong Kong is beginning to be addressed. This process will take some time but it obviously has deep implications for the investigation and prosecution of corruption and organised crime cases. At its most negative, developments in 1999 imply a growing degree of interference by both the Hong Kong government and the PRC authorities in questions of legal process. This may lead to speedy reactions to criminal acts but at the cost of due process; alternatively it may lead to the protection of certain corrupt individuals. This article is not implying that questions of investigation and prosecution were not politicised under British rule (or are not so in Western countries). This was obviously the case, especially as regards controlling corruption in Hong Kong from the 1970s. At issue is, firstly, the degree of politicisation – just how closely are legal decisions and processes connected to specific economic and political interest groups – and, secondly, whether this takes place via due process and can be challenged. It is precisely this debate which informs the next section, which examines the effects of the political economy of Hong Kong on anti-corruption investigations.

THE POLITICAL ECONOMY OF THE HONG KONG SAR

Anti-corruption strategies, and by extension ICAC effectiveness, will be affected by the balance of power amongst various political and economic forces. The Hong Kong police had become an even more powerful social force following their suppression of anti-colonial riots in 1967. But, as mentioned, the split in authority between the metropolitan and colonial government provided the political space to bypass special interest groups and establish the ICAC in the early 1970s. Nevertheless, tackling police corruption was a difficult and complex process. Following the largely successful eradication of syndicated corruption in various parts of the public service (police, public works and so on) in the 1980s the ICAC turned its attention to private sector corruption. However, ICAC effectiveness has been both enhanced and constricted by the lobbying activity of important business sectors.[15] This is true, and only to be expected on a realistic reading, but highlights the often delicate context for anti-corruption policies.

Changes in power between various socio-economic groupings has occurred not only over the last decade but even in the last two years and provides the context for the development and future effectiveness of anti-corruption investigations. The colonial context was one where 'behind the *laissez faire* facade, the British establishment was an elitist coalition of colonial officialdom and tycoon capitalism as evidenced by the memberships, all appointed, of the Executive Council and Legislative Council, the highest organs of administration'. Despite free trade rhetoric, 'official patronage and special preference have dominated in key personnel appointments and decisions on major undertakings, such as public works contracts, aviation rights, monetary and financial measures, professional standards and recognition of qualifications'.[16] Even into the 1980s British corporate interests were overrepresented. Chinese business was split between the larger (ex)Shanghai manufacturers and native Cantonese small scale entrepreneurs, although all were accommodated by a pro-business state.[17] However, in recent years, while the power of the British *hongs* declined Chinese business has gained in influence. Before the handover it could already be argued that

> the increasingly close economic and political ties between Hong Kong's capitalists and the Chinese government, which have been the product of China's economic reforms and open door policy since the 1970s, have fostered the growth of capitalists as a dominant economic and political bloc under the patronage of the future sovereign power.[18]

Chinese business interests were increasingly represented in committees dealing with the handover.[19] Indeed, tycoon Li Ka-shing 'served on every important Beijing appointed body handling Hong Kong's transition to Chinese rule'.[20]

It appears that, since the handover, political power has shifted towards the business class whilst other social and political actors such as pro-democracy political parties and the political elite as represented in Exco and LegCo have declined in influence. One argument goes:

> it is predicted that the Chinese take-over will mean the injection of a political element into business, and *guanxi* (to have the right personal connection) will be crucial in cementing business deals. Corruption is expected to penetrate more deeply into Hong Kong society once more positions in business, the police and other civil services are filled by mainland Chinese.[21]

While this may be an overstatement, since 1997 there has been increased concern about the politicisation of the civil service now that public administration is no longer as insulated from local or mainland pressures,[22] the influence of business, maladministration and corruption.

Policy as regards the recent financial crisis is a case in point. The government's response to the slumping stock and property markets (themselves often related to corruption) has been seen as pro-business, with large economic concerns and property investors receiving public funds and administrative support whilst the public received notice of benefit cuts.[23] The government bought US$15 billion worth of stock to prevent the market crashing, a policy which substantially benefited certain influential families. Further, since Hong Kong depends on 'a vastly overinflated housing market' and property taxes provide a substantial share of government revenue,[24] the government placed a block on land sales and halted its own construction of flats, sustaining property prices and 'the cartels run by the property companies'.[25]

Secondly, the influence of *guanxi* seems apparent in the government's recent decisions to sell real estate at a noticeably low price and to award a property development project worth £1 billion 'without the normal process of public tendering', both to businesses connected to Li Ka-shing, the tycoon with links to Tung Chee-hwa and Beijing.[26] The decision not to prosecute Sally Aw, mentioned above, is another case in point. Perhaps the major public cost of *guanxi* has been the spectacular collapse of the Peregrine investment bank. Established in 1989, the bank cultivated links with the mainland and nearby elites. An unsecured $260 million bridging loan made by Peregrine to Steady Safe, an Indonesian transport company with links to the Suharto family, led to the bank's downfall.[27]

Overall, criticism of the new administration has been based on Tung's centralised rule, inefficiency (as in the problems over the opening of Chek

Lap Kok airport) poor crisis management, and a perceived favouring of indigenous business over other sectors. But these also reflect other more structural concerns such as the fraying of political freedom (with regard to government and mainland ownership or influence over the media) and the rule of law, and thus

> a subtle change in the style of governance and the frame of mind in its administration. It was now a kind of bureaucratic administration without the expected sharpness in dealing with dramatic changes, and the prudence of professional judgement. It was now a kind of paternalism without sensitivity to the needs of the people.[28]

The bases of good governance in the Hong Kong context could be, albeit subtly and slowly, undermined. The independence of the Hong Kong state from mainland pressures is an essential structural variable for the control of corruption and the support of the ICAC. This is obviously the case in the absence of effective corruption control mechanisms at both central and local level in mainland China. The evident capability of the mainland to interfere in Hong Kong governance is also at issue as regards the rule of law. The rule of law is essential not only for the protection of rules of contract, arbitration and general commercial stability but also for governing the operations of the extremely powerful ICAC. Finally, the political economy of Hong Kong has seen an increase in the power of the executive and a shift in power to the business class, both at the expense of other local political and social groups, particularly pro-democracy political parties. The possible effects on anti-corruption policies of this decrease in accountability should be evident to anyone who has studied the experiences of corruption control mechanisms in developing countries which have often politicised and personalised legal and administrative systems. Perhaps accountability could in future arise from below, from media scrutiny or popular activity. Indeed, the ICAC has always made community relations one of the planks of its strategy. However, the restriction of democratic development will constrain this: 'the 1998 electoral arrangements are retrogressive and regrettable not only because they aggravate the limitations to Hong Kong people's political rights but also because they will have negative implications for the long term democratisation of Hong Kong.'[29]

Once again it should be noted that, Patten's term as Governor apart, the British had a similar disdain for democratisation. Further, administration was politicised and subject to influence by powerful interest groups. However, the argument proposed here is that there was still an important difference in the level of politicisation, and a separation of powers influenced by rule of law that constituted a 'liberal authoritarian' style of governance. It is this complex, historically specific set of arrangements that provided the context both for the evolution of corruption and its later control. The remaining sections of this article examine trends in areas which have been or are likely to be the subject of anti-corruption policies: the continuing focus on the public and private sectors; finance, organised crime, and transborder crime. A final section will examine the future of the ICAC in the light of these arguments.

PUBLIC AND PRIVATE SECTOR CORRUPTION

Since the 1980s the ICAC has focused increasingly on private sector corruption. This development sets the ICAC apart from many anti-corruption agencies.[30] Corruption in the private sector should be a target of activity because it is as much a breach of public trust as public sector corruption, and because many corruption cases occur at the interface of the private and public sectors, particularly in jurisdictions such as Hong Kong, where economic activity is in private hands but there is an important and lucrative role played by the government.[31] The 1990s have seen a marked increase in the number of reports of corruption involving the private sector. In 1997, out of a total of 315 persons prosecuted for corruption and related offences, 233 involved the private sector and a further 35 concerned cases where private individuals were charged as a result of their dealings with government/public servants.[32] In 1998, of the 3,555 reports of corruption received by the ICAC, 52 per cent concerned the private sector, 16 per cent the police, 25 per cent other government departments and seven per cent public bodies.[33] The main areas in which corruption is a problem are construction, finance (dealt with below) procurement and, as regards the public–private interface, corruption offences regarding permits/licensing/standards/inspection and so on.[34]

In the public sector the main problem continues to be the police. The large scale syndicated corruption in the police was eradicated during the 1970s by direct attack and also by a simultaneous crack-down on the narcotics trade. This broke the links between the police and triads, centred around lucrative drug trafficking.[35] Police corruption exists, but at a lower level and in a more subtle manner, such as police officers having 'shares' in brothels in return for providing protection, or rigging police internal examinations. Customs will remain a centre of attention, as in all countries, and the large housing bureaucracy continues to be a centre of corruption, with the government controlling a large proportion of Hong Kong's housing stock.

Concerning public and private sector corruption, ICAC strategy will increasingly rest on a pro-active approach. This involves prevention, through providing advice on designing out corruption and investigation through intelligence gathering, the use of informants and undercover operations. Private sector co-operation is of course essential but this will continue to be affected by the relations with the mainland mentioned earlier. If important private sector interests in Hong Kong are either mainland-owned or have mainland links they may effectively be 'off-limits'.

THE POLITICAL ECONOMY OF FINANCE

The rapid development of Hong Kong's financial system was not accompanied by effective regulation or supervision. Financial services, real estate, business services and insurance contributed 25.2 per cent of GDP in 1996, up from 16 per cent in 1985. Following the merger of four existing exchanges, Hong Kong became Asia's second largest financial centre, with the exchange capitalised at HK$3.2 trillion in 1997.[36] Influential business interests ensured the system operated under self regulation, and reforms were often prompted by scandals. The Securities and Futures Commission (SFC) was established in 1989 following scandals in the stock exchanges. A former SFC chairman called the stock exchange 'a private club for brokers', but the SFC itself generally adopted a weak position with regard to financial regulation.[37] The Hong Kong Association of Banks was supposed to regulate the banking sector but the Hong Kong Monetary Authority was established in 1993 with the intention of performing the functions of a central bank.

The government's lenient attitude to regulation was partly a strategy to secure Hong Kong's position as a major financial centre, and partly a result of the fact that many business practices such as insider dealing which are illegal elsewhere are legal, which has arguably created a climate for corruption and crime.[38] 'The colony's total lack of controls on the movement of currency, its guarantees of very tight secrecy for depositors, and a colony-wide banking ethos that gave top priority to the bottom line, allowed government and banking industry officials to strike a see no evil posture.'[39] Money laundering did not become an offence until 1989, and then until 1995 drug traffickers could not be prosecuted for laundering the proceeds of their own trafficking.[40]

During the financial expansion questionable stock dealing practices were evident, and money laundering increased. Further, in the 1990s particularly there was an influx of Chinese companies seeking capital but not offering transparency. These 'red chip' companies were evaluated on political grounds rather than financial soundness. Collapsing companies and instability led to foreign speculation on Hong Kong currency and stocks, leading to the crisis of 1998 in which the government had to prop up the financial system through US$15 billion-worth of purchases.

The crisis has prompted moves to increase regulation, including requiring the disclosure of substantial share purchases, increased penalties for unreported or illegal stock sales and increased regulation of finance companies.[41] But the rules are unclear in practical terms and do not cover offshore companies. Further, there are no plans to introduce general financial legislation clearing up the outdated and partial rules on financial procedures.[42] Perhaps most importantly, the government continues to be committed to self-regulation. In the absence of an independent regulator the ICAC will have to take this role, particularly as following scandals the Stock Exchange has applied to become a public body, which will place it under the supervision of the ICAC and the tougher provisions covering the public sector in the Prevention of Bribery Ordinance.

As regards money laundering, Hong Kong has made progress. It is a member of the Financial Action Task Force and has implemented most of its recommendations. In future, money laundering reforms are expected to be introduced to stress record keeping and customer identification. However, the reporting of large cash transactions has been opposed by the HKMA as Hong Kong is a cash society; the absence of exchange and capital controls remains a spur to the quick movement of cash;[43] the non-banking sector is largely unregulated, and the effective 'underground' banking system also needs to be tackled, in which large amounts of cash are physically moved around the globe by ethnic networks.[44]

The ICAC's capabilities in tackling financial corruption already rest on extensive powers to compel financial officials to provide evidence and testimony and the development of sophisticated techniques. The Commission will require further expansion of intelligence, surveillance and forensic accountancy capabilities. Indeed, 'currently the focus on bribery and corruption in Hong Kong lies in the area of information technology ... to enhance its ability to seize, preserve and analyse data and present such as evidence in court, and to detect and investigate the increasingly complex financial aspects of corruption cases'.[45] But in the absence of effective regulation in Hong Kong, and with the influence of the extremely lax financial system in the mainland, ICAC investigations will be a reactive – and expensive – strategy.

ORGANISED CRIME AND CORRUPTION

Organised crime in Hong Kong takes three, often interrelated, forms: the Triads; more sophisticated organised crime activities which may not involve permanent structures but are based around certain criminal enterprises or single activities (for example smuggling, money laundering, insider dealing and so on); and thirdly low level organised crime groups in the civil service and police. The latter will not be discussed as the large scale syndicated corruption in the police and civil service has mostly been eradicated and current groups are organised on a small level.

Debate as to the influence of triad societies is still evident amongst crime and corruption specialists. According to a leaked police report there are four main triad societies with 30,000 members with an 'outer circle' of 120,000. A leaked ICAC report suggested that half of reported crimes were triad-related. Triad interests run from narcotics smuggling, organised prostitution and racketeering to ventures in property and finance.[46] However, although recently attention has focused on the supposed increasing sophistication of triad activity, 'the preponderance of evidence suggests that the triads and [other] local racketeers are not the principal actors in regional and global enterprise and financial crime'.[47] Triads apparently remain poorly organised and factional, and apocalyptic visions of the development of global Triad–Mafia–Yardie links must be treated with extreme caution. The main new danger in triad activity lies in its participation in enterprise crimes organised by others (see below) and in the alleged links between triad gangs and officials in the mainland in the development of such crimes.[48]

The development of enterprise crime has become an important feature of organised crime. These acts may involve triad participation but they are generally characterised by 'a fluid structure of actors who come together in a given enterprise'.[49] This may be in drug smuggling, counterfeiting, fraud, money laundering, trafficking of people and any number of 'commercial' crimes.[50] For example, the

> sophistication of Chinese criminal groups based in Hong Kong has led to a notable resurgence of credit card counterfeiting in the past few years. Hong Kong based counterfeiting rings were responsible for as much as 40 per cent of the total world-wide counterfeit credit card losses of about $200 million in 1991. While much of the actual counterfeiting is done in such locales as Hong Kong, Thailand, Singapore and Malaysia, the counterfeit cards are now being used in Europe, Australia and North America as well.[51]

Similarly, 'Hong Kong's primary role in the international drug trade is that of a money laundering base. Criminal elements both within and outside Hong Kong use the territory's well developed financial networks to finance and arrange shipments of narcotics originating in Southeast Asia to the US and other markets'.[52] These crimes by nature lead to corruption as they involve the bribery of law enforcement officers, bank officials, customs officers, service sector workers (in the case of credit card theft and copying) government officials and so forth.

Organised crime represents a problem to all law enforcement agencies as it generally involves complex transnational networks and links which may create difficulties in obtaining evidence. As mentioned, the ICAC has increased its training in the areas of forensic accountancy, and other relevant areas such as undercover operations, witness protection, and so on. But central to future operations will be regional and international co-operation, which highlights the final area to be discussed.

TRANSBORDER CRIME

Offences such as counterfeiting, fraud, smuggling and money laundering highlight the fact that transborder crime is often a central part of organised crime. Importantly for tackling corruption in Hong Kong, a major factor here is relations with the mainland. Hong Kong–mainland smuggling has a long history but China's accelerated development has created opportunities for other types of crime, particularly as economic ties between the two jurisdictions have always been close. Trafficking in girls for prostitution in Hong Kong will in all likelihood increase, particularly as the vice industry has exploded in southern China in recent years,[53] and Hong Kong will remain a transhipment point for narcotics and other smuggled goods, whether genuine or counterfeit.

It is believed that triad influence in the growth zone comprising southern China, Macao and Hong Kong is growing, and reports that the triads have links with regional Communist Party officials appear regularly.[54] In 1994 it was reported that 'senior criminal intelligence officers in the Hong Kong police believe that the biggest of the Triad gangs, Sun Yee On, which is thought to have 30,000 members in the colony, now has a stranglehold on the government of Guangdong Province which boasts one of the world's fastest growing economies'.[55] Apart from the triads (whose power, as argued, is often overstated) there are plentiful links between mainland officials and criminals in Hong Kong for the purpose of various transborder offences.[56]

CONCLUSION: CORRUPTION CONTROL AND THE ICAC IN FUTURE

The context of successful corruption control in Hong Kong has rested on important variables: state capacity, favourable relations with the metropolitan power, the rule of law, and the balance of power within the political economy. Since the handover these variables have been seen to be constrained by the mainland to an extent, either through its own interference which began before the handover, or by the choice of actors in Hong Kong, such as the chief executive, the police and business. Closer links between the HKSAR and the mainland will negatively affect corruption control if they lead to a politicisation of decisions of investigation and prosecution.

These are variables the ICAC has little control over. Where it will take pro-active action are in the areas outlined above: in tackling the increased private sector/financial corruption, organised crime and transborder crime. In the past decade or so the ICAC has, like most law enforcement agencies taken a pro-active approach to corruption. One of the reasons for this is the increased sophistication of criminals and criminal acts involving new technologies, complex jurisdictions and the often subtle relationships which underpin corrupt acts. This has necessitated an increased capability in the use of undercover officers, intelligence gathering and assessment and the use of sophisticated techniques to gather evidence.[57] This strategy is of course expensive, and current government plans to reduce public spending will hopefully exclude the ICAC.

International links will be an important factor in ICAC operations, particularly when investigating transborder crime or attempting the extradition of suspects in criminal cases. The ICAC already has extensive links with other law enforcement agencies, including anti-corruption agencies. These include the FBI, UK Metropolitan Police, New South Wales ICAC and so on. These links are assisted by the fact that ICAC officers have often gone on to work in these and other organisations. Developing productive links with local Provincial Peoples' Prosecutorial offices in the Chinese mainland will be a necessity.

The other celebrated prongs of the ICAC strategy – prevention and community relations – will remain important. Community relations will be an interesting variable as apparently the handover has increased a sense of pessimism amongst sectors of the population, and a change in culture may signal more tolerance of petty corruption at least amongst the younger sections of the population.[58]

This paper has not aimed at a comprehensive explanation of the context of the Hong Kong corruption control system and the ICAC's success, but it has sought to highlight some important factors which have governed its operation and which demonstrate the complex – and ever-changing – environment within which such agencies operate. The variables involved in the establishment and long term effectiveness of an anti-corruption agency are complex, a point which must affect any plans to copy the Hong Kong model. For example, the Hong Kong experience suggests that the absence of democracy is not necessarily a drawback to controlling corruption if there is a favourable political context and a functioning rule of law. And, as argued, a favourable political context does not refer to the oft-cited and often meaningless variables such as 'political will' or 'commitment at high levels,' both of which assume what needs to be explained. Rather, it means the practical capacity and realistic motive that a regime may have for controlling corruption. In addition, the balance of power between various interest groups is vital. Political/ideological penetration of the administrative apparatus and legal system, whether in a democratic or non-democratic context, will constrain the adoption of effective corruption control systems.

NOTES

1. A. Block and W. Chambliss, *Organising Crime* (New York: Elsevier, 1981); A. Block and S.P. Griffin, 'The Teamsters, the White House, the Labor Department: A Commentary on the Politics of Organised Crime', *Crime, Law and Social Change*, 27, 1 (1997), 1–30; M. Davis, *City of Quartz* (London: Vintage, 1992); V. Pujas and M. Rhodes, 'Party Finance and Political Scandal in Latin Europe', *EUI Working Paper* No.98/10 (1998); A. McCoy, *The Politics of Heroin: CIA Complicity in the Global Drugs Trade* (USA: Lawrence Hill Books, 1991). On Thailand, see J. Ockey, 'Business Leaders, Gangsters and the Middle Class: Societal Groups and Civilian Rule in Thailand' (Ph.D. Diss., Cornell University, 1992); J. Ockey, 'Political Parties, Factions and Corruption in Thailand', *Modern Asian Studies*, 28, 2 (1994), 251–77; D. Arghiros, 'Political Structures and Strategies: A Study of Electoral Politics in Contemporary Rural Thailand', Occasional Paper No.31 (University of Hull, Centre for Southeast Asian Studies, 1995); A. Laothamatas, 'Business and Politics in Thailand: New Patterns of Influence', *Asian Survey*, 28, 4 (1988), 451–70; on the Philippines, see J.T. Sidel, 'Philippine Politics in Town, District and Province: Bossism in Cavite and Cebu', *Journal of Asian Studies*, 56, 4 (1997), 947–66; J.T. Sidel, 'On the Waterfront: Labor Racketeering in the Port of Cebu', *Southeast Asia Research*, 3, 1 (1995), 3–17; P. Hutchcroft, 'Oligarchs and Cronies in the Philippine State. The Politics of Patrimonial Plunder', *World Politics*, 43, 3 (1991), 414–50.
2. For example, J. Quah's analysis neglects the political and economic context within which anti-corruption policies may be developed. This is particularly the case as regards Singapore, where PAP political hegemony, authoritarian governance and extensive legal controls on social behaviour are important structural variables influencing the specific regime of anti-corruption policies. See J.S.T. Quah, 'Controlling Corruption in City States: A Comparative Study of Hong Kong and Singapore', *Crime, Law and Social Change*, 22, 4 (1995), 391–414.
3. T. Wing Lo, *Corruption and Politics in Hong Kong and China* (Buckingham: Open University Press, 1993).
4. J. Moran, 'Zero Tolerance in Comparative Perspective', *Police Research and Management*, 2, 2 (1998), 43–53.
5. McCoy, *The Politics of Heroin*, Chapter 6; Wing Lo, *Corruption and Politics in Hong Kong and China*, chapter 4; M. Skidmore, 'Promise and Peril in Combating Corruption: Hong Kong's ICAC', *Annals of the American Academy of Political Science*, 547 (1996), 118–30; ICAC, *Annual Report by the Commissioner of the ICAC, HKSAR* (Hong Kong: ICAC, 1998).
6. G. White, 'Corruption and Market Reform in China', *IDS Bulletin*, 27, 2 (1996), 40–48.
7. M. Manion, 'Issues of Corruption Control in Post-Mao China', *Issues and Studies*, 34, 9 (1998), 7–12 at 7. When officials have been targeted it is usually at the lower level: 'Investigations into corruption have recovered more than £1 billion since 1993 and more than 124,000 of the 50 million members of the Communist Party were punished last year for wrongdoing. But despite the huge sums involved there has been only one significant politician prosecuted for corruption.' D. McElroy, 'China Targets the "Big Tigers" in Corruption Purge', *Daily Telegraph*, 17 Jan. 1999.
8. L. Dittmer, 'Hong Kong Returns to China: the Problem of Political Corruption', *Asian Journal of Business and Information Systems*, 2, 1 (1997), 70–71.

9. The oversight has often been weak, but nevertheless enough to be effective and provoke open debate. M. Skidmore, 'Promise and Peril in Combating Corruption: Hong Kong's ICAC', *Annals of the American Academy of Political Science*, 547 (1996), 123–8.
10. B. Wain, 'A Reputation Damaged', *Asian Wall Street Journal*, 5–6 March 1999, 10.
11. J. Gittings, 'Hong Kong Leader asks China to Block Influx of Migrants', *The Guardian*, 19 May 1999.
12. S. Vines, 'Anger as Hong Kong Press Chief Beats Law', *The Independent*, 20 March 1998, 16.
13. B. Gilley, 'Moot Point', *Far Eastern Economic Review*, 2 April 1998, 24.
14. F. Ching, 'Another Place, Another Crime', *Far Eastern Economic Review*, 5 Nov. 1998, 26; S. Vines, 'Luck Runs Out for Big Spender Gangster', *Independent on Sunday*, 15 Nov. 1998; D. McElroy, 'Hong Kong Gang Leader Executed by China', *Sunday Telegraph*, 6 Dec. 1998.
15. T. Wing Lo, *Corruption and Politics in Hong Kong and China* (Buckingham: Open University Press, 1993), Chapters 4 and 5.
16. Both quotes are from M.K. Chan, 'Hong Kong: Colonial Legacy, Transformation and Challenge', *Annals of the American Academy of Political Science*, 547 (1996), 14.
17. Lai Si Tsui-Auch, 'Has the Hong Kong Model Worked? Industrial Policy in Retrospect and Prospect', *Development and Change*, 29 (1998), 66–7; Lo, *Corruption and Politics in Hong Kong and China*.
18. B.K.P. Leung, *Perspectives on Hong Kong Society* (Oxford: Oxford University Press, 1996), 42.
19. Ibid., 42–3; J. Dimbleby, *The Last Governor* (London: Warner, 1998), Chapters 19 and 20.
20. B. Gilley, 'Personal Touch', *Far Eastern Economic Review*, 28 Jan. 1999, 14.
21. Lai Si Tsui-Auch, 'Has the Hong Kong Model Worked? Industrial Policy in Retrospect and Prospect', *Development and Change*, 29 (1998), 74.
22. A. Granitsas, 'Perils of Power', *Far Eastern Economic Review*, 18 Feb. 1999, 22–3.
23. M. Pao, 'Rethinking Self-Reliance', *Far Eastern Economic Review*, 8 Oct. 1998, 14.
24. A. Granitsas, 'Catch 22', *Far Eastern Economic Review*, 11 March 1999, 47.
25. Quoted in D. McElroy, 'Hong Kong's New Chief Falls out of Favour', *Daily Telegraph*, 28 March 1999, 34.
26. Ibid.
27. A. Higgins, 'He Stooped to Conquer', *The Guardian*, 17 Jan. 1998, 28.
28. Tai-Lok Lui, 'Hong Kong Society: Anxiety in the Post-1997 Days', *Journal of Contemporary China*, 8 (1999), 100–101.
29. E. Chan and R. Kwok, 'Democratization in Turmoil? Elections in Hong Kong', *Journal of Contemporary China*, 8 (1999), 65.
30. The ICAC's Operations Department has four branches, two concerned with government and two concerned with the private sector. The 1971 Prevention of Bribery Ordinance contains offences of private sector corruption.
31. Despite the *laissez faire* image of Hong Kong, the government takes a substantial role in infrastructure provision, house building and contracting out various public services to the private sector.
32. ICAC *Annual Report by the Commissioner of the ICAC, HKSAR* (Hong Kong: ICAC, 1998), Appendix 9, 73.
33. ICAC *Corruption Reports 1974–1998*. http://www.cuhk.edu.hk/icac/stat.htm. Accessed 30 March 1999.
34. 'Private sector organisations have been involved in more than 50% of the corruption reports processed by the ICAC in recent years, while procurement issues form about one quarter of the requests for advice. Procurement ... has the potential for serious loss through corruption.' ICAC, *Guidelines for Corruption Prevention: Procurement Practices* (ICAC Corruption Prevention Department, May 1998), 1.
35. McCoy, *The Politics of Heroin*, 400–407.
36. Economist Intelligence Unit, *Country Profile: Hong Kong and Macao 1998–99*, 28–9.
37. Economist Intelligence Unit, *Country Report: Hong Kong and Macao 3rd Quarter 1998*, 26.
38. Leung, *Perspectives on Hong Kong Society*, 106.

39. M. Gaylord, 'City of Secrets: Drugs, Money and the Law in Hong Kong', *Crime, Law and Social Change*, 28 (1997), 93–4.
40. Ibid., 95.
41. Economist Intelligence Unit, *Country Report: Hong Kong and Macao 3rd Quarter 1998*, 17–18; A. Granitsas, 'Taking Charge', *Far Eastern Economic Review*, 8 Oct. 1998, 100.
42. Economist Intelligence Unit, *Country Report: Hong Kong and Macao 4th Quarter 1998*, 2, 17–18; Granitsas, 'Taking Charge'.
43. 'Hong Kong', in *International Narcotics Control Strategy Report 1998: Money Laundering and Financial Crimes* (Bureau for International Narcotics and Law Enforcement Affairs, US Dept. of State, Washington DC, February 1999).
44. A point made by Mike Bishop, ICAC Assistant Director of Operations, Investigation Branch 4, in conversation with the author, 24 March 1999.
45. T. Travers, 'Laws Controlling Corruption – Hong Kong SAR, China', in Nabarro Nathanson (ed.), *Controlling Bribery and Corruption in International Business* (London: Nabarro Nathanson, 1999), 57.
46. S. Vines, 'Chinese Rule Boosts Hong Kong Triads', *Independent on Sunday*, 22 March 1998.
47. R. Godson, 'Criminal Threats to US Interests in Hong Kong and China', *Trends in Organised Crime*, 3, 1 (1997), 44.
48. The Heung family which dominates the Sun Yee On gang were awarded the first contract for a national cinema chain in mainland China. Vines, 'Chinese Rule Boosts Hong Kong Triads'; S. Vines, 'Hong Kong's Gurkhas Guard the Rich', *The Independent*, 5 Nov. 1998, 18.
49. R. Godson, 'Criminal Threats to US Interests in Hong Kong and China', *Trends in Organised Crime*, 3, 1 (1997), 44.
50. For discussion on the conceptual and empirical relationship of organised crime, economic crime and corporate crime, see V. Ruggerio, 'Criminals and Service Providers: Cross National Dirty Economies', paper presented to the 5th Liverpool Conference on Fraud, Corruption and Business Crime, Liverpool, April 1997; V. Ruggerio, 'War Markets: Corporate and Organised Criminals in Europe', *Social and Legal Studies*, 5 (1996), 5–10.
51. Australian Parliamentary Joint Committee on the National Crime Authority, 'Asian Organised Crime in Australia', Australian Parliamentary Joint Committee on the National Crime Authority Discussion Paper 1995, note 11.
52. 'Hong Kong', in *International Narcotics Control Strategy Report 1996: Southeast Asia and the Pacific* (Bureau for International Narcotics and Law Enforcement Affairs, US Dept. of State, Washington DC, March 1997).
53. M. Sheridan, 'Chinese Vice Wave Laps at Hong Kong', *Sunday Times*, 25 May 1997, 21.
54. M. Sheridan, 'Triads Move on Hong Kong', *Sunday Times*, 13 July 1997, 19.
55. Australian Parliamentary Joint Committee on the National Crime Authority, 'Asian Organised Crime in Australia', Australian Parliamentary Joint Committee on the National Crime Authority Discussion Paper 1995, note 66, quoting *Sydney Morning Herald*, 15 Sept. 1994, 15.
56. See, for example, L. Dittmer, 'Hong Kong Returns to China: the Problem of Political Corruption', *Asian Journal of Business and Information Systems*, 2, 1 (1997), 67–8.
57. T. Kwok, 'The Development of ICAC Investigative Capability', paper presented to the ICAC Silver Jubilee Conference, Hong Kong, 22 March 1999. For a general discussion, see ICAC, *Operations Department Review 1997–98* (Hong Kong, ICAC).
58. Tai-Lok Lui, 'Hong Kong Society: Anxiety in the Post-1997 Days'; R. Wong, 'How do Perceptions of Corrupt Behaviour Change? The Hong Kong Experience', paper presented to the ICAC Silver Jubilee Conference, Hong Kong, 22 March 1999. Large scale mainland immigration would also produce a culture shift which might not be positive but the recent decision by the Chinese National People's Congress will make this unlikely.

Combating Corruption in Botswana: Regional Role Model or Deviant Case?

ROBIN THEOBALD AND ROBERT WILLIAMS

In every survey and index of corruption African states are extremely well represented at the lower or negative end of the scale or range.[1] The political and economic consequences of high levels of corruption are well known, but, in the continental catalogue of depredations, there is one apparent exception to the general rule. Botswana has long been seen as an oasis in a desert of corruption[2] and, more recently, the Botswana approach to dealing with corruption has attracted considerable interest from many of its regional neighbours and from farther afield.

This article offers an assessment of the problem of corruption in Botswana, an analysis of the institutional and other methods used to combat it and an evaluation of the applicability of the Botswana experience to other parts of Africa. Assessing corruption and judging the efficacy of methods of controlling it are notoriously difficult tasks. The article will briefly establish a political and economic context before presenting a detailed analysis of the reforms introduced in 1994. The conclusion will re-examine the case for Botswana's exceptionalism in regard to the likelihood of neighbouring states seeking to imitate its legislative and institutional approach to combating corruption.

BACKGROUND

By the mid-1990s Botswana had moved from being among the 25 poorest countries in the world to middle income status, with one of the world's fastest growing economies. The country's GDP registered an average annual growth of ten per cent between 1981 and 1991. Although slowing down after 1991, projected rates for 1997/98 were still in the region of six per cent. In addition, Botswana has acquired a good reputation for sound economic management, strong administrative capacity and public probity. As a major mineral producer, for example, the country confronts all the usual problems of international commodity price volatility. Nonetheless, the

Robin Theobald, Westminster Business School, and Robert Willliams, Department of Politics, University of Durham government has been able to maintain a stable macro-economic environment whilst at the same time promoting agricultural and livestock production.

When diamond prices fell in 1981, the government was able to negotiate a series of potentially unpopular measures including currency devaluation, consumption taxes and a wage freeze. Again, during the first half of the 1980s, a devastating drought resulted in the loss of one-third of the nation's cattle and for five years in succession, 80 per cent of crop production. Despite this, mass starvation was averted as a result of a series of well-managed relief programmes. A serious drought in the early 1990s produced a similar well co-ordinated response. Unlike most sub-Saharan states, Botswana since independence in 1966 has not known military government, has no record of human rights abuses, and has seen a succession of multi-party elections. Although the same party has been in power since independence, there is no evidence of significant electoral manipulation or fraud.

However, Botswana's reputation for good government was severely dented during the early 1990s by a succession of scandals involving powerful political figures. These led to a series of presidential commissions, the first of which concerned itself with the award, to an obscure company under highly dubious circumstances, of a lucrative contract to supply teaching materials to the country's primary schools. The commission revealed several startling errors which resulted in the loss of P27 million (at that time the equivalent of around $13 million). Senior civil servants were held responsible for this loss.

The Second Commission of Inquiry (1991) investigated a number of illegal land transactions in several villages on the periphery of the capital, Gaborone. Evidence was found of misuse of their position for personal gain by a number of parliamentarians and ministers. The vice-president and minister of local government were specifically named and subsequently forced to resign. A third presidential commission examined the activities of the Botswana Housing Corporation, exposing 'gross mismanagement and dishonesty' which had led to 'the loss of tens of millions of Pula'. Ministers and civil servants, it transpired, had used a range of highly dubious projects such as constructing a headquarters for the Corporation as well as a number of high cost houses, for the purposes of self-enrichment.

Even more shocking was the revelation that by late 1993 the National Development Bank – described by the then Minister of Finance subsequently President, Festus Mogae, as a 'pillar of our financial system' – was near to bankruptcy. According to unidentified sources within the bank, prominent among defaulting debtors were not only several ministers but the then President, Ketumile Masire, as well as his brother, Basimane.

These and other scandals strengthened the general perception that rapid economic expansion had brought in its train new and expanding opportunities for fraud, bribery and misappropriation at all levels of the public service.[3]

THE CORRUPTION AND ECONOMIC CRIME ACT, 1994

Against this background of what amounted to moral panic, the CEC Act was promulgated in 1994. The principal objectives of the Act are 'to provide for the establishment of a Directorate on Corruption and Economic Crime; to make comprehensive provision for the prevention of corruption; and confer power on the Directorate to investigate suspected cases of corruption and economic crime and matters connected or incidental thereto'. Included in its strategic plan for the period October 1997 to October 2002 is the Directorate's mission statement: 'We commit ourselves to work together with all communities to combat corruption and economic crime in Botswana, using our resources to provide a high quality, value for money service.'[4]

From its inception DCEC was modelled on Hong Kong's Independent Commission Against Corruption. Indeed, its first director had been deputy director of the ICAC and a number of senior DCEC positions were filled by ex-Hong Kong personnel. One major difference between the DCEC and its Hong Kong template is that the former also deals with economic crime as well as corruption. This decision seems to have been heavily influenced by the perceived high level of fraud in relation to the public sector at the time coupled with the absence of a fraud squad in the Botswana Police Force. The decision to include economic crime (defined as cheating the public revenue) within its remit, was to have major implications for the workload of the Directorate.

Despite this fundamental difference the DCEC adopted the ICAC basic 'three pronged strategy' of investigation, prosecution and corruption prevention and education. Accordingly, as of the end of 1998, the basic structure of the DCEC consisted of a director, a deputy director and five assistant directors. The latter group oversee respectively: prosecutions and training; investigations; intelligence and technical support; administration and financial investigations; and corruption prevention and public education. The establishment at the end of 1998 was 100, including administrative staff, typists, messengers, cleaners, drivers and so on. The Government of Botswana National Development Plan 8 projects the DCEC's establishment to expand to 150. Occupying rented quarters in an industrial estate in Gaborone, the DCEC will move to a new purpose-built headquarters scheduled to be completed by December 1999. In November

1996, the DCEC opened a branch in Francistown in the north of the country.[5]

AN OUTLINE OF OPERATIONS

The DCEC's Report Centre at its HQ in Gaborone processes complaints and information received from any source, including members of the public. The Report Centre is manned from 7am to 7pm weekdays, 7am to 3pm on Saturdays. The centre prepares summaries of received reports for twice weekly meetings of the director and senior colleagues. These meetings decide which reports are to be investigated, which are to be referred to other government departments or parastatals, and which are too trivial to be pursued. With regard to referrals, many complaints do not fall under the legal description of corruption or economic crime, but will be concerned with unnecessary delays, lack of action, uncooperativeness on the part of officials, incorrect or missing information and suchlike on the part of government departments. If considered serious enough, these will be passed to the appropriate department or in some cases ministry for investigation. The DCEC will expect a report back of action taken from the department. The DCEC's standard policy is that the original complainant should always be informed as to what action has been taken in relation to his/her complaint.

For the three years 1995 to 1997 the proportion of reports referred or no action increased from 54 to 79 per cent. This greater selectivity, according to the current director, has been made possible by the increased understanding on the part of government departments of the referral system and a growing willingness to work with it. However, with 68 per cent rise in complaints over these three years, it is likely that the Directorate has had to be more selective with the cases it takes forward for investigation.

Investigations and Prosecutions

When a complaint is authorised for investigation, it will be passed to one of five investigating teams (four in Gaborone and one in Francistown). Each team comprising five to seven officers is led by a principal investigator who is responsible for the prioritisation and supervision of work. If in relation to a complaint sufficient evidence has been amassed that an offence has been committed, this is distilled into a prosecution docket. The docket must then be passed to the Attorney General's office for a decision as to whether a prosecution should be initiated.

Should prosecution be authorised by the Attorney General the case is passed to the (DCEC) Assistant Director Prosecutions. Prosecutions will then normally prepare a case to be presented before a magistrate. Before a reorganisation of the DCEC in early 1997, investigations and prosecutions were joined in the same function so that investigators prepared their own cases. The separation is thought to be more effective as it allows for additional and perhaps more detached scrutiny of the relevant evidence, as well as enabling investigators to concentrate upon their main task.

Intelligence and Technical Support

The basic aim of the intelligence group is to produce, analyse and synthesise, from a range of sources both overt and covert, information about suspect activities, persons, agencies, branches, divisions or even departments of state. Tendering and supplies are typically areas where abuse is at an unacceptably high level. Where appropriate, Intelligence will pass information to investigations. Intelligence is also expected to provide specialised services, most notably covert surveillance. For example, as well as its regular vehicles, the DCEC also operates a covert motor fleet. Telephone tapping and mail intercepts, which are standard practices in the HKICAC, are illegal in Botswana. However, as of the end of 1997, due to a number of factors including the death of a principal investigator in charge of intelligence, this group's activities were largely restricted to recording and collating data. Training in systems analysis and a significant enhancement of its overall systems capacity, especially to coincide with the move to the new headquarters, figure prominently in the DCEC's strategic plan.

Corruption Prevention

The central aim of the Corruption Prevention Group (CPG) is to identify weaknesses and potential points open to abuse and exploitation in the public sector. Identifying weak points arises from two main sources; first, from a review of completed investigations; and, second, from heads of government departments and parastatals who are asked to review their working systems and invite assistance from the group. For example, in 1997 the CPG had *inter alia* produced: a report on the operations of the Motor Vehicle Insurance Fund, a parastatal which handles third party accident claims; a study of the way in which tenders were received, evaluated and awarded for concessions in controlled hunting and photographic areas of game reserves; and a report on the system used the allocation of government pool housing.

The CPG was also compiling a report on the Central Transport Organisation examining areas such as purchase of new vehicles, the receiving and issue of vehicle spares, the purchase and issue of fuel; and procedures for accident investigations. In addition, the CPG is participating in arrangements to include codes of conduct and accountability into a revised General Orders and Public Service Charter. A handbook, *The Standards of Ethical Conduct for all Government Employees*, is in production. CPG also produces information brochures giving concise advice on effective delegation, preventing corruption, ethics in business and codes of conduct. These are aimed at both public and private sectors.[6]

Corruption Education

The Education Group's fundamental aim is to increase public awareness of the evils of corruption and to enlist their support in the fight against it. Its strategy includes advertising on billboards using slogans such as 'We blow the whistle on foul play', as well as the incorporation of appropriate slogans into desk and pocket calendars. Promotional materials such as tee shirts and caps with the DCEC logo have been distributed at trade fairs such as the Botswana International Trade Fair. Members of the group also tour the country giving presentations on the work of the Directorate and advice on corruption prevention to government departments, parastatals and local authorities as well as private bodies. Regular releases are made to the press, citing recent DCEC events and activities, and giving details of the commencement and completion of all prosecutions. DCEC members have participated in talks and phone-ins on the radio and staff members are currently undergoing training in production with a view to expanding output through this medium. The Directorate aims ultimately to expand the presentation of corruption themes as part of the overall moral education of the young in schools. However, because of the predominance of other issues, particularly curriculum development, in the Ministry of Education's current programme, only limited progress has been made in this direction.

Training

Training is currently a joint responsibility of the assistant director of prosecutions. Training for DCEC officers flows primarily from three sources: in-house courses which take the form of short induction courses supplemented by training in more specific skills; courses provided by outside institutions in Botswana, mainly the Department of Public Service Management (DPSM) as well as others such as the Institute of Development Management and the Botswana Institute of Administration and Commerce. The third potential source of training is courses overseas, particularly in the UK. However, as access to these is funnelled through the DPSM, the DCEC is competing for places with other organs of state, most notably the Botswana Police Force.

Administration

The assistant director of administration and financial investigations oversees the standard administrative functions such as accounting, secretarial and typing services, records, supplies as well as other sundry activities such as messengers, cleaners, drivers, storekeepers.

PERFORMANCE

The number of complaints made to the DCEC rose by nearly 70 per cent between 1995, the first full year of operation, and the end of 1997.[7] Whether this reflects an actual increase in the incidence of corruption and/or economic crime or an increasing awareness of the problem is difficult to say. It seems certain that an increasing awareness, including the belief that something can be done about it, is in part attributable to the work and visibility of the DCEC in Botswana. The DCEC Education Group claim that their research indicates that the majority of the population is aware of the DCEC and what it does. However, it is admitted that there are substantial differences along this dimension between urban and rural areas. The fact that three-quarters of the complainants identify themselves may indicate some degree of confidence. (Although we note that the proportion of anonymous complaints increased over the period 1994–97.)

Whilst the DCEC has doubtless played a major role in raising awareness of corruption and corruption prevention in Botswana, the Directorate faces a number of serious difficulties in the near future. These may be divided into two basic categories: operational difficulties and problems of the DCEC's image in Botswana society. A number of serious operational difficulties are identified in the Directors' Reports for the years 1996 and 1997.

Delays in Obtaining Information from Banks

Clearly, details of financial circumstances of suspects are central to many investigations. However, because of inadequate record keeping Botswana's banks have often been unable to supply vital information, leading in some instances to cases having to be dropped. But the efficiency of the banking system has improved and, compared to many other African countries, there are relatively few problems with fraud and money-laundering.

Serious Delays in Attorney General's Chambers

Since the DCEC must obtain authorisation to prosecute from the Attorney General's Office, delays in processing applications in that department retard the process considerably. Such delays have a knock-on effect for the scheduling of court appearances, organising witnesses and so forth. The basic problem is that, following the formation of the DCEC, the volume of cases that had to be processed through the AG's office doubled. However, the AG's staff establishment has not expanded to meet this increase. Although the recruitment of more staff to the AG's office is currently a priority, both reports call for the 'briefing out' of cases to the private bar in order to relieve the backlog.[8]

In the 1996 report the then director complained of serious delays in the processing of cases through the magistrates' courts. In the 1997 report, his successor once again highlighted this problem, affirming that the situation seemed to have deteriorated during that year. Delays are attributable to a number of factors: non-appearance of counsel or deliberate delaying tactics, unscheduled adjournments due to illness, or ritual occasions such as funerals. The judicial process is made more protracted by the archaic practice of magistrates having to take notes in longhand due to the absence of court clerks.[9]

There also seem to be problems over obtaining confessions that can be used in evidence. Under Botswana law confessions are admissible as evidence only if made in the presence of a judicial officer, usually a magistrate (but can also be a district officer). So far as magistrates are concerned, there seems to be reluctance to do this first because the process is extremely time consuming, with detailed statements having to be taken down in longhand. But it also means that the magistrate must first appear in court as a prosecution witness and be cross-examined by another magistrate. Many magistrates seem to want to avoid such situations for reasons of professional status. This problem could be overcome were videotaped confessions admissible – in fact the DCEC already has the technology – but as yet they are not.

It is noted also that the Botswana courts have not adopted the practice under which guilty pleas receive a reduced sentence. This means that there is no incentive to reduce the number of trials. The result is there are too many trials which take too long and sentencing often appears lenient and inconsistent. Overall, court delays are having a serious impact on the number of successful prosecutions. On the surface the DCEC enjoys a high rate of successful prosecutions – around 80 per cent of completed cases. But for the period September 1994 to the end of 1997 only slightly less than half the cases before the courts (207) had been completed.

Recruitment

To the extent that the DCEC is successful in raising public awareness of corruption and economic crime and more especially that something can be done about it, its case load will increase. Since the current case load of investigators is about three times higher (12 active cases per investigator) than the recommended optimum, there is clearly an urgent need for more skilled personnel.[10] The problems of recruiting such skilled individuals as are available is exacerbated by the provision that all new appointments for the DCEC must be channelled through the Department of Public Service Management. The first director criticised these arrangements strongly, finding it 'irksome to involve the Director of Public Service Management in recruitment decisions',[11] and envying the autonomy enjoyed in this respect by the Commander of the Botswana Defence Force and the Commissioner of Police. These concerns are echoed, albeit somewhat more mildly, by his successor. The problem does not seem to be one of gaining permission to appoint but rather of administrative delays in the recruitment process.

PUBLIC IMAGE

Virtually every writer on anti-corruption measures has agreed that prevention is the most cost-effective tactic. Prevention depends upon educating the public and securing their good will and co-operation in the fight against corruption. But good will and co-operation depend upon public trust and the belief that such anti-corruption agencies as exist operate impartially. With regard to the DCEC there is some concern that it is not impartial in the sense that its nets are designed to ensnare only the small fry, leaving the 'big fish' to swim away. Botswana's independent weekly press is not short of stories of the questionable activities and involvements of some politicians and ministers. The substance and accuracy of such stories is difficult to assess. Critics of the government tend to believe 'there is no smoke without fire', while those accused suggest the allegations are mischievous and politically motivated.

However, evaluating this concern – one that is expressed about most anti-corruption agencies – is extremely difficult. The list of initiated and completed prosecutions gives the overwhelming impression of fairly trivial offences involving small sums of money – less than P10,000. The 1997 report, however, cites the conviction of a former acting permanent secretary for fraud and the issue of a warrant for the arrest of the former general manager of Air Botswana. The former permanent secretary received a three-year jail sentence for fraudulently obtaining money from the Motor Vehicle Fund of which he had been general manager. Two of these three years were subsequently suspended, producing a sentence which some observers consider to be somewhat lenient. But the alleged deficiencies of the legal system are not the responsibility of the DCEC, which has itself criticised sentencing practices.

Part of the DCEC's image problem lies in its perceived lack of independence. The fact that it is located within the Office of the President and is answerable only to the President is seen by some as a serious defect. Whilst this location gives the Directorate the authority and clout it may need to deal effectively with other departments of state, such authority can obviously be abused. Under such arrangements the possibility arises that a president might use the Directorate under a weak or compliant director to intimidate or silence critics. For these reasons it has been argued that an agency with this degree of authority should properly report to a parliamentary committee. Conversely, placing an anti-corruption agency at the heart of government might be thought to send a strong political message to the other parts of the governmental system.

Irrespective of the intentions of the President or his aides, the DCEC itself enjoys extraordinary powers. Many of these powers are invested in the office of the director himself, who may authorise any officer of the Directorate

> to conduct an inquiry or investigation into any alleged or suspected offences under the Act; require any person to produce in writing ... all books, records, returns ... and any other documents relating to the functions of any public or private body; require any person ... to provide any information or to answer any questions which the Director considers necessary in connection with any inquiry or investigation which the Director is empowered to conduct under the Act.

Failure to meet these requirements, answer questions or the provision of false information is an offence and liable to up to five years in prison plus a fine of up to P10000. In addition the Director can order an arrest, enter and search premises and seize property all without a warrant.[12]

The extent of these powers has encouraged the view that the DCEC should be made more accountable to an outside review body. Such a body was advocated strongly by the first director basically on two grounds: first, that in the light of the DCEC's extraordinary powers the public needs to be reassured that these are not being abused; and second, that since the Directorate through its Corruption Prevention Group spends a lot of time and energy promoting accountability in other organisations, it needs to practise 'what it preaches'.[13] At this point it is worth noting that the Hong Kong ICAC was subject to several layers of review, including two-yearly inspections by the UK Inspector of Constabulary. The DCEC's second director has also expressed his support for a review body, but to date the proposal does not enjoy governmental support and the issue of independent accountability and scrutiny remains unresolved.[14]

IS BOTSWANA EXCEPTIONAL?

The reputation of the DCEC has spread beyond Botswana's borders. A number of other African countries – Namibia, Swaziland, Malawi, Lesotho and Ghana, for example – have expressed strong interest in the Directorate's operations. The question is does the DCEC offer an approach to dealing with corruption that other African countries may wish to adopt?

In attempting to answer such a question it should be borne in mind that Botswana differs from most other African countries in a number of important respects:

- It is the second wealthiest country in sub-Saharan Africa second only to South Africa (although the global figure masks high levels of poverty as indeed is the case with South Africa).
- With a low level of debt and the highest per capita reserves in the world, Botswana does not have a debt servicing problem. One major consequence of this is that public agencies such as the DCEC are, in African terms, extremely well-resourced.
- It has a very small (1.5 million) population which, although comprising a number of tribal segments as well as minorities, has since independence not produced the serious and often devastating conflicts which have been unleashed in many other LDCs.
- Related to the last point, Botswana emerged from colonialism as a primarily cattle-keeping society in which tribal principles albeit somewhat attenuated, continued to operate. This makes Botswana very different from the complex peasant societies of West Africa and parts of East Africa where relations of surplus appropriation and exploitation were well advanced *before* the onset of European colonialism. As a consequence the predatory tendencies which rise to pathological levels during periods of rapid social and economic change, are almost certainly less deeply embedded in a society like Botswana than say Ghana, Nigeria or Uganda.
- Elsewhere in Tropical Africa, the armed forces have been a major agent of multiple abuse. The fact that Botswana's armed forces have never held political power has hitherto meant that this vital factor in the predatory formula has been absent.

Having made this point about the military, it is important not to exaggerate the 'democratic' character of Botswana politics. On the contrary, one commentator has dubbed the political system as a '*de facto* one-party state' in which a powerful presidency gives free rein to a highly autonomous developmental bureaucracy.[15] This bureaucracy is run by a corps of highly trained specialists recruited according to merit with a significant proportion being well-paid tenured expatriates. This 'mandarin' class has managed the economy since independence, and in the interests of long-term development has been virtually untroubled by political and social pressure. This is primarily for two reasons: first, Botswana's first two presidents, Sir Seretse Khama and Ketumire Masire, would brook no interference with the bureaucracy whether from politicians or such interest groups as existed; and, second, the likelihood of interference or pressure is limited by the underdeveloped nature of Tswana civil society.[16]

Underpinning this underdeveloped civil society lie a number of factors, including the dominant political culture which is a product of the organisation of traditional Tswana tribal society and which emphasises hierarchy and the authority of elders and chiefs. Whilst elders and chiefs were required to listen to the views of kinsmen entitled to speak (that is, senior males), in traditional fora, known as *kgotla*, custom decrees that it is the views of elders and chiefs that should always prevail. This kind of patriarchal ethos has predominated in parliament where, according to John Holm, the role of members has extended little beyond rubber stamping the programmes that emanate from the bureaucracy.[17] Few MPs anyway have the education, sophistication or support staff to challenge complex administrative decisions. Even less do they have the incentive, for electoral support is based primarily upon ethnic affiliation with the result that performance in the House is of little consequence. Since the hitherto dominant Botswana Democratic Party has striven to ensure that every constituency gets its rightful share of resources, a secure base for opposition is difficult to forge.[18]

This is not, however, to argue that the population at large enjoys a high standard of living. On the contrary, the proportion of the population living in poverty may be as high as 47 per cent, which is somewhat odd for a country which is second from the top (position 89) of the World Bank's 'lower-middle-income' economies with a GNP per capita in 1995 of $3,020. This apparently high level of poverty is the result of a deliberate policy of keeping wages down in the public sector, where probably half of the population works. None the less, the consequences of low monetary wages have to a considerable extent been mitigated by large-scale investment in infrastructure, including education, health care and especially low-cost housing. Despite high rates of urbanisation, Tswana towns and cities do not display the sprawling squatter settlements that are a ubiquitous feature elsewhere in Africa. But such dissatisfaction as exists finds it difficult to mobilise against the state on account of the organisational weakness of opposition both within and outside parliament.

Parliament itself was until the 1990s easily dominated by the Botswana Democratic Party (BDP) primarily for three reasons: first, since the BDP has been in power since independence, it has been able to claim the bulk of the credit for the massive economic expansion that has taken place; second, the electoral system is biased towards rural areas where BDP support is strongest. Thus, in the election of 1989 the main opposition party, the Botswana National Front, although garnering 27 per cent of the vote, secured only three parliamentary seats primarily because the bulk of its support lies in the towns. One should also mention here that setting the voting age at 21 – lowered to 18 in 1995 – has hitherto worked in the interests of the BDP as the opposition derives a fair amount of support from the young.[19]

The most serious disadvantage faced by the BNF is the party itself, which is notoriously prone to internecine wrangling and factionalism. In the elections of 1994 the BNF secured 13 of the 40 parliamentary seats (37 per cent of the vote) signifying for some commentators the beginning of the end of BNP hegemony and foreshadowing a possible change of government in 1999. However, this success, far from unifying the party, seemed only to intensify schismatic tendencies to such a level that a special congress held during Easter 1998 had to be dispersed by riot police. There followed a series of court cases involving dissidents against the party's long-standing and, for some, overly autocratic leader, Dr Kenneth Koma, the end result of which was that 11 of the 13 BNF MPs split off to form the Botswana Congress Party (BCP). The BNF has since sought to form a Botswana Alliance Movement (BAM) with other opposition parties but excluding the BCP. But this alliance is very fragile and subject to further splits.[20]

So far as interest groups are concerned a number of factors conspire to inhibit their effectiveness: most have very little in the way of resources both human and material. Accordingly, administrative, research and other support staff are relatively unknown. This makes it very difficult for a relatively poorly educated population to challenge complex administrative decisions which have often been taken in conditions of considerable secrecy. Under such circumstances it is not surprising that most interest groups, even trade unions, have a predominantly non-political agenda engaging primarily in social and recreational activities such as sport, art, music and dance and the like. Such apolitical tendencies are underpinned by traditional Tswana culture and reinforced by the government through often generous financial support. The geography of Botswana, the sheer size of the country (its area roughly that of France) and the thin spread of population makes communications very difficult.

Identifying these weaknesses in Tswana civil society should not allow us to conclude that it is totally supine – far from it. In December 1998, for example, public clamour forced MPs into a partial climbdown over their decision three months earlier to vote themselves a package which allowed them to purchase luxury cars at half price, the other half being paid by the taxpayer. After pressure from such bodies as the Botswana Federation of Trade Unions and expressions of outrage in the independent weekly press, a parliamentary committee agreed to attach a number of limitations to the scheme.[21] In 1999 concerns about the financial links between the Assistant Minister of Finance and Development Planning and a construction company with a large road-building contract led to the resignation of the minister.[22]

Overall, continuing modernisation in the form of urbanisation, the spread of education, developments in mass communications, and, not least, the slowing down of the economy, may be expected to produce a more truculent civil society in Botswana. Events in neighbouring South Africa where trade unions and other interest groups occupy such a high profile in national and local politics will increasingly provide a model for the expression of discontent in Botswana.

CONCLUSION

First, and in relation to the specific issue of the efficacy of anti-corruption agencies in dealing with the problem of widespread abuse, since the Hong Kong ICAC remains the model for this type of body we need to bear in mind that it has been in operation for 25 years; is extremely well resourced (staff establishment alone in the region of 1,300); operates in an environment where legal and financial institutions are extremely well developed; and is subject to a demanding regime of external regulation.

More generally, it is the case that Botswana has until recently enjoyed a reputation as probably the most stable, open, well managed and corrupt free state in Tropical Africa. Despite the scandals of the 1980s and early 1990s, and despite continuing unease about the involvements of politicians, Botswana still does not appear to be afflicted by the rampant plundering which is unfortunately common elsewhere in Africa. On top of this, routine or petty corruption is still minimal. You do not need to bribe immigration officials or customs or police officers or civil servants when you arrive or do business in the country. On the contrary, were you to tender a bribe you would probably be reported to the authorities. This is a remarkable situation which the DCEC bears much of the awesome responsibility to preserve. However, the relative honesty and integrity of Botswana society is threatened from two major sources.

First, some politicians have ongoing involvement in, if not actually illegal, highly questionable dealings which are believed to have led to unacceptably high financial gains. If this is permitted to continue unchecked, particularly in a country where 47 per cent of the population is held to be living in poverty, there is a serious danger that these practices will have a corrosive effect upon public morals in general. Botswana could slither down a slope such as Tanzania has descended over the last two decades or so. In the 1970s Tanzania had a reasonable record on corruption, but economic collapse and rampant inflation since has unleashed pervasive rent-seeking from the top politicians and officials down to lowly clerks, nurses, teachers and policemen.[23] More encouraging is the recent ministerial resignation which suggests that Botswana's leaders are responsive to press allegations of improper conduct and potential conflicts of interest.

Botswana is unlikely to face economic collapse in the conceivable future. On the contrary, with a still expanding economy and possibly the highest foreign exchange reserves per capita in the world, the near future seems reasonably assured. But, paradoxically, economic expansion, as we have seen, is also associated with an upsurge of abuse. The opportunities for self-enrichment on the part of those who occupy critical positions at the public/private intersection will not therefore diminish. Accordingly, the DCEC needs to be seen to be doing more about the dubious interests of sections of the Botswana political elite. The problem is that many of the involvements of parliamentarians and ministers that have led to excessive material gains are not strictly illegal under the Corruption and Economic Crime Act. However, this does not rule out action aimed at producing much-needed greater transparency in the dealings of elected officials. In his 1996 report the then director noted a paper that had been submitted to the clerk to the National Assembly recommending the declaration of the financial interests of the president and members of parliament. This had been accepted and a bill to this effect is under consideration. Any extended delay in the declaration of financial interests will fuel speculation about the government's motives.[24]

The second major source of danger for Botswana is that, however committed the country's leaders are to curbing corruption and economic crime within its borders, these efforts can be seriously undermined from outside. Admittedly, every state in the world is to some degree inserted into the global economy, which means that corruption, wherever it appears, necessarily has an international dimension. In Botswana's case, however, a particular source of possible contagion flows from the country which has by default always had considerable influence upon what passes within its borders, its neighbour South Africa. Not only is South Africa an economic giant compared to Botswana but the current downturn in the South African economy is likely to lead to increased targeting of opportunities for profit in neighbouring states, not least Botswana. Already Botswana's Financial Assistance Policy, which aims to stimulate entrepreneurial activities through government grants, is a major target for fraud, much of it perpetrated by South African nationals. Accordingly, the decision taken in 1994 to include economic crime within its remit could well lead to an already stretched DCEC being seriously overloaded with fraud investigations.

Whatever happens, the case load of the DCEC is not going to decline in the immediate future. On the contrary, the DCEC will be a victim of its own success: the more effective its educational programmes, the more complaints it is likely to receive. This highlights the seriousness of the problem that faces most LDCs – a serious shortage of skilled personnel. We are here concerned not just with the DCEC or the police force, but at all levels, not least within the judicial system. Were there, for example, to be marked improvements in the Directorate's investigatory and prosecutorial skills base, without corresponding gains elsewhere, this would yield at best only insignificant increases in overall throughput.

Hitherto, Botswana institutions, both public and private, have dealt with the skills shortage through the employment of expatriates. In the case of the DCEC, for example, the deputy director and four of the five assistant directors are expatriates. The employment of expatriates has a number of advantages in addition to the benefits that flow from their skills experience. The fact that they are to a greater extent insulated from the cut and thrust of politics, particularly organisational politics, can endow policies and decisions with a greater degree of objectivity. But expatriates are, of course, expensive. They are normally paid additional allowances, which usually means that overall they are earning more than their local peers and perhaps even superiors. In an overall situation in which good accommodation is in extremely short supply, expatriates must be housed at a standard which is commensurate with their expectations. More important, from a political point of view, a dominant and highly visible expatriate community is, in the long term, unacceptable. As more formally qualified indigenous personnel move onto the labour market, the pressure for 'localisation' will increase. It is thus not surprising that in his 1997 report the director announced that a major development during 1997 was the commencement of 'complete localisation'.[25] Informally there is the view that all expatriates will have left the DCEC by 2005. The pursuit of such a policy will, without doubt, place a heavy burden on training, particularly operational training. Training for anti-corruption activity is scarce and specialised and it is questionable whether Botswana can address such training issues from its own resources. The DCEC is a high-profile organisation which has attracted attention from many of its regional neighbours. Its effectiveness is difficult to assess with precision because success in implementing anti-corruption strategies is not to be measured simply in quantitative terms by counting prosecutions or investigations. Anti-corruption strategies founded solely on detection and punishment may have some short-term deterrent effect but the more likely consequence will be to overload the court system. If this is the outcome in Botswana, the prospects in countries with more limited legal and financial resources do not appear good. In the long term, anti-corruption strategies need to address opportunities, incentives, attitudes and rewards. The DCEC has begun work on corruption prevention and education, but much more needs to be done.

It remains the case that, despite the 'moral panic' which provoked the creation of the DCEC in 1994, levels of corruption in Botswana were low and remain low by continental standards. It is also the case that, despite some economic difficulties, the Botswana economy is built on relatively stable and solid foundations. In a sea of conflict and turmoil, Botswana remains an island of political stability. It is this political and economic stability which facilitates the orderly functioning of government and which, in particular, provided the DCEC with a secure base from which to operate and plan for the future. It is too soon to say what the long-term prospects for the DCEC are, but it is clear that any attempt at simple replication of its organisation and functions by other states is fraught with difficulty.

In favourable circumstances, the DCEC is an organisation which is stretched by its workload. Given that other countries in the region do not enjoy similar levels of economic and political stability and require substantial donor assistance, the prospects for replicating the DCEC elsewhere are not promising. In countries where the incidence of corruption is much higher, where economic security is a remote aspiration and where political stability is fragile and temporary, an anti-corruption agency like the DCEC would simply be overwhelmed.

NOTES

The authors wish to express their thanks to Director Timon M. Katlholo and the officers of the Directorate on Corruption and Economic Crime, Botswana, for their generous co-operation and assistance during the DFID-funded field research in Botswana. They would also like to thank the founding director of the DCEC, Graham Stockwell, for much useful background information. The views and opinions expressed here are solely those of the authors.

1. According to the 1998 Transparency International Corruption Perception Index (TICPI), Cameroon is ranked 85th out of 85 countries included, with Tanzania and Nigeria at 81, Kenya at 74, and Uganda at 73. The TICPI is available at http://www.transparency.de.
2. K. Good, 'Corruption and Mismanagement in Botswana: A Best Case Example?', *Journal of Modern African Studies*, 32, 3 (1994), 499–521; R. Charlton, 'Exploring the Byways of African Political Corruption: Botswana and Deviant Case Analysis', *Corruption and Reform*, 5, 1 (1990), 1–28.
3. See Good, 'Corruption and Mismanagement in Botswana'.
4. *Annual Report 1997*, DCEC, Botswana, 8.
5. Ibid., 4, 5.
6. Ibid., 17–19.
7. Ibid., 13.
8. Ibid., 7. See also *Annual Report 1996*, 11.
9. Ibid., 11.
10. *Annual Report 1997*, 6.
11. *Annual Report 1996*, 9.
12. *Corruption and Economic Crime Act, 1994* (Gabarone: Government Printer, 1994), 94–8.
13. *Annual Report 1996*, 25.
14. *Annual Report 1997*, 12.
15. See John D. Holm, 'Development, Democracy and Civil Society in Botswana', in Adrian Leftwich (ed.), *Democracy and Development* (Cambridge: Polity Press, 1996), 97–113.
16. See Patrick P. Molutsi and John D. Holm, 'Developing Democracy when Civil Society is Weak: The Case of Botswana', *African Affairs*, 89, 356 (1990), 323–40.
17. Holm, 'Development, Democracy and Civil Society in Botswana', 102.
18. Ibid., 105.

19. Ibid., 105.
20. See 'BAM Splits', front-page story in the *Botswana Guardian*, 23 April 1999.
21. See 'The Gravy Train Stops Here', *Botswana Guardian*, 4 Dec. 1998.
22. See 'Nkate in the Bull's Eye', *Botswana Guardian*, 23 April 1999, 4.
23. The Warioba Commission, set up by Tanzania's president at the beginning of 1996, identified 'rampant corruption' in the public service that had escalated at an alarming rate over the past 20 years. Both grand and petty corruption were found to be pervasive afflicting all areas of government. *The Warioba Report*, Government of Tanzania, 1996.
24. *Annual Report 1996*, 5; *Annual Report 1997*, 12.
25. Ibid.

Democracy, Development and Anti-Corruption Strategies: Learning from the Australian Experience

ROBERT WILLIAMS

Corruption was once thought of as peculiarly and inextricably linked to underdevelopment. It was believed that, after the 'take-off' into economic growth, many of the characteristics of poverty would, like a snake shedding its skin, be cast off. Development would eradicate poverty, reduce political instability and violence and limit the opportunities for corruption. As countries developed, they would pass from a corrupt phase to a less corrupt one. The history of developed states like the USA and UK seemed to lend credence to such a view. The decline and eventual disappearance of rotten boroughs in British electoral politics and the gradual extinction of the political machine in American cities confirmed the judgement that corruption flourishes at particular stages on the road to modernity. When that stage was passed, corruption would decline in political and economic significance.

The mechanisms and processes that effected the transformation from vice to virtue were not obvious. But as literacy levels rose, they encouraged the growth and spread of newspapers and magazines. If corruption flourishes in conditions of secrecy, then subjecting the conduct of politicians and officials to external and independent scrutiny is likely to deter all but the most rapacious. In some contexts, this was accompanied and reinforced by the extension of the franchise and so the newly enfranchised and educated citizenry were better able to hold their political masters accountable for their stewardship of public resources. Corruption, in this view, is best reduced by development and democratisation. Economic, social and political maturity are thus often seen as preconditions for controlling corruption.

There is some evidence to support the view that corruption flourishes in conditions of underdevelopment. The league table of corrupt states maintained by Transparency International is consistently headed by countries in Africa, Asia and Latin America.[1] Some states in the south have,

Robert Williams, Department of Politics University of Durham in effect, been privatised. The long awaited 'economic take-off' has been indefinitely postponed. Many African countries are so ravaged by corruption that it has brought about acute civil violence and state collapse. In conditions of mass illiteracy, acute poverty and civil strife, the delicate flower of democracy is not able to take firm root. Thus, if corruption peaks in circumstances of dictatorship and underdevelopment, does it follow that developed democracies are less likely to experience endemic or institutionalised corruption? Where democracy is well established, where there is economic prosperity and where there are independent mass media, the prospects for controlling corruption appear to be good. Where these conditions are absent – notwithstanding the efforts of international agencies, donor countries and national governments – signs of sustained progress in combating corruption are rare. Apart from the recent recognition that companies in the developed world play a significant role in generating corruption in the trading activities of the south,[2] corruption has largely been seen as a problem which afflicts the economically and politically dispossessed.

But this is a caricature of reality: corruption is equally prevalent in many developed democracies. Corruption is endemic in the American electoral system, nepotism flourishes in French government and the Italian political system collapsed under the weight of the corruption that permeated it. If corruption is a phase that countries go through before they reach maturity, much of the developed world seems to be experiencing a second childhood. But if corruption is a chronic condition rather than a disease of childhood, is it like viral infections which lie dormant for periods and then flare up for no discernible reason and is it possible to identify the factors which encourage and sustain it in supposedly democratic and developed environments?

CONTEMPORARY AUSTRALIAN CORRUPTION SCANDALS

One of the most sensational episodes in recent Australian history took place in Victoria in the 1970s and 1980s and concerned the relationship of the Federated Ship Painters and Dockers Union (FSPDU) with politicians, officials and businessmen. In its 1982 report, the commission investigating the FSPDU dramatically described it as 'a state within a state' and suggested that the 'painters and dockers have assumed to themselves a position outside the law'.[3] The union was, in effect, a criminal organisation. Most of its officeholders in Victoria had significant criminal records (across a range of offences, including violence) and many of their activities were fraudulent in character. Having exposed the major frauds of the FSPDU – the so-called 'bottom of the harbour' schemes involving bogus companies and disappearing accounts – the commissioner, Frank Costigan, turned his attention to the question of why such activities had been allowed to continue for so long. Costigan appeared to suggest that his efforts to break organised crime syndicates were frustrated by the ability of rich and powerful suspects linked to them not just to buy the best legal and financial advice but, more worryingly, to buy protection from corrupt politicians, judges, police officers and officials.

Law enforcement agencies are a potential threat to organised crime and, if they are not intimidated, there is always the option of bribery. In Australia, as elsewhere, the operation of extensive criminal businesses such as supplying drugs or running illegal gambling operations is not practicable without reaching an accommodation with law enforcement officers. In the past 20 years there have been major investigations of police corruption in New South Wales, Queensland, Victoria and Western Australia. The corruption of those responsible for law enforcement is therefore a prime tactic of those engaged in substantial criminal enterprises, but the corruption can reach upward from the police to include judges, juries and even the bribing of government ministers.

The 1987 corruption scandal in Queensland was triggered by media allegations that the Queensland police had persistently ignored and implicitly condoned criminal activity relating to drugs, gambling and prostitution. Previous efforts to investigate allegations of police corruption had been largely frustrated by a combination of political and trade union opposition together with a closing of ranks within the police force. As the scale of illegal activities increased, so too did the funds available for bribery. The Fitzgerald Commission[4] found systematic corruption in the police force, and one of the consequences of the inquiry was the conviction and imprisonment for bribery of Terence Lewis, Queensland's Commissioner of Police. The 'wall of silence' which had successfully rebuffed previous inquiries was broken by the liberal use of immunity granted to a 'whistle blower' within the police force. But the most important distinguishing characteristic of the Queensland case was not the conviction of senior public figures but rather the commissioner's emphasis on political and organisational principles, structures and procedures which is discussed below.

The scandals of Victoria and Queensland had their contemporary counterparts elsewhere in Australia, and in New South Wales the Labour government of Premier Neville Wran found itself under a barrage of media and political criticism for its seeming indifference and ineffectiveness in dealing with allegations of corruption.[5] There was growing public concern about the integrity of public administration in the state. This concern was fuelled by particular scandals, including the imprisonment of a chief magistrate and a cabinet minister for bribery, trials of senior officials and an inquiry into the police force, leading to the discharge in disgrace of a Deputy Commissioner of Police. The image of the Wran government was tarnished by the spate of scandals and contributed to its 1988 electoral defeat. The new Liberal administration headed by Nick Greiner had swept into office on a wave of anti-corruption rhetoric and there was a demonstrable political need to be seen to be doing something substantial about corruption. The substance proved to be the creation of the Independent Commission Against Corruption (ICAC).[6]

Four years after it was established, the ICAC delivered a report which found that Premier Nick Greiner and another minister had engaged in conduct which violated part of the ICAC Act and which constituted a breach of trust in relation to a public appointment.[7] Greiner appealed the finding but resigned as premier of New South Wales before the matter was judicially resolved because of censure by the Legislative Assembly. The initiator of the ICAC was, in effect, driven from office by his own creation.

CORRUPTION INVESTIGATIONS: CONTEXT, REFORMS AND THEMES

These diverse illustrations of corruption in Australia all share an important characteristic in that the political authorities in question refuted or denied the charges. In all the cases, they made counter-accusations against their accusers and protested their innocence. Such protestations may appear self-serving but the image of virtuous accusers and villainous accused is simplistic and misleading. It suggests both that charges of corruption constitute powerful ammunition in Australian political wars and that the combatants may be using inconsistent and incompatible notions of corruption.

Neville Wran's Labour government in New South Wales dismissed the corruption allegations of then opposition leader Nick Greiner as partisan mischief making. When Premier Greiner himself was later under attack, he saw it as political opportunism by the Labour Party in a context of a finely balanced Legislative Assembly. In Queensland, the long serving premier, Sir John Bjelke-Petersen, said he had nothing to confess and expressed his confidence that 'history will vindicate me'.[8] While denial and counter-attack are parts of the political armoury, it seems that these episodes suggest deeper tensions and divisions within Australian political culture. These conflicts are not to be dismissed as part of the rough and tumble of Australian politics, but should be seen as manifestations of competing and contrasting conceptions of liberal democracy.

To exaggerate the point, it is possible to see commissioners Costigan and Fitzgerald and the ICAC as representing a purist, even puritanical, approach to corruption in public life. They are repelled by the 'dirty' world of politics in which pragmatism normally triumphs over principle. In this view, politicians and public officials must, like Caesar's wife, be above suspicion. They exhibit what might be termed zero-tolerance of corruption and are concerned not only to root out corruption but to eliminate even the appearance of corruption. In this sense, they are 'men on a mission', zealots who have absolute confidence in the righteousness of their cause. By implication, those who oppose them are at best protecting the guilty and at worst are guilty themselves. They reject the suggestion that the pursuit of absolute integrity can prove incompatible with other important goals and values.

Thus the Costigan investigation of the excesses of the FSPDU in Victoria developed into an inquiry into serious business fraud and subsequently into a broad-ranging inquiry into organised crime and its possible links to political, police and business figures. Those subject to Costigan's attentions were quick to claim that not only had he hugely overstepped his brief but he had also abused the powers of the royal commission. Most obviously, a royal commission is protected by privilege and, therefore, if it makes potentially defamatory statements about individuals, they have no legal redress through an action for libel. Furthermore, such commissions are not courts of law and are not bound by legal procedure. There is, for example, no obligation to prove charges beyond reasonable doubt and neither is there a requirement to inform an accused person of the allegations against them or give them an opportunity to explain their conduct. One of those targeted by the Costigan commission, the prominent businessman, Kerry Packer, claimed that Costigan 'has disgraced the institution of royal commission, and his own profession as a lawyer. The Costigan report has indelibly demonstrated that substantial power invested in a person prepared to use it in a warped, arbitrary and unprincipled way can decimate individual rights and totally over-ride basic principles of justice'.[9]

Commissioner Costigan rejected Packer's complaints about his investigations, but it is clear from his reports and other documents that he and his staff were unhappy about the difficulties they encountered in their efforts to assemble evidence against powerful and resourceful people. They were dissatisfied with the limitations imposed on their investigations by concepts of natural justice and, in particular, by the presumption of innocence. In effect, Costigan argued that normal concerns for civil rights and liberties were inappropriate in certain kinds of cases. He asserted that the balance of the criminal justice system in Australia was tilted in favour of the corrupt and the criminal. His investigations were delayed and disrupted by court proceedings initiated by some of the subjects of his inquiries. To Costigan, this was unacceptable because, he noted, the commission was only taken to court 'by the wealthy and intelligent, by the type of person who is potentially the greatest threat to the civil liberties of the citizen'. For Costigan, protecting the civil liberties of criminals damages the civil liberties of law-abiding citizens. The pursuit of the corrupt and the criminal therefore justifies invading privacy and infringing the civil liberties of suspects. Where the threat of organised crime and the corruption it engenders is acute, Costigan argues that exceptional and draconian steps are justified. This view was not generally shared and it caused concern in circles beyond those of the criminal and corrupt. The Federal Director of Public Prosecutions warned of the threat to civil liberties from over-zealous actions intended to curb organised crime and corruption. One newspaper concluded that Costigan 'employed the methods of the Star Chamber, not of a democratic society under the rule of law'.[10]

While Frank Costigan was anxious to seek out and punish guilty individuals, Tony Fitzgerald's ambitions were much wider. The central thrust of his inquiry into corruption in the Queensland police was towards a restructuring of the entire political system of Queensland. This restructuring was aimed at bringing to Queensland different and superior forms of parliamentary government and democratic accountability. Fitzgerald was not so much interested in testing the truth or falsity of particular allegations or punishing particular individuals, but rather was concerned to expose and analyse the pattern, nature and scope of the misdeeds he had uncovered. He was appalled by the extent of wrongdoing revealed, under protection of immunity, by some key witnesses. In Fitzgerald's words, the inquiry 'began by pulling a few threads at the frayed edges of society. To general alarm, sections of the fabric began to unravel'.[11]

What started as an inquiry into alleged misconduct by sections of the Queensland police developed into a thesis on the characteristics and virtues of good government whose central pillars were accountability and openness. Fitzgerald had little patience with the 'rotten apples' theory of corruption, but placed the blame on the political structures and culture of Queensland public life. His determination to point the way towards creating a cleaner system of parliamentary democracy is evidenced by the fact that the section of his report dealing with the political context of corruption is significantly larger than the section describing the alleged misconduct. Within six months of reporting, the opposition Labour Party came to power in the state elections, bringing to an abrupt end 32 years of ultra-conservative rule. Corruption in public life was the main campaign issue and the Labour leader, Wayne Goss, committed himself to implementing the

Fitzgerald recommendations. The Fitzgerald Report is thus one of the rare examples of an investigation of corruption that produced a political transformation.

The core of the Fitzgerald Report is the proposition that the 30-year dominance of the National–Liberal coalition under the leadership of Bjelke-Petersen was based on an electoral fraud. It was based less on the support of a majority of the electorate than on the workings of a zonal electoral system which effectively over-represented rural areas where National–Liberal strength was concentrated. Fitzgerald essentially contended that the government which appointed him to investigate corruption was itself illegitimate. In his words, 'a government which achieves public office by means other than free and fair elections lacks legitimate political authority over that system'.[12] He drew a direct correlation between the consequences of this distortion of democracy and the growth of corruption. Fitzgerald's prognosis is that 'the institutional culture of public administration risks degeneration if, for any reason, a government's activities ceased to be moderated by concern at the possibility of losing power'.[13] Put more directly, where governments rig the electoral rules to ensure permanent control of power, accountability evaporates and those in office are free to abuse their positions without fear of discipline or punishment.

Fitzgerald's prescription for Queensland's ills involved an electoral and administrative review commission which he said should have a priority agenda to include the following: reviewing electoral boundaries; the composition and appointment procedures of public bodies; the introduction to a system of parliamentary committees; an enhanced role for the auditor-general; freedom of information legislation; and the adequacy of provisions for regulating political donations and financial disclosures. If this were not enough, he further recommended the establishment of a criminal justice commission to review, initiate and co-ordinate the reform of criminal justice administration. Its role would include monitoring police performance and it would have responsibilities for public sector misconduct. As if to demonstrate that he had not entirely forgotten the catalyst for his inquiries, Fitzgerald also advocated sweeping reforms of the Queensland police force. In the commissioner's judgement the political, administrative and law enforcement systems of Queensland had been tried and found wanting. Although he did not go as far as providing a blue-print for the new systems, because these were matters for the parliament and the Queensland people, Fitzgerald made it clear what he saw as the characteristics of a virtuous government .

In New South Wales, the Liberal-National Party victory in the 1988 elections was partly due to the campaign waged against the Labour government's apparent inability or unwillingness to stem the rising tide of corruption. The creation of the ICAC was a response to the issues of the campaign but, only four years later, Premier Nick Greiner was to find himself driven from office by an ICAC report condemning his conduct. Greiner had called an election in 1991 in the expectation that he would increase his majority. The results were disappointing and his government had only a wafer-thin majority which depended on the support of a number of independent MPs. The following year, after talks with the Greiner administration, one of these MPs, Tony Metherall, resigned his seat and was simultaneously appointed to a senior position in the New South Wales public service. The timing and manner of this appointment provoked widespread and intense media criticism and prompted an ICAC investigation.

The ICAC report[14] found that the conduct of Greiner and others in the Metherall appointment and resignation amounted to the partial exercise of official functions and constituted a breach of trust. Corrupt conduct is broadly defined in the ICAC Act.[15] It commonly involves conduct of any person that adversely affects or could adversely affect, directly or indirectly, the honest or impartial exercise of official functions by any official or public authority. The definition includes the misuse of information by a public official or any other breach of public trust. But conduct does not amount to corrupt conduct unless it could also constitute or involve a criminal offence, a disciplinary offence or reasonable grounds for dismissal. In the case of conduct of a Minister of the Crown or a Member of a House of Parliament, corruption should involve a substantial breach of an applicable code of conduct. This final specification is not helpful as there was no code of conduct in force in parliament in 1988 when the act was passed and nor was there at the time of the Metherall affair. Despite an amendment to the act in 1994 providing for a draft code to be presented within 12 months, it remained the case in 1998 that no code of conduct for members had been implemented.

The direct outcome of the Metherall affair was the resignation of Greiner because of parliamentary censure. He appealed the ICAC's finding against him and, in August 1992, the Court of Appeal confirmed that the conduct met the criteria for corruption in the 1988 Act but a majority opinion held that it did not constitute reasonable grounds for dismissal.[16] This curate's egg of a judicial decision satisfied neither party. Greiner was resolute that he had done nothing corrupt and the ICAC remained convinced that what was done was so serious as to merit removal from office.

A number of important themes run through the Victoria, Queensland and New South Wales cases. The first concerns the fundamental conflicts between commissioners dedicated to rooting out corruption and the political authorities which appointed them to office. A second theme is the differing perceptions of the protagonists about the character and seriousness of the conduct under review. A third is the disputes over the measures necessary to deal with the alleged misconduct. A fourth is the contrasting conceptions of commissioners and politicians about what constitutes legitimate political conduct. And the fifth is the conflict between idealised notions of public life and parliamentary democracy and the political realities faced by politicians. At times, the exchanges between the commissioners and their state governments reveal a gulf in language, priorities, values and understanding. Whereas the commissioners represent themselves as impartial enemies of corruption, the politicians interpret their zeal as anti-political and even anti-democratic.

In his response to the censure motion against him, Nick Greiner argued that, if his conduct was judged to be corrupt, it would be 'for practical purposes, the death of politics in this State'. Greiner's position was that the ICAC was trying to introduce new rules into the political game without the approval of the players. It was not just that politicians were being judged by rules they rejected but that new standards were being applied to past conduct. From his perspective, taking patronage out of politics was equivalent to taking parties out of politics.

An epidemic of corruption scandals often induces moral panic and over-reaction. In such contexts, corruption commissioners can almost seem to act as modern witchfinder-generals, playing on popular fears and asserting guilt where there was once a presumption of innocence. They deem customary political behaviour to be improper and they reject the legitimacy of established electoral systems. They rewrite the rules of politics and government and they do so without regard to the damage to individual reputations or to the practical workings of democracy. They encourage a climate of suspicion and distrust, thus undermining confidence and public trust in public figures and the wider political system. They do what they do in the name of the public interest or common good but none is elected, none are directly answerable to the public and none is responsible for ensuring the formulation, enactment or implementation of public policies.

Frank Costigan seemed to view attempts to limit his inquiries and to resist his call for a reversal of the burden of proof as evidence of a political cover-up. When the corruption investigators describe the situations they find in the gravest terms, political logic dictates that government remedies must be quickly agreed to avoid charges of indifference, complacency or even collusion. Tony Fitzgerald made large claims about the illegitimacy of the Queensland electoral system. These claims formed the basis for his call for the reconstruction of representative democracy. But there are reputable analysts who believe that his critique of the electoral system was misconceived and misleading.[17] The New South Wales ICAC found the state premier guilty of corruption for engaging in the kind of informal employment practices which have many precedents in the administrations of various parties. From one perspective, the corruption commissioners act in the name of a cleaner, better form of democracy where integrity and accountability are the priorities. From another perspective, they represent an unelected threat to the elected representatives of the people and established ways of conducting political business.

CONCLUSION

The literature on explaining corruption is substantial and one of the most popular approaches of the 1980s and 1990s is principal/agent analysis. Its strength is explaining how and why officials betray the trust of their political masters. It is rather weaker in explaining how political leaders' actions can be explained and characterised.[18] The reason for this weakness is evident from the case studies considered in this article. In the Australia case, those who have passed judgement on politicians are employing criteria and frames of reference which are different to and incommensurate with those used by politicians. Where Corruption Commissioners stress the need for impartiality, the stock in trade of party politicians is partiality. Where public officials are expected to treat members of the public without discrimination, party politicians expect to receive preferential treatment from their party colleagues. Where public appointments are concerned, independent assessments based on merit are expected, but, when political promotion is concerned, a range of other considerations come into play. Presumably, if all cabinet appointments were made on strict criteria of merit, then all cabinets would be made up of members of several parties unless the claim could be sustained that the governing party had a monopoly of talent. In short, politics and public administration are different and it is where they intersect that the collision of competing value systems occurs.

Reformers sometimes give the impression that they think political systems should, in some sense, be neutral, that there should be a 'level playing field' for political competition. There is also the suggestion that the sole motivation and reward of public office should be the clear conscience that comes from dedicated service to the public. But politics everywhere is a rough business. Politicians are not all altruistic ascetics and a firm adherence to principles can prove more of a handicap than an advantage in a political career. Patterns of political conduct are established and legitimised by long practice and by the informal acquiescence of opposition parties.

Politics is, on one level, about winning elections and many politicians are motivated by the maxim, 'to the victor the spoils'. If contradicted, they might ask in puzzlement, 'So what is it about?' Politicians learn to build support among followers by tending to their specific and partial needs. They rise in party hierarchies by building networks, exchanging favours, lending and withholding support, rewarding supporters and punishing enemies, and by manoeuvring for tactical advantage over political opponents and rivals. They acquire disciples, foot soldiers and fair-weather friends and they learn that party loyalty and cohesion take precedence over ideological purity and personal integrity. The rules of politics are neither identical with nor necessarily consistent with the ethical standards, guidelines and codes of conduct which emanate from anti-corruption commissions.

The important question in a representative democracy is what happens when different ethical codes collide? Is all party political activity corrupt, almost by definition? Or are politicians special cases and exceptions to the ethics rules? Are politicians subject to the same or modified rules as civil servants or to parliamentary rules of their own devising? The outcome of the Greiner episode suggests that the appeal court believed that Greiner had engaged in improper conduct amounting to corruption under the 1988 Act but it did not think that it merited dismissal because, when Greiner acted as he did, he did not intend acting corruptly and was not aware that he was acting corruptly. To this extent, the court recognised the special role of ministers as 'principals' in that they have obligations and commitments beyond their responsibilities to act in the public interest. The 'contract' between politicians and their electorates has many facets and to remove a state premier is a very large step to take. Electorates have the power to remove politicians they do not trust and, when corruption is a major issue, they do, as both Wran in New South Wales and Bjelke-Petersen in Queensland discovered. Between elections and in the absence of serious criminal charges, the dismissal of a state premier on grounds of violating standards of which he was unaware and which were determined by an extra-parliamentary body should lie in the realm of constitutional possibility rather than political reality.

Taken at face value, concepts such as development and democracy are unhelpful in assessing the nature and role of corruption. Economic development does not presuppose the parallel development of a purist or puritanical political culture. Australia lays claim to being a democracy but so too does Denmark and their political cultures and experience of corruption are very different. The case studies discussed here show how the increased saliency of corruption as a political issue has created conflicts and tensions within the distinctive political traditions of Australian states. In the conflict between corruption crusaders and politicians, who is to judge? Are these legal or political issues? In any democracy, presumably all public servants are ultimately judged in the court of public opinion but it raises further issues of how to assess weight, how to respond to divisions in opinion and how to cope with disjunctions between public opinion and public behaviour. The 'public' do not believe or expect their elected representatives to be candidates for canonisation but nor do they expect them to be habitual thieves and compulsive liars.

Political parties are generally regarded as indispensable features of developed democracies but we know that the funding of parties raises concerns about improper influence.[19] In the absence of comprehensive state funding, we expect parties to raise money from private individuals and organisations but purists argue that such contributions should only be given for altruistic reasons. Yet self-interest, whose pursuit lies at the heart of principal/agent analysis, is clearly an important motive in all aspects of politics. We expect politicians and their parties to serve both the public interest and their private interests. We suspect that politicians are sometimes 'economical with the truth' and that they seek office for a range of complex and not always wholly admirable reasons.

Our understanding of political activity in a developed democracy is clearly interwoven with an understanding of what constitutes improper conduct by our elected representatives. The ICAC found that Premier Nick Greiner had overstepped a line which to him and many of his counterparts in Australia and his predecessors in New South Wales was blurred if not invisible. The appeal court concluded that Greiner had not knowingly engaged in corrupt conduct and subsequent judgements of the ICAC have been informed by considerations of intentionality as well as conduct. Corruption is normally associated in the public mind with personal benefit or enrichment yet the ICAC never alleged that Greiner had made any personal gain in the Metherall affair. One student of the affair suggests that it looks like a case of 'institutional' rather than personal corruption,[20] but goes on to suggest that 'institutional corruption' is a deeply contestable concept that offers no clear criteria for distinguishing between proper and improper political conduct.[21] Within any democracy, there are often competing notions of corruption at work and there are no easy or simple ways of resolving conflicts between them. The process of development can help remove some of the incentives and opportunities for corruption, but others remain. As democratisation takes hold, political competition becomes more formal and structured and the contestants develop sets of rules and understandings to regulate and moderate their rivalries. The participants in democratic political processes are attuned to shifts in public moods and priorities and, when concerns about corruption in Australia increased, opposition politicians made political capital at the expense of the incumbent parties. Allegations of corruption are inexpensive forms of campaigning which invariably attract media attention. Greiner understood this in opposition in New South Wales but, when the weapon was turned against him in government, he dismissed it as media hype and a political tactic by the Labour Party.

If political parties remain the preferred vehicles for mobilising and organising public opinion both in emergent and developed democracies, they will continue to seek political donations and they will continue to jostle for party advantage in national and local assemblies. Treating political parties as if they were simply another form of public service organisation is a mistake. It will always be difficult to take the politics out of government and it may be unwise to try. The 'moral panic' that led to the establishment of the ICAC in New South Wales and the political transformation of Queensland has now passed. Labour are once again out of power in Queensland but back in power in New South Wales. Nick Greiner became Chairman of the Sydney Olympic Committee and the ICAC complains of progressive reductions in its funding. In democratic polities, corruption has the obvious potential to become a key electoral issue, but maintaining long term public and political support for a high profile anti-corruption strategy is rather more problematic. The imperatives of democratic politics will contrive to complicate the quest for integrity in public life for the foreseeable future.

The case studies suggest that democracy is not a panacea for controlling corruption. It is, of course, important to consider the nature of political institutions and their forms and roles. It is also important to consider the balance between state power and civil liberties. But reforming institutions, changing laws and creating new public bodies to control corruption do not in themselves easily, quickly or completely transform the political cultures of states. No doubt Victoria, Queensland and New South Wales needed institutional and procedural reform but effective reform requires a consensus on the nature and severity of the problem, a willingness to act in a sustained fashion, agreement on the mechanisms to be employed and a common set of political values. Every form of democracy depends more on shared understandings and commitments than on any particular set of institutional arrangements. Where there is misunderstanding and values are contested, attempts by international financial institutions in Africa or corruption commissioners in Australia to impose new democratic procedures and structures are fraught with difficulty.

NOTES

1. Transparency International Corruption Perception Index (TICPI), available at http://www.transparency.de.
2. See, for example, the OECD Convention on Combating Bribery.
3. Royal Commission on the activities of the Federated Ship Painters and Dockers Union (Commissioner: Frank Costigan QC) Interim Report, No.4, 109 and 110 (the Costigan Commission), Australian Government Publishing Service, Canberra, July, 1982). The inquiry and associated issues are discussed in Robert Williams, 'Crime and Corruption in Australia', *Corruption and Reform*, 1, 2 (1986), 101–14.
4. Report of a Commission of Inquiry Pursuant to Orders in Council: Commission of Inquiry into Possible Illegal Activities and Associated Police Misconduct (Fitzgerald Report), (Brisbane: Government Printer, 1989). See also, Robert Williams, 'Corruption in Queensland: The Fitzgerald Inquiry', *Corruption and Reform*, 6, 1 (1991), 53–60.
5. For discussions of corruption in New South Wales in the 1970s and 1980s, see Bob Bottom, *Connections* (Melbourne: Sun Books, 1985), and Evan Whitton, *Can of Worms* (Marricksville: Fairfax, 1986).
6. Ian Temby 'The Setting Up of an Anti-Corruption Agency in New South Wales', in *Fourth International Anti-Corruption Conference Report* (Australian Government Publishing Service, 1990).
7. Ian Temby, ICAC Commissioner, Report on Investigation into the Metherall Resignation and Appointment (Sydney: ICAC, June 1992).
8. Quoted in *Brisbane Courier-Mail*, 5 July 1989, 1.
9. Quoted in *The Bulletin*, 13 Nov. 1984, 30.
10. Quoted in ibid., 28.
11. Fitzgerald Report, 4.
12. Ibid., 127.
13. Ibid., 127.
14. See the useful discussion in Mark Philp, 'Defining Political Corruption', *Political Studies*, 45, 3 (1997), 43–69.
15. The charter, obligations, definitions of corrupt conduct and functions of the ICAC are set out in the *ICAC Annual Report, 1997–98* (Sydney, 1998), 10–11. For further information, see the ICAC website: http://www.icac.nsw.gov.au.
16. *Greiner v. Independent Commission Against Corruption* (1992) 28 NSW LR 12 at 134–5.
17. See, for example, Malcolm Mackerras, 'A Revisionist Interpretation of Queensland's Electoral Scheme', *Australian Journal of Political Science*, 25, 2 (1990), 339–49.
18. For a discussion of the weaknesses of principal/agent analysis, see Robert Williams, 'New Concepts for Old', *Third World Quarterly*, 20, 3 (1999), 492–4.
19. See Robert Williams (ed.), *Party Finance and Political Corruption* (Basingstoke: Macmillan, 1999).
20. See Dennis Thompson, *Ethics in Congress: From Individual to Institutional Corruption* (Washington, DC: Brookings, 1995).
21. Philp, 'Defining Political Corruption', 439.

Conclusion: Prospects for Reform in a Globalised Economy

ROBIN THEOBALD

In the preceding chapters we have discussed in some detail the problem of corruption, examined a wide range of policies and strategies aimed at containing it, and considered the relevance of a democratic political system and the process of democratisation to these strategies. What conclusions may we reach, if any? What is the role of democratisation in the crusade against corruption, or, for that matter, vice versa?

Whilst overall anti-corruption strategy in a given country is usually an admixture of a range of policies, these tend to coalesce around three central elements: the establishment of an anti-corruption agency, the general reform of the public sector and the promotion of a strong civil society. Since each of these dimensions has already received considerable attention both by the contributors to this collection and elsewhere, we confine ourselves in this brief conclusion to highlighting certain key themes.

First, in so far as a country's anti-corruption strategy expresses itself in the establishment of a dedicated anti-corruption agency (ACA) – and it increasingly does – we note that this is often a consequence of an upsurge of moral panic following revelations of high level scandals (Hong Kong, Botswana, New South Wales). As Williams has pointed out above, when examining anti-corruption strategies, we need constantly to bear in mind the political potency of anti-corruption discourse. Accusations of corrupt practices, that is, provide a convenient metaphor for discrediting those in power just as declaimed commitment to an anti-corruption crusade affirms a regimes's moral integrity as well as providing ammunition which can be directed at critics. Even when there is a genuine desire to do battle against corruption, as there frequently is, the creation of such bodies is often driven more by the need to be seen to be 'doing something' than being the product of a carefully considered strategy. In other words, insufficient attention may be given to the long-term resource implications which, as we shall now see, are likely to be considerable.

Robin Theobald, Westminster Business School, University of Westminster

Second, for ACAs to have a meaningful impact, they must be extremely well resourced in terms of both material and human capital. This means that they obviously need adequate office space, office equipment such as word processors, computers, reprographic, library and data storage facilities, an efficient telephone system and so forth. Given the topographical characteristics and communication difficulties of many LDCs, such bodies particularly need a fleet of reliable four wheel drive vehicles. For the purposes of vital intelligence gathering and surveillance, a separate covert fleet must be operated and maintained.

The demands of ACAs on human capital are stringent. Investigating corrupt behaviour which, by definition, is usually covert, gathering sufficient evidence to secure a successful prosecution, is an extremely painstaking and time-consuming activity. It is also an activity which requires highly specialised skills, skills which in LDCs tend to be in short supply. These are also skills which are difficult to inculcate through short-term training. Not only must ACA officers be highly skilled, they must also be adequately motivated, which in the first instance means well paid with pension rights and probably other allowances, not least for adequate housing. High level salaries are needed not only to sustain optimal levels of motivation but also honesty. ACA officers, like some of their counterparts in the police service, tend to have access to highly sensitive information which they could turn to their own advantage in a variety of ways. They may, therefore, be seen to be in need of additional inducements to remain honest.

As Theobald and Williams point out above, such agencies tend to be victims of their own success. To the extent that they are able to raise public awareness of the problem of corruption and, more important, the fact that something can be done about it, complaints and demands for action will obviously increase. One major consequence of this is likely to be escalating pressure for branches to be established in the provinces. In societies where communications are difficult, where there are low levels of literacy and consequently a heavy reliance on face-to-face interaction, the existence of a single branch in the capital seriously limits access. But additional branches call for additional resources and so demand spirals.

The general point is, of course, that whereas in all societies such resources are in short supply, in less developed states they are invariably acute. In this respect, the ACA will be competing with other public bodies, especially the police service and the system of justice. In a situation of escalating crime, these agencies may demand and receive priority. We return to the question of the overall availability of resources below.

Third, in order to be effective ACAs must be endowed with considerable legal and administrative powers. Considering legal powers first, investigations will often involve covert operations where suspects have to be kept under surveillance, their premises surreptitiously searched, their telephones tapped and so forth. In an era of globalised operations where large sums of money can be transferred out of a country at the push of a button, speed of action will be at a premium. Accordingly, powers of search and arrest without a warrant may be deemed essential. Such powers, together with the abandonment of the presumption of innocence, which are normally seen to be necessary by such agencies, are likely to come into conflict with the accepted notions of civil rights which prevail in a democracy. Such powers are obviously open to abuse.[1]

So far as administrative authority is concerned, ACAs will have to deal with all departments of state, whether to investigate maladministration, corruption, or merely to advise on corruption prevention. Whatever the case, ACAs need the authority to require – in the final analysis compel – potentially all areas of government to co-operate, respond to enquiries, yield information, implement reforms and so forth. The necessity for this kind of administrative clout is often taken to mean that such agencies need the strongest possible backing, perhaps even that of the head of state. Here we are not talking merely about enthusiastic declarations of support but a direct line of authority. But this, of course, raises the problem of accountability, of who 'guards the guards'? As we saw, the ICAC in Hong Kong was subjected to several layers of inspection, whilst its counterpart in New South Wales reports to a parliamentary committee. The DCEC Botswana, however, is responsible to, and reports only to the Office of the President, and although the need for the establishment of some form of review body is formally acknowledged, action on this has yet to be taken.[2] Such a situation is undesirable for two reasons: it obviously permits political interference in ACA operations, perhaps protecting the machinations of kin and cronies, at the same time targeting regime critics and opponents; and, second, even where actual political interference is minimal, in the absence of appropriate levels of transparency, the public perception will be that the ACA is a only a token organisation which spends most of its time trying to net the small fry. The issues of accountability and transparency are thus of paramount importance.

Fourth, as has previously been pointed out,[3] ACAs are heavily dependent upon a strong institutional environment, especially in immediately ancillary areas such as the police service and the judiciary. No matter how effective their investigatory arm, ACAs will achieve little in the public eye if they cannot secure an acceptable level of prosecutions because of a grossly over-stretched or deeply corrupt judicial system. The need for strong institutions is obviously not confined to the police and judiciary, but applies to the public service generally. Concerted attempts to track down financial irregularities in government will be relatively fruitless if most departments are seriously in arrears with submitting their accounts to the auditor general's office.[4] Efforts to combat, say, the illegal diversion of teachers' salaries will yield little if the department of education is unable to maintain accurate and up-to-date records of its staff establishment. Attempts to curtail urban land speculation by politicians and their cronies will be seriously impeded by the unavailability of records in the land registry. This dependence upon strong institutions extends increasingly to the area of finance, particularly the banking sector, whether this be public or private. Much corruption and fraud comes to light because of the discovery of inexplicably large sums of money in private bank accounts. But if banking records are inadequate, not only may malfeasance remain undiscovered, but even when it is unearthed, such gaps can seriously impede investigation and prosecution because of difficulties with evidence.

We have now moved to our second major dimension of what appears to become the standard anti-corruption strategy – the general reform of the public sector. To be sure, advocates of ACAs among IFIs and many donors generally see their introduction as only one component of a comprehensive programme of reform of the public sector in general.[5] But this of course solves neither the problem of the huge volume of resources needed, nor the awesome conundrum of assigning priority. As has been frequently observed, less developed states face the enduring problem of appropriating through taxation sufficient resources to support their administrative apparatus. But the very condition of economic underdevelopment, augmented by the typical LDC configuration of economic activities, yields little in the way of surplus which can be directed to institution-building.[6] Thus LDCs are caught in the familiar vicious circle of administrative underdevelopment: low levels of administrative capacity limit the state's ability to appropriate resources; but limited ability to appropriate resources, in turn, severely inhibits the development of administrative capacity.[7] To this disability has been added, in many cases, the burden of often chronic indebtedness. This, of course, means that a significant portion of what the state is able to appropriate must be set aside for debt servicing rather than being employed to build up much-needed capacity. To the issue of this crucial link between overall institutional weakness and the condition of economic underdevelopment we return below. Let us first consider the third major element in a typical anti-corruption strategy: civil society.

Given the anti-state rhetoric of the neo-liberal worldview, it was probably inevitable that the emphasis should eventually shift to civil society. In the neo-liberal scenario, the state surrenders voluntarily, under pressure or of necessity, those areas which it can no longer service. Civil society associations then move to occupy the political and economic space vacated by the state. Civil society thus, in a sense, comes to the rescue of the state. But will it?

A considerable amount of academic attention has been devoted to the analysis of civil society both generally and specifically in relation to LDCs. Such is the volume of this output that even to attempt to summarise it here would be ludicrous. We merely reiterate the main arguments made by the contributors to this volume. These are that the outlook for a vigorous civil society in less developed states is not encouraging. Poverty, low levels of literacy, geographical and social isolation, and, probably most important of all, the unrelieved burden of surviving from day to day, hardly conduce to participating in and organising those associations that will constitute an effective check on the actions of government. In addition to the objective situation endured by the citizens of the south must be added the carrot and the stick from above. The carrot may take the form of an expediently significant hike in public sector salaries, usually on the eve of elections;[8] or the provision of new school buildings or a dispensary in an area of marginal support. Or it may involve the selective sponsoring and funding of civil society organisations, perhaps giving priority to those with a manifestly traditional orientation.[9] The stick may entail the compulsory registration and perhaps heavy government involvement in the operations of key associations, especially trade unions, political parties and human rights groups. And, of course, the stick may, and unfortunately often does, amount to no less than uninhibited intimidation, persecution, imprisonment, torture, terror and murder. On this point, it is salutary how highly mobilised and urbanised civil societies in developed Latin American states with strong democratic traditions, such as Argentina and Chile, were for many years cowed into silence by ruthless and determined military governments. It is even more disconcerting how states that have existed for more than a century and a half have generally failed to confine their militaries to the narrowly constitutional role this agency allegedly performs in developed states.[10] The reasons for this are complex and clearly beyond the scope of this Conclusion. Suffice it to note that a major consequence is the perpetuation of a culture of political violence under which Latin American militaries and paramilitaries are routinely deployed against dissidents. Thus, although Mexico has never endured military government since the ascendance of the Partido Revolucionario Institucional 70 years ago, this regime has always relied heavily on the army to deal with serious opposition.[11] Even in the now formally democratic Argentina, critics of the regime of Carlos Menem continue to be harassed and in some cases murdered.[12]

In the case of states that display significant ethnic/regional differences, the stick and carrot can be combined in the deliberate exploitation of these differences by ruling elites. Such tactics have been particularly apparent in the 'new' states of sub-Saharan Africa where time-serving autocrats such as Mobutu Sese Seko have been chillingly adept at displacing hostility onto suitable minorities and 'strangers'. If we look at the regime presided over for 21 years by Kenyan president, Daniel Arap Moi, we encounter a government that is subject to considerable opposition internally as well as good deal of external pressure from IFIs and donors. Yet by an astute combination of manipulation and repression Moi has successfully and consistently divided and fragmented the opposition. A central feature of Moi's strategy has been to stir up ethnic hostilities in order to demonstrate that free elections would be destabilising.[13] This brings us to a key point, which is that the fundamental structures of power within a given state will be almost certainly be replicated within its civil society. Accordingly, in a state where structures of authority and power are articulated primarily through patriarchal and clientelistic-type ties, it is inevitable that such relationships will penetrate civil society associations. And, of course, the resulting tendency for such societies to be compartmentalised into vertical blocs will be seriously reinforced where the state is fragmented by ethnic, regional, religious and other similar formations. The pervasiveness of what are usually referred to as patrimonial or neo-patrimonial relationships and their articulation with primordial segments in many if not most of the new states (or 'empires'), is pivotal to the issue of the abuse of office.[14]

However, not wishing to strike an overly pessimistic note, we must concede that mobilised civil societies throughout the world have made significant gains, particularly over the past decade. From the global wave of upheavals which followed the collapse of the Soviet Bloc to the election of Kim Dae-Jung in South Korea, of a civilian government in Guatemala, the return of a kind of democracy in Nigeria, to the overthrow of Suharto (but possibly not of 'Suharto Inc.'), democracy would seem to be well and truly 'on the march'. As Adrian Leftwich has pointed out, the percentage of formally democratic states in the world grew from a mere 25 per cent in 1973 to 68 per cent in 1992.[15] However, the extent to which these 'formal democracies' have been transformed into ongoing institutionalised democratic systems of government, with all that this entails, is a matter of some controversy. It is also a matter of some considerable complexity.[16] Therefore, since this question has already been be addressed by a number of commentators, including Doig in this volume, we confine ourselves to highlighting three key themes.

First is the issue of the perennial funding of the political parties which are almost universally seen as a key component of democracy: in the absence of a mass membership, newly launched or newly revived parties tend to be dependent upon and be bankrolled by wealthy individuals, 'big men', business consortia not excluding interests overseas, as well as, increasingly, organised crime. This, of course, raises the usual problems of favouritism, cronyism, string pulling, of the assertion of covert and illegitimate interests generally. Such problems, as we saw in the 'Introduction' to this volume, are in no sense confined to less developed states. But precisely because of the fragility of the democratic process in LDCs, the fact that this process can more easily be hi-jacked by strategically placed individuals and elites renders the funding question that much more critical.

Second, the loosening of controls which accompany liberalisation and democratisation has been noted to produce an upsurge of corruption. In this volume, David Stasavage has shown how the decline of FRELIMO controls contributed to an increase and diffusion of corruption in Mozambique. In an extremely detailed study of South Africa, Tom Lodge has demonstrated how this problem is likely to be particularly acute in a society where a significant proportion of the population, in this case a majority, is living in conditions of desperate poverty. In such a situation the removal of restraints induces a virtual frenzy of opportunism, some of which is inevitably directed at the public sector.[17]

This last point brings us to the third major aspect of the process of democratisation, which entails the consequent upsurge of pressure on the state and the services which the state is expected to provide from education to security, from health to all-weather roads. Here the less developed state is ill-equipped, to put it mildly, to handle the escalation of demands which invariably deluge upon it in the wake of *glasnost*. Thus we return yet again to the enduring dilemma of the less developed state's inability to garner the resources to institutionalise required levels of administrative capability. It is hard to see how such states can break out of the vicious circle without significant economic development. Whether such a development is likely to be forthcoming is yet again an extremely complex question to which we cannot address ourselves in this context. However, it does seem to be the case that levels of development needed are unlikely to be achieved in the face of a vigorous and strident civil society. At this point, we would make the familiar observation that the historical experience of now developed societies yields very few examples of the establishment of democratic political system prior to or even in the early stages of industrialisation. In the UK even full adult suffrage – a fairly minimal condition – was not conceded until 1928, nearly a century and half after industrial take-off. If we turn to the examples of the Asian 'tigers' – which LDCs were once strongly urged to emulate – in none do we encounter the kind of civil society that provides the model that we meet in governance discourse. On the contrary, the militarisation of South Korea, the degree of regimentation and control imposed upon citizens and employees in Hong Kong, Singapore and Taiwan seriously collide with Western liberal notions of citizen rights. In the light of these examples, it is difficult to disagree with Young and Kante's observation that 'the effort to promote democracy in the midst of acute economic distress is historically unprecedented'.[18]

Accordingly, there appears to be a fair degree of tension between the goals of state building on the one hand and promoting democracy on the other. In this respect the prevailing anti-corruption discourse with its emphasis on good governance contains something of a contradiction. This is possibly because this discourse is based upon conceptions of 'democracy', 'civil society' and 'public administration' which are rooted in a specific historical conjuncture under which western European states and the US industrialised and modernised. Although the respective routes to modernity displayed important variations between these states, certain key common elements obtained: two of the most significant were *nationally* organised capitalist development which produced, second, a large class-conscious, albeit generally reformist, working class. This industrial proletariat spearheaded the push for full rights of citizenship,[19] culminating in the welfare capitalist regimes that dominated western Europe from the end of World War Two until the mid-1970s. It was this conjuncture that gave us the metaphor of the administered economy responding efficiently and effectively to the needs and interests of a well articulated civil society.

But less developed states facing problems of economic stagnation, often pervasive political corruption, escalating crime and violence, and political instability are locked into a totally different phase in the development of the global economy. As we saw in the 'Introduction', the concatenation of globalisation, along with the revolution in information technology, which *inter alia* permit the free movement of capital; the break-up of the Soviet bloc; the awesome increase in crime, together with growing poverty and inequality, do not augur well for the reform of the invariably fragile, in some cases virtually collapsed, states of the south. If the tidal waves of globalisation can undermine the foundations of the once apparently impregnable fortresses of Japan and South Korea, what are the prospects for Brazil and Mexico, let alone Mozambique and Uganda?

The global context of corruption, stagnation and instability obviously raises very large questions. All one can attempt to accomplish in a context such as this is to signpost possible ways forward. Bearing in mind Doig's emphasis (above) on the sequencing of reform, in so far as one can assign priority, the emphasis has to be upon state building or, rather, rebuilding. This is not to argue that the promotion of civil society should be consigned to the backburner. On the contrary, a vigorous civil society is the ultimate safeguard of basic human rights and the final bulwark against the depredations of death squads. Consequently, continued support for civil society must be driven by moral as well as mere development policy imperatives. However, an observation made by several commentators is worth repeating at this point: an effective civil society depends upon a strong and stable public order in the sense of a well institutionalised and differentiated state. Civil society, that is, requires the administrative apparatus to uphold and operate according to the principles which underpin the judicious and fair distribution of public resources. Not least, civil society depends upon the state to mediate between the constituencies of which it is composed.[20] An over-mighty civil society can swamp even relatively institutionalised states with administrative paralysis as the result.[21]

The essence of the neo-liberal solution to the problem of low state capability has been a combination of slimming down and more effective management of what is left: a 'leaner and fitter' state! Whilst acknowledging the need for economies, the evidence seems to suggest that such an approach alone does not constitute a long-term solution, that rebuilding will need substantial extra resources.[22] Where these resources will come from is truly a massive problem. It has been suggested here that they are unlikely to be generated from within. Much-needed debt relief tied to designated administrative reform programmes, although controversial, could constitute a beginning. But only a beginning: it seems clear that the problem of corruption, and the more general abuse of power of which it is a manifestation, will ultimately be contained only as part of a comprehensive programme of reform. That is to say, a programme which addresses the fundamental roots of economic backwardness and inequality. For, contrary to the drift of a good deal of current policy wisdom, corruption is a symptom rather than a cause of underdevelopment.

NOTES

1. See, for example, J.S.T. Quah, 'Singapore's Experience in Curbing Corruption', in A.J. Heidenheimer, M. Johnston and V.T. LeVine (eds.), *Political Corruption: A Handbook* (New Brunswick: Transaction Publishers, 1989), 841–54.
2. See *Annual Report 1997* (Botswana: Directorate on Corruption and Economic Crime, 1998), 12. An article in the independent Botswana weekly, *Midweek Sun*, 5 May 1999, described the DCEC as 'wanting, as its functions are under the supervision of politicians. It is the lack of total independence that leads many to believe that it cannot police its own masters.' See *TI Newsletter*, June 1999, 5.
3. See, for example, A. Doig, 'Good Government and Sustainable Anti-Corruption Strategies: A Role for Independent anti-Corruption Agencies?', *Public Administration and Development*, 15 (1995), 151–65.
4. An Indian government report in 1994 listed 779 public companies and corporations whose accounts were seriously in arrears. Personal communication from a former Accountant-General of Kerala state.

5. See, especially, F. Stapenhurst and P. Langseth, 'The Role of Public Administration in Fighting Corruption', *International Journal of Public Sector Management*, 10, 5 (1997), 311–30.
6. For an early statement of this problem, see N. Kaldor, 'Taxation for Economic Development', *Journal of Modern African Studies*, 1, 1 (1963), 7–23. See also M. Bratton, 'Beyond the State: Society and Associational Life in Africa', *World Politics*, 41, 3 (1989), 407–29; R. Sandbrook, *The Politics of Africa's Economic Recovery* (Cambridge: Cambridge University Press, 1993); and W. Little, 'Political Corruption in Latin America', *Corruption and Reform*, 7 (1992), 41–66. J.S. Migdal's *Strong Societies and Weak States* (Princeton, NJ: Princeton University Press, 1988) includes an interesting appendix, 'Assessing Social Control', which addresses the problem of tax capacity in less developed states.
7. See H. Bienen, 'The Economic Environment', in G. Hyden, R.H. Jackson and J.J. Okumu (eds.), *Development Administration: The Kenyan Experience* (Nairobi: Oxford University Press, 1970), 43–62.
8. See D. Green on Ghana where in 1992 the Rawlings regime was to a certain extent able to 'buy' the election by agreeing to pay accrued end-of-service benefits to workers dismissed from state-owned enterprises, and by granting increases of 70–80 per cent to public servants and many other workers: 'Ghana: Structural Adjustment and State (Re)Formation', in I.A. Villalon and P.A. Huxtable (eds.), *The African State at a Critical Juncture: Between Disintegration and Reconfiguration* (London: Lynn Rienner, 1998), 202.
9. See, for example, K. Good, 'Authoritarian Liberalism: A Defining Characteristic of Botswana', *Journal of Contemporary African Studies*, 14, 1 (1996), 29–51.
10. For a concise appraisal of the 'professionalism', or the lack of it, of Latin American militaries, see J.S. Fitch, *The Armed Forces and Democracy in Latin America* (Baltimore, MD/London: Johns Hopkins University Press, 1998).
11. According to Jose Saramago (Nobel prizewinner for literature, 1998), the Mexican government currently has nearly 60,000 troops – around one-third of the army – in effective occupation of the state of Chiapas, location of the 1994 Zapatista Army rebellion. 'Chiapas de douleur et d'espoir', *Le Monde Diplomatique* (March 1999), 12, 13.
12. C. Gabetta, 'Coup de Semonce pour le President Argentin', *Le Monde Diplomatique* (Dec. 1997), 11. See also M. McCaughan, 'Police Brutality Cowes Argentinians', *The Guardian Weekly*, 21 Feb. 1999. On rising police brutality, including summary executions, in Brazil, see C. Gabizon, 'Meurtrière Police de Rio', *Le Monde Diplomatique* (July 1999), 19.
13. C. Clapham, *Africa and the International System. The Politics of State Survival* (Cambridge: Cambridge University Press, 1997), 202–3. See also G. Prunier, 'Des Habits Neufs pour le Vieux Despote Kenyan', *Le Monde Diplomatique* (Jan. 1997).
14. In a seminal piece written over 30 years ago, Guenther Roth likens many new states to premodern empires such as Austria-Hungary and the Ottoman Empire: 'Personal Rulership, Patrimonialism and Empire-building in the New States', *World Politics*, 20 (1968), 194–206.
15. A. Leftwich, 'On the Primacy of Politics in Development', in A. Leftwich (ed.), *Democracy and Development* (Cambridge: Polity Press, 1996), 3–24.
16. According to Jonathan Fox, a number of states, which held elections in the early 1990s, have failed to reach a democratic threshold: Mexico, El Salvador, Guatemala, Colombia, Peru, Taiwan, Thailand, Malaysia, the Philippines, Nigeria, Ghana, Kenya, Serbia as well as several of the former Soviet republics, are examples. 'The Difficult Transition from Clientelism to Citizenship. Lessons from Mexico', *World Politics*, 46 (1994), 151–84.
17. T. Lodge, 'Political Corruption in South Africa', *African Affairs*, 97, 387 (April 1998), 157–88.
18. C. Young and B. Kante, 'Governance, Democracy and the 1988 Senegalese Elections', in G. Hyden and M. Bratton (eds.), *Governance and Politics in Africa* (London: Lynne Rienner, 1992), 52.
19. See T.H. Marshall, *Citizenship and Social Class* (Cambridge: Cambridge University Press, 1950); and B. Turner, (ed.), *Citizenship and Social Theory* (London: Sage, 1993).
20. See especially J. Keane: 'without the protective, redistributive and conflict mediating functions of the state, struggles to transform civil society will become ghettoized, divided and stagnant, or will spawn their own, new forms of inequality and unfreedom.' 'The Limits

of State Action', in J. Keane (ed.), *Democracy and Civil Society* (London: Verso, 1988), 385. See also S. Nolutshungu: 'Democratization cannot abstract away or bypass, the task of state construction, the consolidation of state authority, the building of institutions and ... a certain ascendance over "civil society" that circumscribes the domain of private interests, placing it within the compass of social policy and the law.' 'Africa in a World of Democracies: Interpretation and Retrieval', *Journal of Commonwealth and Comparative Politics*, 30, 3 (1992), 331.

21. For example, see A.K. Campbell on the difficulties of bringing disciplinary action in a US city bureaucracy: 'Civil Service Reform as a Remedy for Bureaucratic Ills', in C.H. Weiss and A.H. Barton (eds.), *Making Bureuacracies Work* (London: Sage, 1979), 113–29.
22. On the need for 'rebuilding' as opposed to the neo-liberal obsession with 'overhauling', the primary aim of which being 'getting more for less', see O.P. Dwivedi, *Development Administration: From Underdevelopment to Sustainable Development* (London: Macmillan, 1994), ch.6.

Abstracts

In the State We Trust? Democratisation, Corruption and Development,
by Alan Doig

This article provides the context for the contributions in this volume by looking at the relationship between democratisation and the state. While the state has been a major source, and resource, for corruption in developing and transitional countries, it is also the means by which democratisation moves beyond the issue of the vote to delivering those services and processes which democratisation promises. Refocusing or realigning the state, as well as pre-empting the potential for corruption that is also inherent in the process of democratisation, requires careful sequencing and co-ordination while re-engaging public participation must be undertaken by the state in ways that supplement a reliance solely on the party system to achieve the *purpose* of democratisation.

Democratisation or the Democratisation of Corruption? The Case of Uganda, *by David Watt, Rachel Flanary and Robin Theobald*

This article examines the extent to which the country's structural changes implemented since 1986 are helping to reduce corruption and thereby alleviate poverty and generate economic growth. The examination will involve an analysis of key elements in Uganda's turbulent history since independence, a mapping of the political, economic and social inheritance of the National Resistance Movement (NRM), an examination of the NRM's proposed reform programme and the initiatives actually implemented in support of democratisation. The critique will consider whether the resultant changes are reducing corruption, merely shifting where it impacts or are actually creating new opportunities for corruption to flourish.

Mozambique in Transition: Causes and Consequences of Corruption, *by David Stasavage*

This article attempts to measure the level of corruption in Mozambique at a particularly important point during its economic transition programme (1995–96), to examine what might account for the presence of corruption, and to assess the effect of corruption on the economy. While data on corruption in Mozambique (as anywhere) are scarce, there is partial evidence to point to a dramatic increase in the level of corruption in recent years. This seems attributable to a change in the basic conditions for deterrence of corruption highlighted by principal-agent theory: bureaucrats retain extensive control rights over economic activity, structures for monitoring bureaucrats have been weakened during the recent political transition, and trends in wages have created incentive problems. The effects of corruption on the Mozambican economy involve both a distorting effect on government trade and tax policies and a disincentive effect with regard to investment, particularly for smaller firms. It underlines the implications of poor economic reform on state performance and income if, as is discussed elsewhere in this volume, the state is to be in a position to respond to the expectations of democratisation.

The Changing Context of Corruption Control: The Hong Kong Special Administrative Region, 1997–99, *by Jonathan Moran*

Increasing attention has been focused on the analysis of corruption in its historical, social, political and economic context. While this is not a new development, recent studies have attempted to analyse corruption as a dynamic phenomenon, part of specific national and regional patterns of state–society relations, developmental trajectories, international linkages and political-economic structures. If these approaches can provide important explanations for the development of corruption, they can also apply to studies of anti-corruption policies. This approach informs the analysis contained in this article, which discusses the context for anti-corruption strategies in the Hong Kong Special Administrative Region (SAR), and the role of the Independent Commission Against Corruption (ICAC), following the transfer of sovereignty from Britain to the People's Republic of China in 1997.

Combating Corruption in Botswana: Regional Role Model or Deviant Case? *by Robin Theobald and Robert Williams*

This article offers an assessment of the problem of corruption in Botswana, an analysis of the institutional and other methods used to combat it and an evaluation of the applicability of the Botswana experience to other parts of Africa. Assessing corruption and judging the efficacy of methods of controlling it are notoriously difficult tasks. The article briefly establishes a political and economic context before presenting a detailed analysis of the reforms introduced in 1994. The conclusion re-examines the case for Botswana's exceptionalism in regard to the likelihood of neighbouring states seeking to imitate its legislative and institutional approach to combating corruption.

Democracy, Development and Anti-Corruption Strategies: Learning from the Australian Experience, *by Robert Williams*

This article explores some aspects of the relationship of democracy and development to corruption in Australia. It illustrates how notions of development, democracy and corruption have to be unpacked in particular circumstances. Australia enjoys one of the highest standards of living in the world. It has a stable, multi-party democracy and it is free from the acute societal strains found in many parts of the South. Yet, in the past 20 years, Australia has experienced a series of problems with corruption. This article addresses some of these problems, the strategies employed to combat them and the implications for explaining and tackling corruption.

Index

accountability 2, 15, 16, 32, 38, 65, 79, 84, 85, 100, 135, 140–46, 144, 151
  in Botswana 126
  in Hong Kong 107
  in Uganda 44, 46–9, 57, 58
aid 1, 37, 70, 72, 74, 85, 90, 91
  and corruption 72, 74–5, 90–91
Amin, Idi 39–40
Annan, Kofi 1
anti-corruption 11, 29, 55–6, 98, 101, 125, 138, 156
  in Uganda 57–62
anti-corruption agencies (ACAs) 42, 55, 99, 113, 125, 130, 133, 149–52
  in Australia 137, 142, 143, 146
  in Botswana 10, 119–26, 131–3, 151
  in Hong Kong 9–10, 53, 99–100, 101–2, 103, 105, 107, 108, 110, 111–13, 119, 121, 130, 151
anti-corruption policies 98, 105, 132
  in Hong Kong 98, 101, 107, 108
anti-corruption strategies 2, 41, 60, 105, 132, 147, 149, 152
aid 1, 26, 74, 85
  corruption in 72, 74–5, 90–91
Argentina 8, 153
audit 25, 37, 42, 50, 69, 74, 91
Australia 11, 17, 102, 136
  and democracy 138, 143, 144, 146
  and fraud 136, 139, 141
  and organised crime 137, 139, 140
  and police corruption 137–8, 139, 140, 141
  Independent Commission Against Corruption (ICAC) 138, 142, 143, 146

Bangladesh 11, 135
Bank of Credit and Commerce International (BCCI) 7
Benin 6
Bhuto, Benazir 4
Block, Alan 98
Botswana 10, 149
Botswana Democratic Party (BDP) 128–9
  Directorate on Corruption and Economic Crime (DCEC) 10, 119–26, 131–3, 151
    and accountability 126
    independence of 125–6
    powers of 119, 126
  Corruption Prevention Group 121–2, 126
  political culture 127–8

Brazil 156
bribery 2, 5, 66, 67–8, 70, 72, 73, 75–7, 81, 85, 86, 90, 99, 110, 119, 130, 137–8
Burundi 4
business environment 10
business regulation 72–4, 78, 79–80, 89–90
business sector 19, 39, 68, 69, 72, 76–8, 102, 105–6, 107

Cameroon 88
Centre for the Promotion of Investment (CPI) 73, 75–6, 90, 94
Chad 6
Chile 8, 153
China 27
  and Hong Kong 100–102, 103–4, 105–6, 107, 109, 111, 112, 113
CIETinternational 46, 59
citizenship 14, 17
civil service *see* public service
civil society 9, 16–17, 18, 19, 22, 25, 27–9, 30–32, 127, 152–3, 154, 156
  in Uganda 51–3, 56
clientelism 22, 26, 48–9, 60, 154
Cockroft, Lawrence 23
codes of conduct 54–5, 58, 122, 142, 145
cold war 7
colonialism 22–3, 42, 70, 79, 89, 99, 100, 127
  in Uganda 38–9, 40
Commercial Crime Bureau 100
conflict of interest 49–50
Congo, Democratic Republic of 58, 61
Constitutional Commission 42–3
corruption 1–5, 7, 10–11, 24, 41, 65, *see also* anti-corruption
  control of 51, 53–6, 59, 60, 31, 41–2, 99, 102, 107, 112–14, 147
  and business 72–4, 79–80, 89–90, 105–6, 107, 109
  and customs 68, 70–72, 75, 78, 86–9, 92
  decentralisation of 48–9, 57
  grand corruption 3–5, 7, 58
  impact of 13, 24, 62, 66–8, 75, 92, 95
  investigation of 112, 120–21, 123, 139–44, 150–51
  level of 24, 37, 46, 60, 65, 68–75, 86, 117, 132
  petty corruption 3, 5–6, 113, 130
  and private sector 108–9, 113
  and public sector 8, 24, 44, 48, 59, 67, 70,

79, 85, 95
    in Uganda 37, 41–2, 46, 48–50
Costigan Investigation 137, 139–40, 143
crime 5, 104, 109, 111, 150, 156 *see also*
    organised crime
criminal justice 99, 139, 141
Crook, Richard 32
cronyism 5, 61, 151, 152, 155
customs 6, 66, 108
    in Mozambique 68, 70–72, 75, 78, 86–9,
    90, 92

Davis, Mike 98
Davis, Peter 11, 153
decentralisation 25, 32–3, 91
    of corruption 48–9, 57
    in Uganda 42, 46–9
democracy 9, 14, 15, 20, 56, 135, 136, 145,
    149, 154, 156
    in Australia 138, 143, 144, 146
democratisation 13, 14, 15, 17, 19, 20–21,
    24, 25–33, 41, 135
    in Uganda 56–9
Denmark 145
Department for International Development
    (DFID) 2, 41, 45
deregulation 8, 25
development 9, 13, 15, 135, 145, 155
Dicklich, Susan 52
Directorate on Corruption and Economic
    Crime (DCEC) 10, 119–26, 131–3, 151
Doig, Alan 9, 154, 156
drugs 8, 137
    in Hong Kong 99, 108–9, 111, 112

economic crime 119–20, 123, 124, 131 *see*
    also crime
elections 14–15, 22, 29–30, 38, 43, 57, 61,
    84, 85, 94, 118, 129, 141–2, 145
elites 14, 22, 23, 27–8, 61, 77, 154
European Commission 4, 94

factionalism 41, 59, 129
financial control 47
financial sector 102
financial system 19, 109, 110, 118
Flanary, Rachel 10
Foreign Corrupt Practices Act (FCPA) 2
France 98, 136
fraud 4, 24, 111, 118, 119, 131, 152
    in Australia 136, 139, 141
    investigation of 131
FRELIMO 11, 65, 70, 75, 77, 83–4, 87
Furley, Oliver 43, 57

Ghana 25, 126, 127

good governance 9, 10, 26, 29, 107, 118,
    140, 156
governance 9, 15, 21, 24, 155
Greiner, Nick 138, 142–3, 145, 146–7
Guanxi 19, 106
Guatemala 154

Holm, John 128
Hong Kong 9–10, 53, 149–56
    and accountability 107
    anti-corruption policies 98, 101, 107, 108
    corruption and business 105–6, 107, 109
    and China 110–12, 103–4, 105–6, 107,
    109, 111, 112, 113
    and drugs 99, 108–9, 111, 112
    and financial crisis 106
    guanxi 106
    Independent Commission Against
    Corruption (ICAC) 9–10, 53, 99–100,
    101–2, 103, 105, 107, 108, 110, 111,
    112, 113, 119, 121, 130, 151
    and money-laundering 109–10, 111, 112
    and organised crime 103, 104, 110–12,
    113
    and police corruption 99, 100, 105, 108,
    110, 111
    and private sector corruption 108–9, 113
    rule of law 99, 100, 102–4, 112, 113, 114
Houphouet-Boigny, Felix 4
House of Commons 5

Independent Commission Against Corruption
    (ICAC)
    in Australia 138, 142, 143, 146
    in Hong Kong 9–10, 53, 99–100, 101,
    102, 103, 105, 107, 108, 110, 111,
    112, 113, 119, 130, 151
Indonesia 78, 88
informants 109
Inspectorate of Government (IG) 46, 51,
    53–5
institution building 140
integrity 144, 147, 149
International Monetary Fund (IMF) 2
investigation, of corruption 112, 120, 121,
    123, 138–44, 150–51
Italy 98, 136
Ivory Coast 60

Japan 99, 156
judicial system 28, 37, 45, 46, 65, 79, 84–5,
    101, 124, 131, 142, 150, 151

Kenya 154
Klitgaard, Robert 84

law enforcement 8, 14, 113, 141
law, rule of 16, 29, 57, 59, 65, 99, 100, 107,
    140
    in Hong Kong 99, 100, 102–4, 112, 113,
        114
Leftwich, Adrian 24–5, 154
legitimacy 26–7, 42, 43, 102, 139, 143
Lesotho 126
less developed countries (LDCs) 9, 18, 127,
    131, 150, 152, 153, 155
liberalisation 77, 79
Lodge, Tom 155

Machel, Samora 70, 84
Malawi 25, 60, 126
Malaysia 82
Mali 71
Mamdani, Mahmood 61
Manor, J. 32
Masire, Ketumile 118, 127
Maxwell, Robert 7
McGregor, Allister 11, 153
Mazdoor Kisan Shakti Sangathan (MKSS) 31
media 27, 30, 52–3, 55, 85, 98, 102, 136, 146
Mexico 8, 153, 153, 156
mismanagement 118
Mobutu Sese Seko. 4, 7, 154
Moi, Daniel Arap 154
money-laundering 109, 110, 111, 112
Moran, Jonathan 10
Mozambique 10, 65, 156
    and business–government relations 76–8
    and business regulation 72–4, 79–80,
        89–90
    and corruption increase 65–8, 69–70
    and civil war 86
    and customs 68, 70–72, 75, 78, 86–9, 92
    and foreign aid 72, 74–5, 90–91
    FRELIMO 11, 65, 70, 75, 77, 83–4, 87
Mugenyi, M. 58
Museveni, Yowei Kaguta 10, 39, 40, 42, 43,
    52, 56, 59, 61

Namibia 126
National Resistance Army (NRA) 39, 40, 43,
    46, 61
National Resistance Movement (NRM) 10,
    40–41, 43, 44, 46, 50, 53, 57, 59
nepotism 3
Niger 6
Nigeria 6, 27–8, 31, 127, 154
non-governmental organisations (NGOs) 2, 4,
    11, 32, 33, 74
    in Uganda 52–5
Nzongola-Ntalaja, G. 33

Obote, Milton 38–9, 40, 43, 59
OECD 2
organised crime 10, 20, 98, 155 see also
    crime
    in Australia 137, 139, 140
    in Hong Kong 103, 104, 110–12, 113

Pakistan 4, 60
patrimonialism 23, 45, 154
patronage 26–7, 58, 105
patron–client relations 19, 154
pay 37, 44, 45, 65, 67, 78–9, 80, 83, 95, 150
Peru 8, 32
Philippines 31, 82, 98
police 8, 23, 41, 59, 65, 79, 100, 103, 122,
    150, 151
    corruption in 6, 105, 108
        Australia 137–8, 139, 140, 141
        Hong Kong 99, 100, 105, 108, 110,
            111
political culture 127, 138, 145, 147
political elites see elites
political parties 28–9, 42–3, 56–7, 145, 146,
    147
political will 26–7, 60, 113
Portugal 79
poverty 8, 9, 39, 117, 127, 130, 136, 153,
    155, 156
    eradication of 52, 135
principal-agent 65, 67, 86, 144, 146
private sector 22, 27, 67, 72, 78, 82, 84, 85,
    89, 100, 155
    corruption in 108–9, 113
privatisation 18, 77, 88, 142
    in Uganda 49–50, 51, 58
public order 99, 157
public procurement 2
public sector 8, 18, 23, 27
    corruption in 8, 24, 44, 48, 59, 67, 70, 79,
        85, 95
public service 23, 41, 59, 60, 83, 100, 110,
    119
    pay 37, 44, 45, 65, 67, 78–9, 80–83, 95, 150
    reform of 11, 44–6, 60, 83, 95, 142, 149

Rajasthan 31
reform, of public service 11, 44–6, 60, 83,
    95, 149
Regan, Anthony J., 57–8
regulation 69, 70, 83, 110
    of business 72–4, 78, 79–80, 89–90
rent-seeking 1, 4, 31, 65, 88, 130,
    in Bangladesh 142
rule of law see law
Russia 20, 67, 79

Saleh, Salim 49, 50, 53
Scott, James.C. 138
Schonwalder, G 32
self-enrichment 4, 30, 49, 84, 118, 131
Senegal 25, 60
Shleifer, Andrei 77, 87
Singapore 82, 98, 99, 155, 156
sleaze 5
Smith, Hedrick 5
smuggling 88, 92, 104, 111–12
social capital 32
social inequality 8
South Africa 131
South Korea 82, 154, 156
Spain 98
Stasavage, David 10, 155
structural adjustment 8, 10, 25–6, 33, 44, 65
Sudan 61
Swaziland 126

Taiwan 82, 156
Tanzania 39, 71, 130
tax 3, 24, 47, 66, 68, 90, 92, 95,
    evasion of 20–21, 24, 70–71, 86
    limited capacity to 48, 142
ten-point programme 40–41
Thailand 31, 78, 98
Theobald, Robin 10, 150
Togo 6
transnational corporations (TNCs) 3, 7
transparency 2, 15, 49, 56, 109, 131, 151
Transparency International (TI) 2, 6, 37, 60, 135
Turkey 8

Uganda 10, 127, 156
    accountability in 44, 46–9, 57, 58
    anti-corruption in 57–62
    civil society in 51–3, 56

colonialism in 38–9, 40
corruption in 37, 41–2, 46, 48–50, 57–62
decentralisation in 42, 46–9
democratisation in 56–9
Inspectorate of Government 46, 51, 53–5,
    60
non-governmental organisations 52–5
privatisation in 49–50, 51, 58
public service reform in 44–56, 60
Uganda Human Rights Commission (UHRC)
    42, 53, 55, 59
Uganda People's Congress (UPC) 38, 43
Ukraine 60
United Kingdom 4, 5, 100, 101, 102, 104,
    105, 135, 155
    Department for International
        Development (DFID) 2, 41, 45
United Nations 1–2, 8, 24
United States 4, 5, 98, 135, 136, 156
Uruguay 8
urbanisation 16
USAID 85, 136

Vishny, Robert 77, 87

Wade, Robert 31
wages see pay
Watt, David 10
White, Gordon 28
Williams, Robert 10, 11, 150
World Bank 1–2, 37, 47, 49–50, 79, 82, 84,
    128
World Trade Organisation 2

Xiaoping, Deng 101

Zambia 71
Zimbabwe 60

Books of Related Interest

Democracy in Argentina
Hope and Disillusion

Laura Tedesco, *University of East Anglia*

This book is a study of the social, political and economic development
that took place in Argentina under President Raúl Alfonsín, offering a
new approach to the democratisation process and economic adjustment
of the 1980s. The objective of this book is to analyse a period in
Argentina's history that contains the key to understanding the changes
undergone by the Argentinian state and economy in the 1980s. The
book argues that the crisis of the Argentinian state deepened under
Alfonsín due to a particular combination of economic and political
circumstances. The run on the austral in February 1989, followed by
hyper-inflation, imposed a specific restructuring which was eventually
undertaken by the Peronist Menem government. The author argues that
President Carlos Menem was able to carry this out because Alfonsín
had failed to impose an alternative restructuring to that of the 1976
military dictatorship. To understand Alfonsín's failure, the book
analyses the political factors that influence economic decision-making
and the way such factors are inextricably interrelated. In Argentina the
important political factors were: the trade unions, international creditors
and the Armed Forces.

Although the Radical government of Alfonsín was unable to resolve the
crisis of the Argentinian state, this book suggests that as a result of its
policies on human rights violations, which undermined the political role
of the Armed Forces, it was able to set Argentina on the path towards
consolidating democracy.

240 pages   1999
0 7146 4978 3 cloth
0 7146 8094 X paper

FRANK CASS PUBLISHERS
Newbury House, 900 Eastern Avenue, Ilford, Essex, IG2 7HH
Tel: +44 (0)20 8599 8866 Fax: +44 (0)20 8599 0984 E-mail: info@frankcass.com
NORTH AMERICA
5804 NE Hassalo Street, Portland, OR 97213 3644, USA
Tel: 800 944 6190 Fax: 503 280 8832 E-mail: cass@isbs.com
Website: www.frankcass.com

The Resilience of Democracy
Persistent Practice, Durable Idea

Peter Burnell, *University of Warwick* and
Peter Calvert, *University of Southampton* (Eds)

If the past is any guide, many of the new 'Third Wave' democracies can be expected to fall by the wayside. Moreover, a significant part of the world's peoples do not enjoy democratic government. This volume brings together studies of many of the small number of previously established states that have retained and/or restored democracy despite – in many cases – formidable economic, social or political challenges. It seeks to establish common themes, whether or not they appear to fit a grand causal theory. It is, after all, the very adaptability of democratic systems that characterises their persistence, durability and resilience.

304 pages   illus   1999
0 7146 4965 1   cloth
0 7146 8026 5   paper
A special issue of the journal Democratization

Civil Society
Democratic Perspectives

Robert Fine and Shirin Rai, *both at the University of Warwick* (Eds)

Civil Society examines the idea of civil society in its historical and contemporary dimensions. It provides a clear, comprehensive and critical mapping of the idea, the burden of expectation that it has carried, and the intellectual and political dimensions that surround it.

184 pages   1997
0 7146 4762 4   cloth
0 7146 4313 0   paper
A special issue of the journal Democratization

FRANK CASS PUBLISHERS
Newbury House, 900 Eastern Avenue, Ilford, Essex, IG2 7HH
Tel: +44 (0)20 8599 8866 Fax: +44 (0)20 8599 0984 E-mail: info@frankcass.com
NORTH AMERICA
5804 NE Hassalo Street, Portland, OR 97213 3644, USA
Tel: 800 944 6190 Fax: 503 280 8832 E-mail: cass@isbs.com
Website: www.frankcass.com

Civil Society and Democracy in Africa
Critical Perspective

Nelson Kasfir, *Dartmouth College, USA* (Ed)

This book provides a careful and broad critique of the conventional
wisdom in applying the concept of civil society to politics in sub-
Saharan Africa, and particualry to democratization. It examines the
ideological roots of the conventional concept, the reasons for the failure
of civil society actors, such as the churches, to play their expected roles,
the exclusion of marginalized actors, the inability of civil society
organizations to act independently of the state and the failure of civil
society to contribute effectively to democratizing the African state.

160 pages   1998
0 7146 4908 2 cloth
0 7146 4453 6 paper
A special issue of the journal Commonwealth & Comparative Politics

FRANK CASS PUBLISHERS
Newbury House, 900 Eastern Avenue, Ilford, Essex, IG2 7HH
Tel: +44 (0)20 8599 8866 Fax: +44 (0)20 8599 0984 E-mail: info@frankcass.com
NORTH AMERICA
5804 NE Hassalo Street, Portland, OR 97213 3644, USA
Tel: 800 944 6190 Fax: 503 280 8832 E-mail: cass@isbs.com
Website: www.frankcass.com

Democratization and the Media

Vicky Randall, *Essex University* (Ed)

While there is widespread agreement that the mass communications
media play a potentially crucial role both in democratization and in
ensuring democracy's survival, this insight remains remarkably under-
researched or theorized. The essays especially commissioned for this
volume together analyse differing aspects of the complex relationship
between the media and democracy in a diverse range of national
contexts.

Specific contributions examine the consequences of the media for
privacy and for internal party democracy in Britain; the implications of
the new information media for democracy; the media's role in
democratization in eastern Europe, the Middle East, Africa and Asia
and in the ostensibly democratic politics of France and the US. In her
introductory comments, the editor helpfully sets out the main underlying
questions and draws upon the individual essays to suggest some broad
comparative themes and conclusions.

264 pages   1998
0 7146 4894 9 cloth
0 7146 4446 X paper
A special issue of the journal Democratization

FRANK CASS PUBLISHERS
Newbury House, 900 Eastern Avenue, Ilford, Essex, IG2 7HH
Tel: +44 (0)20 8599 8866 Fax: +44 (0)20 8599 0984 E-mail: info@frankcass.com
NORTH AMERICA
5804 NE Hassalo Street, Portland, OR 97213 3644, USA
Tel: 800 944 6190 Fax: 503 280 8832 E-mail: cass@isbs.com
Website: www.frankcass.com